SHOW US YOUR WEIRD!

Do you know of a weird site found somewhere in the United States, or can you tell us about a strange experience you've had? If so, we'd like to hear about it! We believe that every town has at least one great tale to tell, and we're listening. It could be a cursed road, haunted abandoned site, odd local character, or bizarre historic event. In most cases these tales are told only in the towns in which they originated. But why keep them to yourself when you could share them with all of America? So come on and fill us in on all the weirdness that's lurking in your backyard!

You can e-mail us at: Editor@WeirdUS.com,
or write to us at:
Weird U.S., P.O. Box 1346, Bloomfield, NJ 07003.

www.weirdus.com

Al's Acknowledgments

Sincerest appreciation is hereby expressed to the following people and organizations who helped me on my personal Weird Oregon journey, whether providing leads, helping with research, or simply offering encouragement: the Silverton Chamber of Commerce, the Silverton Public Library, Cottage Grove Library, Cottage Grove Historical Society, Steve Williams, Rock-n-Rogers Diner, King County Library System (Washington), Tacoma Library (Washington), Vancouver Library (Washington), Walter "Yashah" Collins, Renee Rank (site manager, Hotel Oregon), Liz Devine of the McMenamins marketing department, the Oregon Historical Society, Robyn Rawls of the Hillsboro Parks and Recreation Department, and Susan Vaslev and the staff of Enchanted Forest.

An especially big thank you to our Weird Oregonians—the generous bunch profiled on the previous two hundred–plus pages—who opened their homes, lives, and personal materials to the cause. We hope you find the end result worthy of your participation.

Further gratitude to my family and friends, too numerous to list by name, who are weirder than they may think (except for my wife, Tammy, who knows exactly how weird she is)!

And, as always, heartfelt thanks to Cooper the dog, who taught me that wrestling breaks are the perfect antidote to writer's block.

PHOTO CREDITS

WEiRD

OREGON

Your Travel Guide to Oregon's Local Legends and Best Kept Secrets

By AL EUFRASIO and JEFF DAVIS

Mark Sceurman and Mark Moran, Executive Editors

STERLING

New York / London

WEiRD OREGON

STERLING and the distinctive Sterling logo are
registered trademarks of Sterling Publishing Co., Inc.

Published by Sterling Publishing Co., Inc.
387 Park Avenue South, New York, NY 10016
© 2010 Mark Moran and Mark Sceurman
Distributed in Canada by Sterling Publishing
c/o Canadian Manda Group, 165 Dufferin Street
Toronto, Ontario, Canada M6K 3H6
Distributed in the United Kingdom by GMC Distribution Services,
Castle Place, 166 High Street, Lewes, East Sussex,
England BN7 1XU
Distributed in Australia by Capricorn Link (Australia) Pty. Ltd.
P. O. Box 704, Windsor, NSW 2756, Australia

10 9 8 7 6 5 4 3 2 1

Manufactured in China.
All rights reserved.

Photography and illustration credits are found on page 270
and constitute an extension of this copyright page.

Layout and production by bobsteimle.com

Sterling ISBN: 978-1-4027-5466-1

For information about custom editions, special sales, premium
and corporate purchases, please contact Sterling Special Sales
Department at 800-805-5489 or specialsales@sterlingpublishing.com.

CONTENTS

Our weird journey began a long, long time ago in a far-off land called New Jersey. Once a year or so we'd compile a homespun newsletter to hand out to our friends called *Weird N.J.* The pamphlet was a collection of odd news clippings, bizarre facts, little-known historical anecdotes and anomalous encounters from our home state. The newsletter also focused on the kind of very localized legends that were often whispered around a particular town but seldom heard outside the boundaries of the community where they first originated.

We had started the publication with the simple theory that every town in the state had at least one good tale to tell. *Weird N.J.* soon become a full-fledged magazine and we made the decision to actually do all of our own investigating and see if we couldn't track down just where all of these seemingly unbelievable stories were coming from. Was there, we wondered, any factual basis for these fantastic local legends that people were telling us? Armed with not much more than a camera and notepad we set off on a mystical journey of discovery. Much to our surprise and amazement, much of what we had initially presumed to be nothing more than urban legend actually turned out to be real, or at least contained a grain of truth that had originally sparked the lore.

After about a dozen years of documenting the bizarre, we were asked to write a book about our adventures, and so *Weird N.J.: Your Travel Guide to New Jersey's Local Legends and Best Kept Secrets* was published in 2003. Soon people from all over the country began writing to us, telling us strange tales from their home states. As it turned out, what we had first perceived to be a very local-interest genre was actually just a small part of a more universal phenomenon. People from all over the United States had strange tales to tell that they believed to be true, and they all wanted somebody to tell them to.

When the publishers of the book asked us what we wanted to do next, for us the choice was simple: "We'd like to do a book called *Weird U.S.*, in which we could document the local legends and strangest stories from all over the entire country," we told them. So for the next twelve months we set out in search of weirdness wherever it might be found in these fifty states.

In 2004, after *Weird U.S.* was published, our publisher asked us once more where we wanted to go next. In the year that had taken us to put together *Weird U.S.*, we had come to the conclusion that this country had more great tales waiting to be told than could be contained in just one book. We had discovered, somewhat to our surprise, that every state we researched seemed to have more fascinating stories to offer than we actually had pages to accommodate. Everywhere we looked we found unwritten folklore, creepy cemeteries, cursed locations, and outlandish roadside oddities. With this in mind, we told our publishers that we wanted to document it *all*, and to do it in a series of books, each focusing on the peculiarities of one particular state.

The first person we looked to for help when it came to documenting all that is weird in the northwest corner of the country was Jeff Davis. Jeff is without question one of the most knowledgeable people around when it comes to hauntings of the Pacific Northwest. He is the author of several books on the subjects of ghosts and other mysterious creatures that lurk in the shadows of Washington and Oregon. Jeff also contributed some of his strange stories to our *Weird Hauntings* book in 2006, so we'd collaborated with him already and knew what a pleasure he was to work with.

The next person we invited to come onboard, for our *Weird Washington* project, was Al Eufrasio, who actually grew up in our home state of New Jersey before relocating to the Pacific Northwest. Living three thousand miles away didn't stop him from contributing his unique brand of demented illustrations and stories to *Weird N.J.* magazine and *Weird Washington* book. Our friendship with Al grew over the years and he was always one of our go-to guys whenever we needed artwork that was humorous, provocative, and insightful all at the same time. When it came time to find an author to point out the lighter side of a state's myriad oddities, we knew Al would be the perfect guy for the job.

Both Jeff and Al did an extraordinary job on *Weird Washington.* The book published in 2008, was a tremendous success and a great addition to the Weird series. So when it came to choosing authors to collaborate with on a *Weird Oregon* volume, there was really no question in our minds who to turn to. Both Jeff and Al possess what we refer to as the "Weird Eye." The Weird Eye is needed to search out the sort of stories we were looking for. It requires one to see the world in a different way, with a renewed sense of wonder. And once you have it, there is no going back——you'll never see things the same way again. All of a sudden you begin to reexamine your own environs, noticing your everyday surroundings as if for the first time. And you begin to ask yourself questions like, "What the heck is that thing all about, anyway?" and, "Doesn't anybody else think that's kind of weird?"

So come with us now. Let Jeff and Al take you on a tour of the Beaver State, with all of its ghostly haunts, legendary locations, and unusual characters. It is a state of mind we like to call *Weird Oregon*.

—*Mark Moran and Mark Sceurman*

Well, here we go again. You know what lies ahead if you read our previous tome, *Weird Washington*. (And if you haven't, why not? It complements this book rather well, so grab a copy ASAP!)

In *Weird Oregon*, we aim to continue proving what most locals already know: that the Pacific Northwest, though sometimes considered low key, resonates with colorful history and unique legends. The quirky vibe so often perceived by visitors is akin to an initiation. "You wanna hang with us, you've gotta think differently for a while." Those who do so quickly understand the Northwest's appeal, and usually return home with a bemused but glowing assessment of the region.

There is a metaphor for this somewhere in the reaction to our previous book. *Weird Washington* was a much bigger success than we anticipated. The frequent requests we've gotten to do book signings, presentations, and interviews verify that there is widespread interest in the stranger, more mind-boggling tales around us.

One question we are constantly asked at these events is, "Which state is weirder—Washington or Oregon?"

Our standard answer has been, "We'll leave that for the readers to decide." Is this just a way to avoid alienating one group of readers? Certainly not. Like beauty, weirdness is oftentimes in the eye of the beholder. (That said, we're confident that our selections herein merit the distinction.)

One reminder before you leave on your mental or literal road trip: We fully encourage reader participation. If you have something to add to one of our stories, know of something that we did not include, or feel that we got a detail or two wrong, please write in and let us know. You might just see yourself published (with credit) in a future volume. Contact information is provided in the back of the book.

Is Oregon weirder than Washington? You tell us!

—*Al Eufrasio*

Welcome to Weird Oregon, the second book I cowrote in the Weird U.S. series for Mark Moran and Mark Sceurman. At one point, I was not sure I would get this assignment. Have you ever received a forwarded e-mail several pages long, requiring you to scroll down through the statements from various other people? I received an e-mail like that before I signed the contract for *Weird Washington*. There was an exchange between Mark Moran and someone else, and it went something like this, "Mark, are you sure you want to hire an archaeologist for this book? After all, they are pretty boring authors."

Mark did, and I got the job. *Weird Washington* became a best seller at many Barnes & Noble stores across the state. Some people bought it for light reading, or for ideas on holiday trips. It was also recommended by the Washington State Librarians, to aid educators in teaching state history. What was the appeal? I think it was partly the rapport between me and my co-author, Al Eufrasio. Being weird guys, we might know what appeals to others like us across the Pacific Northwest. And trust me, there are plenty of us around!

So which state is weirder: Washington or Oregon? I cannot answer that, but Oregon's weirdness began long ago, with the world's oldest running shoes, found in a desert cave that had been an inland ocean thousands of years ago. Oregon's Native Americans told stories about many places as part of their rich tradition, but it was the coming of the Europeans that left the weirdest mark on Oregon. This history began with a possible lost colony founded by Sir Francis Drake, and buried treasure in Oregon's Coast Range.

Later, the pioneers who took the Oregon Trail left a legacy that continues to this day. Along the way nearly one in ten people died before reaching Oregon. Those who made it were changed by the experience, becoming a no-nonsense folk who spoke their own minds. For better or worse, Oregonians stuck to their beliefs and opinions, no matter what someone else thought. Today, do not ask people from the Oregon what they think if you do not want to hear the answer. These rugged individualists did things their way.

Through the years, Oregon has had visits from explorers, authors, outlaws, and future presidents. While Portland may be the vortex of Oregon's weirdness, there are many weird places to see across the state. You just have to go find them. There are peculiar properties, like a gas station restroom that looks like cowboy boots. There's a man flying across the state in a lawn chair tethered to a bunch of helium balloons. How about that "city" in eastern Oregon with a year-round population of zero to two, depending on whether anyone gets trapped in the snow. There are natural wonders found nowhere else, like the Oregon Caves, and the stunning Chateau hotel.

Remember, seeing weird things does not always mean going far away to see new things. It also means seeing things around you with new eyes.

—*Jeff Davis*

Local Legends

Much of Oregon's unique character shines through in the stories passed around of places, things, and events that have, in one way or another, affected specific areas of the state. The beauty of these stories is how they tend to take on a life of their own, enhanced as they are with varying degrees of exaggeration and truth. The subjects gain an almost mythical quality from repeated, and sometimes altered, tellings.

This mythical quality can be applied to the one-time criminality of pinball, which led competing crooks in Multnomah County into a flurry of one-upmanship for control of the local pinball market. It can apply equally to unconfirmed historical rumors, such as that of the lost Blue Bucket Mine. Even more dubious tales, such as reports of a mind-control device that was disguised as a video game and secretly tested in Portland, have widespread circulation.

The Oregon coast certainly has its share of these kinds of odd stories, from glowing sand to ancient forests to an exploding whale.

In many ways, some of these entries could easily be categorized in other chapters. There is a certain element of uniqueness to them, however, that sets them apart and earns them each a mention here. See if you agree as you read these items of highly varied focus and veracity, which we collectively refer to as local legends.

A Waxy Buildup in Nehalem

In December 2007, Loretta LeGuee was walking along the sand near Gold Beach after a storm when she spotted a large object that turned out to be a ten-pound chunk of beeswax. Her find re-ignited interest in a centuries-old mystery of the Oregon coast involving the origin of thousands of pounds of what appears to be beeswax that many people have collected over time. Most historians believe the wax came from one or more shipwrecks, but other people believe they're waxlike minerals that could lead to a fortune hidden under the sands near the Nehalem River.

European explorers and later settlers found there were no native wax-producing bees in North or South America, so they had to import beeswax. The Spanish, who had several rich colonies in Central and South America from the 1500s to the 1700s, in particular required beeswax candles to celebrate Catholic Mass. Ocean currents between California and the Philippines enabled them to set up a network of ships (called Manila galleons by some) that sailed the route from 1572 to 1817, establishing trade of goods from the New World and bringing in important Old World supplies, including beeswax for candles. Several of these ships were wrecked or simply went missing, and it seems common sense that at least one, laden with beeswax, wrecked off the Oregon coast.

Native Americans might have been collecting the beached wax for some time to use in trade. Early explorers spoke of the Clatsop Indians and other costal tribes trading beeswax with them. Sgt. John Ordway of the Lewis and Clark Expedition mentioned trading for some "small fish and a little bears wax" (some historians have corrected the spelling to "bees wax"). And American settlers arriving in Oregon traded with Native Americans for large quantities of the wax before they found deposits on the beaches near Nehalem themselves.

In the mid- and late 1800s, the people around Nehalem collected this waxy material, which was usually encrusted with sand. Some found what looked like candles with missing wicks, others found fist-sized pieces, and a lucky few found chunks weighing up to 150 pounds. There were strange symbols on some of these pieces, a few resembling Arabic characters and others that were more arcane. Historians' estimates of the total amount recovered ranged from 1,500 pounds to over 100 tons.

Between 1890 and 1916, locals scavenged wood from a shipwreck exposed near the site where most of the wax was recovered. This seemed to prove the shipwreck theory. Or did it?

In 1893, a piece of what was commonly called Nehalem wax was on display at the World's Columbian Exposition in Chicago. When the commissioner in charge of a nearby Austrian mineral display saw the Nehalem wax and examined a piece, he declared it to be a natural mineral called ozokerite, a petroleum product related to paraffin. Even though other chemists analyzed more Nehalem wax and said it was beeswax, many people still believed that it was ozokerite, suggesting that there was simply too much Nehalem wax taken out of the ground to have come from a ship.

For more than a decade, word spread among geologists and potential investors across the country, as ozokerite is sometimes found in and around oil deposits. Several petroleum engineers were convinced that if ozokerite were lying just below the sands of Nehalem, a rich oil deposit might lie only a few more feet down. Between 1909 and 1910, promoters sold mining stock to investors and erected an oil derrick over a spot where locals said huge deposits of wax had been recovered. The investors gathered a safe distance away and cheered as the drill bit cut into the sand. They waited all day for the gusher of oil that would make them all rich. And they waited the next day, and the day after that. It didn't take long for the money and their spirits to run out.

Reactions were mixed. Some wanted to cut their losses and put the whole boondoggle behind them. Others claimed fraud and tried to get their money back. Nobody was satisfied, and the only ones who made money were the people who owned the drilling rig.

After that no one seemed to doubt that the Nehalem wax really was beeswax, and the history behind it faded into a local curiosity until recently. A group of volunteers and archaeologists began researching the Nehalem wax deposits and have conducted investigations, looking for the old wreck. As *Weird Oregon* goes to press, they haven't found it yet, but they are still looking. A search of records helped them pinpoint two likely candidates for the ship that wrecked along Oregon's shores. According to reports of the Naga Research Group, it seems likely that the Nehalem shipwreck was that of the Manila galleon *San Francisco Xavier*, lost at sea in 1705. It's possible, but *Weird Oregon* has heard about some interesting investment opportunities, drilling for offshore oil in Oregon . . .

To see pieces of Nehalem wax, visit the Tillamook Pioneer Museum in Tillamook and the Naga Group Web site (www.nagagroup.org).

The Witch's Castle at Macleay Park

Forest Park, a five-thousand-acre reserve just west of downtown Portland, provides a dramatic change of scenery from the urban sprawl surrounding it. Entering it is like being swallowed into another, more primeval world. Extending for eight miles along the Willamette River, it is the largest urban forest in the United States. A portion of its southern end is designated as a separate area, Macleay Park. The entire expanse boasts more than seventy miles of trails for walking and biking, but one spot in particular has become the prime destination for many seekers of the weird.

Walking about a mile on the Lower Macleay (aka Balch Creek) Trail from Macleay Park will lead you to the gutted ruins of a stone building popularly known as the Witch's Castle. Weathered and moss laden, it certainly looks as creepy and foreboding as its name implies. The legends surrounding it are appropriately unnerving.

Stumping the Balches

Part of the mystique surrounding the Witch's Castle, called the Stone House by the Portland Parks and Recreation Department, is inspired by events involving the original landowners more than 150 years ago.

In the 1850s, Danford Balch and his wife, Mary Jane, lived with their five sons and four daughters in a cabin on 350 acres of the surrounding forest, which they'd acquired in a land claim. In October 1858, Balch hired a young laborer from Vancouver, Washington, named Mortimer Stump to help him clear some land. Stump temporarily moved in with the family and immediately became smitten with fifteen-year-old Anna Balch, the eldest daughter. Anna returned his affection, so one day Stump asked Balch for Anna's hand in marriage.

As Stump's employer, Balch thought of himself as socially superior to Stump and his kin. He refused Stump and then evicted him. After Mortimer Stump and Anna Balch eloped in Vancouver on November 4, Anna moved in with the Stump family.

On November 18, the couple, along with Stump's father and brother, took the Stark Street Ferry to Portland to pick up some supplies. They ran into drunken Balch, who belligerently insisted that Anna go home with him. Cuthbert Stump, the father, remarked, "You are making a great fuss about your child; she is an ordinary little bitch and I do not know what the hell you want of her!" Balch retrieved his double-barreled shotgun at home and returned in time to catch the Stumps boarding the ferry back to Vancouver. Balch followed them onboard. Whether deliberately (as the Stumps claimed) or by accident (as Balch insisted), his double-barreled shotgun went off, blasting Mortimer Stump in the face and killing him.

Witnesses quickly disarmed and subdued Balch, and he was arrested. A trial was scheduled for the following spring, but soon after his arrest, Balch escaped and hid in the forest around his homestead. Evidence suggests that Balch tried faking his own death, because Mary Jane identified a drowning victim as her fugitive husband. Yet police found him eight months after his escape, on July 23, 1859.

When the case finally went to trial, several neighbors testified against Balch and even implicated Mary Jane, who they said was just as angry about Anna's elopement. According to the witnesses, she constantly nagged her hard-drinking husband to fulfill his oft-repeated vow to kill Mortimer Stump. For Balch's part, he denied even knowing the witnesses, insisting that he was being set up. In the end, Balch was convicted of murder and sentenced to hang.

On October 17, 1859, Danford Balch earned the dubious honor of becoming the first person executed in the state of Oregon. An apocryphal story has his daughter Anna attending the hanging with the Stump family.

Ghost Wars and Satanism

By 1897, real estate developer Donald Macleay owned a portion of the former Balch property. Frustrated with the taxes on the impractical forested hillside, he donated it to the city of Portland and its name became Macleay Park. Other surrounding properties were converted into parks in subsequent years.

Among the legends derived from the Balch–Stump conflict is the (probably mistaken) belief that Danford Balch's hanging happened somewhere in the park. Many people also believe the Witch's Castle to be the remains of the old Balch home. Actually, the eerie structure is what's left of a Depression-era public restroom.

It's said the restless spirits of the Stump and Balch families dwell around here, feuding for eternity in midnight "ghost wars." Over the years a few curious people who came here in the dark of night supposedly disappeared, perhaps into a ghostly netherworld. Others were eventually found wandering on the park trails, as lost in mind as they were in direction. The rest were apparently spared, perhaps so that they could warn others away from the Witch's Castle . . . or perhaps to lure them there. These otherworldly tales allegedly attract other sinister activities, such as late-night satanic rituals that include torture and human sacrifice.

Plumbing of the Freaky and the Undead

Growing up in southwestern Portland, I recall hearing tales of a mysterious stone structure in Macleay Park (within the larger Forest Park) where satanists and ghosts hang out—a sort of social club for the freaky and the undead. I made a trip to this place—the "Witch's Castle," or the "Stone House"—one February Sunday.

Based on its ominous name and the vague rumors I'd heard years back, I was expecting to find the house tucked away in a dark corner at the end of a poorly maintained park trail. I figured I'd wind up lost, wandering in circles for hours, and then magically the building would appear in front of me. Inside, a bubbling cauldron would no doubt be waiting.

In reality, the Stone House sits beside the popular trail, on a small hill overlooking a stream. Even in broad daylight it is freaky-looking. All that is left of the second floor is a ceilingless husk covered in moss, with faded red paint covering spots on a wall. The oddest detail: a bent safety bar. Who or what did this? Your guess is as good as mine, but my money is on a sledgehammer. A small doorway downstairs leads to a dark room covered in graffiti and broken glass. At some point, someone had used it as a hobo hostel.

According to Portland Parks and Recreation, the house's lease was never in the hands of a kiddie-chomping witch or a depraved recluse; it was a restroom built by the Works Progress Administration during the Depression. Over the decades it was heavily vandalized, and out of service since the 1962 Columbus Day storm that ravaged it. —*Brandon Hartley*

Saucer Celebration in McMinnville

Sometimes when a local legend brings recognition to an area, enterprising individuals will capitalize on it in ways that also become legendary. A case in point: McMinnville's annual UFO Festival. The Trent flying saucer photos (see the Unexplained Phenomena chapter) are a huge source of civic pride in town. Considered milestones of ufology, the photos' importance to the community is most evident during this two-day event, held in mid- to late May.

Attending the UFO Festival for the first time may be a little intimidating. At first glance, it appears that McMinnville is in the midst of a full-scale space invasion. Heed the immortal advice of novelist Douglas Adams: Don't

panic! Chances are that the scores of aliens (and men in black) milling about are just human partygoers in costume. The UFOs cruising down Third Street are probably just parade floats. The familiar tune in the air is most likely coming from human musicians, not the *Star Wars* cantina band. The festival attracts a wide assortment of attendees, ranging from true believers to skeptics, and all manner of fun seekers in between. And we can't entirely discount the presence of a real alien or two.

The festival originated in 2000, when Oregon's well-known pub-and-hotel outfit McMenamins celebrated the fiftieth anniversary of the Trent photos at the Hotel Oregon. Locals and tourists attended in droves. The first party was such a success that it was embraced as an annual event. The city leadership soon realized the profit potential and expanded on the UFO Festival with a city-sponsored event called Alien Daze.

Now most local businesses join in the festivities, adorning their storefronts with alien- and UFO-themed decorations. The Mack Theater holds screenings of sci-fi movies and awards "Alien Oscars." Local restaurants sell "ice cold alienade," while snack stands offer "alien ears." Ironically, a Mutual UFO Network member at the festival, taking issue with the word *weird*, chided us for "trivializing" the UFO phenomenon by writing about it in this book!

Despite the abundance of whimsical references to little green men, the festival also caters to serious enthusiasts. McMenamins arranges lectures by well-known UFO experts, as well as documentary screenings.

The event even attracts those whose primary interests lie elsewhere within the unexplained. While scoping out the goings-on, we spent quite some time speaking with two members of the Oregon Bigfoot Society. Their assessment of the festival? Weird . . . in a good way!

McMENAMINS 5TH ANNUAL
2004
UFO FEST
ufofest.com
confidential

Friday, May 14
& Saturday,
May 15

HOTEL OREGON

FRIDAY EVENTS
FREE AND OPEN TO ALL AGES
UNLESS OTHERWISE NOTED.

UFO EXHIBIT HALL
5 P.M. TO 7 P.M. & 9 P.M. TO 11 P.M.

SPEAKER'S FORUM
WITH BUDD HOPKINS
& ERIC BYLER
7 P.M. TO 9 P.M. • $7 PER PERSON.........

SPEAKER'S RECEPTION & BOOK SIGNING
9 P.M. TO 11 P.M.

Featured Speakers
**BUDD
HOPKINS**
INTERNATIONALLY RENOWNED
UFO ABDUCTION RESEARCHER

ERIC BYLER
OREGON UFO REVIEW

SATURDAY EVENTS
FREE AND OPEN TO ALL AGES UNLESS OTHERWISE NOTED........

UFO EXHIBIT HALL • 10 A.M. TO 5 P.M.

ALIEN ABDUCTION WORKSHOP
& TRENT CASE DOCUMENTARY • 10:30 A.M. TO 12:30 P.M.

3RD ANNUAL UFO COSTUME PARADE • 1 P.M.

WILLAMETTE RADIO WORKSHOP
PERFORMING 2 EPISODES OF FLASH GORDON • 2:30 P.M.

ALIEN COSTUME BALL • WITH REGGAE BY 1 & 1 • 8 P.M. TO MIDNIGHT • 21 & OVER ONLY.....

UFO LODGING PACKAGE AT HOTEL OREGON
INCLUDES LODGING FOR TWO, ADMISSION TO THE SPEAKER'S FORUM AND ALIEN COSTUME BALL, AND BREAKFAST THE
FOLLOWING MORNING. $139 TO $155 PER COUPLE. CALL (503) 472-8427 FOR RESERVATIONS.

McMENAMINS HOTEL OREGON
310 N.E. Evans • McMinnville, Oregon • (503) 472-8427 • ufofest.com
no. 125 • 4/13/04

McMENAMINS SIXTH ANNUAL
ufo festival

All events are at Hotel Oregon and are free,
unless otherwise noted.

FRIDAY, MAY 13, 2005
Speaker's Forum with Keynote Speaker Dr. Roger Leir
and Terry Halstead's Trent Case Documentary
Mack Theater • 7 p.m. to 9 p.m. • $7 per person

Live music with SNEAKIN' OUT
7 p.m. to 10 p.m.

Speaker Reception and Book Signing • 9:30 p.m.

SATURDAY, MAY 14, 2005
Live music with JACKSTRAW, kids
UFO Exhibitor Tent
activities and more
10 a.m. to 8 p.m.

UFO Workshop with Dr. Roger Leir and
Peter Davenport • 10:30 a.m. to 12:30 p.m.
$7 per person

3rd Annual UFO Costume Parade
Historic Downtown McMinnville • 1 p.m.

Willamette Radio Workshop Performance
Mack Theater • 3:00 p.m.

TheUFOStore.com Film Festival
2 p.m. to 5 p.m.

Alien Costume Ball with GAYLE FORCE AND
THE WINDBREAKERS
8 p.m. • 21 and over

Tickets & lodging packages available

ufofest.com
McMENAMINS HOTEL OREGON
310 N.E. Evans • McMinnville, Oregon • (503) 472-8427

---

mcmenamins
**9th annual
UFO
Festival**

**SCREENING OF
STAR DREAMS
& Q&A**

with
Robert Nichol
**SATURDAY,
MAY 17, 2008**
Doors at 9 a.m.
Screening at 9:30 a.m.

$10 per person
All ages welcome

McMinnville
Community Center
325 N.E. Third St.
McMinnville, OR

ufofest.com

Weird Science on the Oregon Coast

Beachconnection.net, an Oregon coast tourism Web site, offers a look at several oddities along the shore. Among our favorites are the following items with a scientific bent.

Ghost Forests

Proposal Rock is a forest-topped sea stack in the tiny beachfront community of Neskowin (fifteen miles north of Lincoln City). The basalt giant, an undisturbed natural haven for sea birds, serves equally well as backdrop for an adjacent natural attraction. Appearing on the beach only during minus tides are the remains of an ancient forest, two thousand to five thousand years old. The sitka spruce trees, which stood majestically so many eons ago, are reduced to rocklike stumps, choked with seaweed and barnacles.

Another similar ghost forest can be found in Arch Cape, on the northern Oregon coast. Geologists have carbon dated these particular stumps to about four thousand years. Along with sitka spruce there are the remains of cedar and perhaps redwood trees.

Geologists have developed a sound theory on how the ghost forests came to be. They surmise that about four thousand years ago, coastal sand rose so rapidly that the trees were buried and protected from conditions that would normally cause decay. Geologic shifting may have also dropped the forests about two dozen feet. Their reappearance in recent years has worried a few locals, as it may indicate increasing land erosion.

Singing Sand

Then there's the strange cacophony of "singing" sand. Sands in the Oregon Dunes National Recreation Area (see the Ancient Mysteries chapter) and near Cannon Beach can make a singing or violinlike noise when stepped on or otherwise rubbed together.

The squeaking sound happens on some stretches of sand that have recently dried, mostly within one hundred feet or so from the shore. Grain size, density, shape, and other factors contribute to the particular tone of the "singing."

Remember, kids: Just because it's weird doesn't mean it can't be educational!

The Green Flash

The "green flash" at sunset along the coast is a relatively frequent event. According to Beachconnection.net, "The green flash is defined as a small, greenish blob you see just above the setting sun, just a second or so before it dips away below the horizon. Certain conditions must exist for you to see it, mainly that it is clear, with no clouds or fog, between you and the horizon." The flash is essentially an airborne mirage caused by the refraction of light from the sun at the horizon through layers of moist air. Because green and blue light are at the tail end of the visible spectrum, and because green light is easiest to perceive, we see it for a little longer than the rest of the spectrum of setting sunlight.

Battlefield Oregon

Japan's attack on the U. S. Navy at Pearl Harbor, Hawaii, marked America's entry into World War II. Immediately after December 7, 1941, Americans were hot for revenge, and they got their first taste of it on April 18, 1942. The Doolittle Raid, named after its strategist and leader, Lt. Col. James Doolittle, involved sixteen B-25 bombers striking military and industrial targets in several Japanese cities, including Tokyo. At the time, the offensive was considered to be of little tactical advantage; its main goal, which it achieved, was to boost American morale.

Planned as a one-way operation, the planes had been launched from an aircraft carrier 650 miles from the Japanese coast. (Lacking fuel capacity to return to the carrier, most of the planes were crash-landed in China or Russia.)

The United States would later realize that the raid garnered some strategic significance, after all. The Japanese, surprised by the attack, assumed that the United States had developed a new kind of long-range bomber. As a result, they reassigned many of their fighter planes to protect the home islands, limiting their air capabilities elsewhere.

Japanese leaders staged retaliatory strikes, without combat aircraft, on the American mainland—three of them in Oregon. They all became unlikely historical milestones.

The Shelling of Fort Stevens

Shortly after the Doolittle Raid, Japan sent two submarines to disrupt shipping along the western United States and Alaska. One of them, named I-25, torpedoed a freighter off Neah Bay, Washington, and then proceeded south. At about 11:30 P.M. on Sunday, June 21, 1942, the sub's commander, Meiji Tagami, ordered his crew to fire on Fort Stevens.

As the submarine's huge deck gun boomed, pandemonium broke out in the fort. Maj. Robert Huston, the senior officer in charge, realized that almost all of the incoming shells were landing harmlessly on the beach or in the surrounding marshland. Major Huston figured that even if the submarine were in range (which it was, but a hasty assessment suggested it wasn't), why shoot back and give the Japanese a better idea of where to aim? So he never gave the order to return fire.

In all, submarine I-25 fired at Fort Stevens seventeen times before departing in a westerly direction just before midnight. The most significant damage it did was nicking some phone cables that later rusted and had to be replaced. Shortly after, the sub suffered from a fatal case of mistaken identity (see "Aquatic Anomalies: The Tragedy of Tommy Turtle" in the Beaver State Beasts chapter). The short-lived attack on Fort Stevens was the only assault on a military base in the continental United States during World War II, the first since the War of 1812.

Firebombing the Klamath Mountains

Submarine I-25 returned to the Oregon coast later that year, on the foggy morning of September 9. The new Japanese tactic was to create a national emergency that would panic Americans and, hopefully, divert priorities and resources from the war. A massive forest fire might produce

pandemonium, and the Klamath Mountains, in Oregon's southwestern corner, were chosen as the site.

A small seaplane was launched from the submarine. Pilot Nobuo Fujita flew about five miles inland toward Mount Emily and dropped an incendiary bomb on Wheeler Ridge. Howard Gardner, a local forest ranger, heard the explosion and noticed the plane, then filed a report at a ranger station. However, his report was dismissed, as it was common for military patrols to fly over the area.

When the fog lifted later that morning, Gardner and a coworker found a circle of smoldering forest about fifty to seventy-five feet wide, complete with fused earth, melted rock, and a crater measuring three feet in diameter in the center.

The Forest Service had thought the crater had been caused by a lightning strike until they noticed fragments of bomb casing and thermite pellets scattered around and embedded in surrounding trees. Even so, they reasoned that the bomb had to have been accidentally dropped from an American plane. The military soon confirmed otherwise and tried in vain to suppress news reports of the incident. They needn't have worried: The first bombing of the continental United States by an enemy aircraft only strengthened America's—and Oregon's—resolve. The site of the bombing was added to the National Register of Historic Places in 2006.

The plot to start a massive fire never did succeed. Nobuo Fujita flew a second firebombing mission later that month. It failed too.

BALLOON BOMB'S MECHANISM

BAG - 34 ft. IN DIAMETER

FLASH-BOMB TO DESTROY BAG AFTER DESCENT

MECHANISM WHICH RELEASES BALLAST BAGS AND BOMBS IN SEQUENCE.

BALLOON'S MECHANICAL "BRAIN."

BOMB WHICH DESTROYS WHOLE DEVICE ON CONTACT WITH GROUND.

INCENDIARY BOMB

ANTI-PERSONNEL BOMB

A Seattle artist's sketch from a description of the balloons which the Japanese are launching by the hundreds from their home islands against continental United States. They take an average of four days to make the crossing and the direction and height is controlled by an ingenious device that releases sand bags or gas upon reaching a certain low level and a complex mechanism that drops incendiary and anti-personnel bombs when the balloons have traveled a certain distance. A great amount of meteorological study was put into the aerial devices, which have done little harm and taken a very limited number of lives. If you see a balloon of this type or a mechanism of this general appearance, remain at a distance and telephone authorities. (International)

Balloon Bomb Tragedy at Gearhart Mountain

On May 5, 1945, Pastor Archie Mitchell drove east of Bly with his wife, Elsie, and several children from his Sunday school class (ages eleven to fourteen), intent on fishing and picnicking near Gearhart Mountain. Elsie, who was five months pregnant, exited the car with the children and walked off into the woods while Pastor Mitchell parked. Moments later, as Pastor Mitchell was walking up to meet them, Elsie called out, "Look what we found, dear!" Almost immediately, a gut-wrenching explosion killed her, their unborn child, and five youngsters in their charge. A stunned Pastor Mitchell drove back to Bly to report the incident.

What the unfortunate group had found was the latest—and weirdest—weapon in Japan's arsenal: the Fu-Go, or balloon bomb. Fu-Gos consisted of a large, spherical balloon, about a hundred feet in diameter, made of impermeable mulberry paper and filled with hydrogen. Tethered beneath it were thermite bombs and other high explosives.

The method of delivering Fu-Gos to their intended target was particularly innovative for the time. The Japanese did early research in meteorology and were the first to discover the jet stream, a series of fast-traveling easterly air currents about six to nine miles above Earth. The Fu-Gos traveled along the jet stream toward North America. A series of sandbags were used as ballast; an altimeter triggered electric charges that would drop them, two by two, if the Fu-Go dropped below a certain altitude. The intent was for the balloons to descend in North America, with bombs exploding as they hit the ground.

Fortunately, Fu-Gos were unreliable, as there was no way to guarantee where the bombs landed or that they would explode. Of about nine hundred Fu-Gos intended for the United States, only about a third of those have been accounted for; the rest were probably lost at sea.

The relative lack of public awareness of the balloon bombs is due to government efforts at playing down their threat. The news media briefly covered the incidents, but the federal government quickly discouraged any further reports. They did not want Japan getting the impression that the Fu-Gos were in any way effective, especially since

they could so easily be adapted to biowarfare. That bit of strategic censorship worked, and Japan phased out its Fu-Go program.

The relative ineffectiveness of the Fu-Gos lends an especially sad and random tone to the deaths of Elsie Mitchell and the children. They were simply investigating an unfamiliar object and accidentally triggered the bomb. Curiosity made all the difference in what had essentially been a failed bid to spread terror. Today, a bronze plaque on a stone marker at the site serves as a monument to the victims, the only people killed by enemy actions in the continental United States during World War II. It is located in the Mitchell Recreation Area, a small picnic ground adjacent to Leonard Creek.

Portland's Pinball Wars

Until recent decades, Portland was known as a hotbed of vice. Even the 1948 election of Mayor Dorothy "No Sin" Lee, a zealous reformer, did little to dent the city's long-established illegal businesses. The problem was that many local officials, especially within law enforcement, were all too willing to accept hush money from the Rose City's underworld.

Gambling was big business back then, and at the time, pinball machines were considered gambling devices on par with slot machines. The bars and clubs used them as games of chance in the same way a modern-day football pool might be operated: Participants would wager on whether a player could achieve a specific goal, such as winning free games or lighting up certain combinations on the backglass. Some pinball machines could be mechanized for record keeping and making the odds of a payoff adjustable.

A notable rivalry emerged between two racketeers over pinball machines. Their story was reinvigorated in 2001 by *Portland Tribune* columnist Phil Stanford. He later compiled several articles detailing their "pinball wars" in his book *Portland Confidential.*

Jim Elkins and Stan Terry had both been bootleggers during Prohibition and both had moved on to coin machines, distributing their slot and pinball machines to various clubs in the area. Between them, they dominated the local market, Elkins in Portland and Terry elsewhere throughout Multnomah County. "Pinball King" Terry had the edge in the 1940s, and Elkins was determined to dethrone Terry by just about any means.

At various times, Elkins's hired thugs visited gambling dens to vandalize, burglarize, or outright steal Terry's machines. Terry didn't seem fazed. Business was good, and not even these setbacks prevented him from expanding his operation.

By 1954, Elkins was exasperated with Terry's resilience. He met in Seattle with a few criminal confederates and cooked up a more refined solution. They organized a pinball owners' association, the Coin Machine Men of Oregon, affiliated with the Teamsters union. This was a calculated move designed to deny Terry membership, thus putting him at odds with the Teamsters.

In early 1955, the Teamsters picketed the Mt. Hood Café—a Portland eatery—for hosting Terry's now "nonunion" pinball machines. The café's Teamster owner, in an uncomfortable position with his own union, faced dire financial consequences. Terry and Hy Goldbaum, a Las

Vegas "bill collector" of some renown, reached a financial settlement with the Teamster boss and the picket was quickly called off.

A few months later, possibly under duress from the Teamsters, Elkins sold Terry his share of Portland's pinball racket. Shortly thereafter, Herman "Bugsy" Burns, late of the Washington State Penitentiary, paid Elkins a visit. Bugsy had worked for him on and off, mostly delivering heroin between Portland and Seattle. Now, per Elkins's request, Bugsy brought along two friends from the hoosegow. Posing as deliverymen, the thugs schemed to steal all of Terry's machines: They would collect all Terry's "outdated" machines, ostensibly for newer models that would arrive later in the day. But before they could even pull off the job, Bugsy and his pals were arrested as they attempted to rob a supermarket.

In 1956, defeated and disliked, Elkins began ratting out Portland's organized-crime figures, including city officials and Teamsters. He provided enough material for a series of articles in the *Oregonian,* which resulted in Elkins, Terry, and others being subpoenaed to testify before the Senate Labor Rackets Committee. On the federal committee was an up-and-coming senator from Massachusetts named John F. Kennedy. His brother Robert was the committee's chief counsel.

Faced with ever-increasing scrutiny, Portland began cleaning up its reputation. Police suddenly started enforcing the city's pinball ban, technically in effect with Dorothy Lee's mayoral term. Terry briefly petitioned to overturn the ban, but the Supreme Court upheld it. Terry phased out his pinball empire and, like Elkins, focused on other illicit enterprises.

By the 1970s, pinball had mostly overcome its seedy reputation, and by the 1980s, the new kids in town— video games—almost completely overshadowed pinball. Before too long, rumors began spreading about one video game in particular—a rare and sinister coin-op that purportedly ruined more lives around Portland than pinball ever did . . .

From Pinball King to Patriotic Shepherd

In 1967, years after his reign as Multnomah County's Pinball King, Stan Terry fell off a ladder and fractured his skull. After recovering, some who knew him swore that it affected his personality, making him more of a character than he already was. Now, with an appetite for politics, he ran—unsuccessfully—for mayor of Portland, among other city, county, and state offices. Terry was disqualified as a mayoral candidate because he was not a Portland resident.

A few locals still relate other Stan Terry stunts, such as this one: After getting into a land-use dispute with the city of Lake Oswego, Terry bought a flock of sheep; dyed them red, white, and blue; and let them graze on his property. Soon, the unmistakable odor of sheep manure permeated downtown Lake Oswego. When the city and neighbors complained, Terry sportively explained that he was only expressing his patriotism. Eventually, he and the city came to an agreement and the sheep—colors, smell, and all—were removed.

The Purported Perils of Polybius

While early video games like Space Invaders, Pong, and Pac-Man are familiar to most people, hardly anyone remembers Polybius.

A scant few descriptions of the game have turned up over the years. Most amount to little more than vague memories of an abstract shooting game released around 1981. The graphics, cutting-edge at the time, should have garnered it more recognition, but the games appeared in only a few Portland-area arcades (possibly in Beaverton and Hillsboro). Official-looking men in black suits were said to stand silently within sight of the machines, observing players. On occasion, they would access the machines to collect data rather than quarters—precisely what kind of data, nobody seems to know.

Why was a possibly state-of-the-art game so poorly distributed, and why were mysterious agents keeping watch over it?

Whispers soon circulated that Polybius was an experimental mind-control device. A few minutes of zapping enemies would trigger a special strobe light and/or on-screen activity designed to disrupt the player's brain waves. Teenagers allegedly became unwitting guinea pigs for some sort of conspiratorial psi-war research. Many wound up, it was said, either amnesic, catatonic, or hopelessly insane.

Rational explanations were offered: Polybius was really a prototype of Tempest, a game that fits the hazy descriptions of Polybius rather well. Tempest was released by Atari in

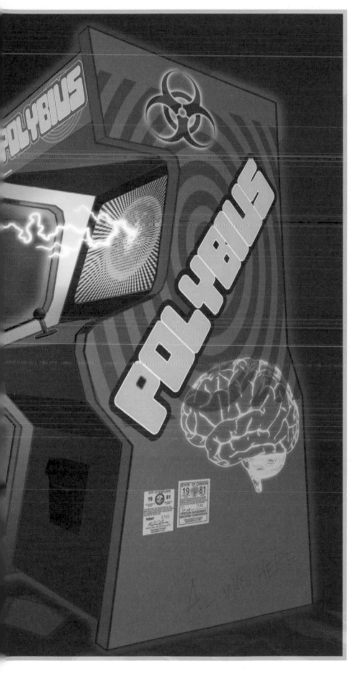

1981, using a new video technology composed of strange, angular objects flipping and crawling at a furious pace across geometric playing fields.

The theory went that, while playing Tempest's supposed prototype, an epileptic youth had a seizure from staring at the colorful video mayhem. This speculation is valid only insofar as strong visual stimuli are indeed known to trigger epileptic seizures. Word of the incident may have spread, eventually developing into the rumor of a mind-control experiment.

A few years ago, a person calling himself Steven Roach offered another explanation via the Internet. He claimed to have cofounded a German software company, hired by a South American firm, to develop a video game that would showcase an advanced proprietary graphics technology. According to Roach, the game was test-marketed in the Portland area because of demographics. Company representatives briefly hung around to evaluate player reactions to Polybius, explaining where the stories of "men in black" came from.

It's highly doubtful that a game developer would release a prototype to arcades for "testing" purposes. And why would South American and German business partners test-market a game in Portland instead of somewhere closer to home?

Rare and mysterious—and possibly nonexistent—Polybius has captured the imaginations of many gamers over the years. Pictures of a purported arcade cabinet and a single image of the supposed title screen have made the rounds but have been met with some skepticism. At least one independent Polybius "remake" has been produced, either from memory or the creators' own impression of what the game could have been like. The legend has even inspired a low-budget independent film titled *VectorZone.*

Maybe Polybius really existed. Maybe it really was a sinister mind-control device. On the other hand, maybe it's just a fictional cautionary tale devised by some misguided crusader, the video game equivalent of heavy metal music leading to teen suicide, or comic books causing juvenile delinquency.

The overriding message of the legend is clear enough: Video games will fry your brain.

Of Treasure and Tragedy: The Blue Bucket Mine

In 1848, the discovery of gold in California triggered a westward rush of highly competitive prospectors. Many of them also ventured north into Oregon, where their search for gold sometimes paid off. To a group of settlers who headed west just three years earlier, the prospectors' success provided a disappointing epiphany: The fight for survival during their westward migration probably caused them to walk away from a fortune without even realizing it. Their story spread quickly and initiated the enduring legend of the Blue Bucket Mine.

In 1845, a four-hundred-person wagon train left Iowa for Oregon. After 1,500 miles of hard travel in ox-drawn wagons, the migrants arrived at the Malheur River at the Idaho-Oregon border. The exodus had been rough: Several oxen died en route from blood poisoning, as did a physician, Dr. Fisher, who got sick after examining one of the carcasses. Their hard journey would only get worse.

As with other groups of migrants, their plan was to take the Oregon Trail northwest along the Columbia River to The Dalles. Stephen Meek, a mountain guide hired by the immigrants in Montana or Idaho, insisted that he knew of a better route, located south of the main branch of the Oregon Trail. Roughly half of the wagons split off to try his supposed shortcut across the Cascade Mountains.

For more than a week, the migrants moved westward along the Malheur River and across the rocky bluffs beyond. West of Castle Rock, the journey became substantially harder. The oxen and wagons could barely handle the terrain, and the pioneers found themselves in the desert. Meek led them to Malheur and Harney Lakes, which he knew of from an earlier trip. Unfortunately, both lakes were mostly dry, and the brackish water that remained was fit for neither human nor animal. The people had little choice but to press on.

Farther along in the Harney Valley, several oxen wandered off. A three-man scouting team went searching for them. The oxen were found near a small freshwater spring. Thrilled at having found drinkable water, the men filled a few blue wooden buckets to take back with them. They also found some peculiar rocks clumped together in one spot in the spring. As an afterthought, they grabbed around fifteen to twenty of them to show their fellow travelers. Their shiny yellow hue looked almost metallic.

They were just lumps of copper, concluded a few of the travelers who handled the samples, nothing important. Asked how many such rocks there were, one of the discoverers said at least enough to fill one of their blue buckets. The spring was used until it turned to mud, and the group moved on, taking only a few of the "copper" nuggets.

Misfortune, disease, and death continued plaguing the pioneers as they struggled to find their way. Morale diminished, tempers flared, and Stephen Meek (below) escaped a lynching only by the grace of a few level heads. Fearing for his life, he eventually took off alone to find help.

In the end, the survivors reached The Dalles without further assistance from Meek. All told, the trip took well more than a month, and twenty-three people of all ages succumbed to illness, malnutrition, and dehydration along the way. A fair number of oxen and other livestock shared a similar fate. Most of the survivors recuperated in The Dalles. Some settled there, and others continued on, far more cautiously, to other areas. All were doubtlessly glad to put their hellish journey behind them.

After all the hardships the travelers suffered, the gold rush of 1848 must have seemed like one last kick in the pants from Lady Fate. Some of the wagon train survivors began wondering if the "copper" they came across was something more valuable. The matter was put to rest by Dr. Fisher's widow, who had kept one of the rocks as a souvenir.

Upon examination, it was found to indeed be gold.

Many of the pioneers, along with other prospectors, ventured back to the site, on a tributary of the John Day River, to search for the so-called Blue Bucket Mine. (Gold mania of the day had inflated rumors of a few nuggets into an entire mine.)

The influx of prospecting to the area helped tame the Meek Cutoff, as the arduous route came to be known. It became a viable route for travelers as camps and other resources sprouted up. Ultimately, it paved the way for settlements in eastern Oregon.

Other than what the pioneers found during their migration, no other yield has come from the site. This does not eliminate the possibility that unknown members of the wagon party clandestinely returned for the gold themselves, or that the later prospectors didn't look in the right place. In fact, gold was found farther east in the 1860s, which may lend credence to the stories.

While the truth about the Blue Bucket Mine is technically lost to history, its legend endures, both as a symbol of financial optimism and as a tribute to perseverance under the most challenging of circumstances.

Cetacean Detonation Frustration

Wikipedia defines *viral videos* as "video clip content which gains widespread popularity through the process of Internet sharing." Distributed via Web sites, e-mail, and other means, these often funny clips have become a common, even legendary, Internet phenomenon. One such video, a news story from Portland TV station KATU, has become an all-time classic and was the fifth most-watched viral video in 2006 according to a BBC study. Shot by cameraman Doug Brazil and featuring reporter Paul Linnman, it chronicles a whale of an error in judgment.

It happened on November 12, 1970. A few days earlier, an eight-ton, nearly forty-six-foot-long, and very dead gray whale had washed ashore in the coastal town of Florence. Locals considered it an interesting novelty, but the stench of rotting flesh was becoming too much to bear. After some discussion, responsibility for its disposal was foisted on the Oregon Highway Division, whose officials were as confused as anyone about how to get rid of it. A clever plan—or so they thought—was devised after consulting with the navy.

In the video, Linnman, standing near the enormous dead mammal, elaborates: "The Highway Division decided the carcass couldn't be buried because it might soon be uncovered [by the changing tide]. It couldn't be cut up and then buried, because nobody wanted to cut it up, and it couldn't be burned. So dynamite it was, some twenty cases,

or a half ton of it." The dynamite was positioned on the side of the whale opposite the ocean, the intent being to blow most of it out to sea. Presumably, seagulls would scavenge the small bits that would be left over, making for a relatively easy cleanup.

Curious spectators were moved to sand dunes a quarter of a mile away to avoid injury. Meanwhile, George Thornton, the lead engineer in charge of the project, expressed confidence in the Highway Division's explosive strategy. He cautioned, however, that it might take a second detonation to finish the job.

Observers and Highway Division employees held their collective breath as the seconds ticked down. . . .

In the video, a large cloud of misty red sand suddenly engulfs the whale, followed by a thundering boom. Indeed, at this point it's the audio that's most telling. Cheers are heard, but they abruptly stop. It takes but a second to realize the implications of the repeating splats and the sounds of grossed-out, panic-stricken bystanders. As Linnman alliteratively put it, "the blast blasted blubber beyond all believable bounds!"

Smelly whale giblets of all sizes rained down on Florence, spattering fleeing onlookers and smashing a parked car well beyond the supposed quarter-mile "safe zone." The area quickly became a disgusting, stinky mess.

To make matters worse, George Thornton's caveat came true: Half a ton of dynamite just didn't cut it. Huge chunks of whale were left on the beach. That they were too big for the seagulls to carry off was a moot point; the gulls were nowhere in sight, scared off by the explosion. The remaining pieces had to be buried after all. The only silver lining to this whole fiasco was that, remarkably, nobody was hurt.

As Linnman dryly put it, "It might be concluded that should a whale ever wash ashore in Lane County again, those in charge will not only remember *what* to do, they'll certainly remember what *not* to do." Nine years later, a pod of forty one dead sperm whales washed ashore nearby. This time they were burned and, tide be damned, buried.

Thanks to KATU's news report, the dead disintegrated whale achieved immortality. Dubbed tapes of the broadcast circulated for years, and in 1990 humorist Dave Barry wrote a column about it, sarcastically suggesting that we ought to "get hold of the folks at the Oregon State Highway Division and ask them . . . to give us an estimate on the U.S. Capitol." The essay struck a chord with readers and was itself widely circulated. Meanwhile, someone digitized the video and posted it on an electronic bulletin board. From there, it jumped onto the Internet. The exploding whale had hit the big time.

And so, too, did Paul Linnman, who has become inexorably linked with the incident. A few years back, he was interviewed by BBC News when a dead whale exploded in Taiwan (from natural causes). Once, while in Newport doing a news segment on Keiko the whale (from the movie *Free Willy*), his presence apparently caused some anxiety. "You're the person who blows them up," an elderly lady accused him. "What are you doing here?"

As he commented to *Weird Oregon,* "I've learned to live with the whale since it has come up, in one way or another, every day for nearly thirty-seven years now!" Linnman's firsthand account of this most messy miscalculation can be found in his memoir, titled *The Exploding Whale: And Other Remarkable Stories from the Evening News.*

Of Glowing Sand and Brown Blobs

From sea monsters to blocks of wax washing ashore, the Oregon coast has long hosted a variety of strange goings-on. The advantage to enthusiasts is that, whether or not you come across something truly weird, the coast is always worth visiting for its "normal" merits. Still, one bit of weirdness there may be closer than you think—just look down.

If you're lucky, you might see a legendary coastal phenomenon: glowing sand. That's right—your footsteps may ever so briefly light up the sand around your feet with a blue-green glow! (Naturally, this is best seen at night.)

How does this happen? Are there supernatural forces at work? Is it magic? Actually, no; there is a scientific explanation. Technically, it's not even the sand that glows.

Phytoplankton are microscopic marine plants at the very bottom of the food chain. They are eaten by small fish, which are in turn eaten by bigger fish, and so on. They are also a key part of whales' diets. Phytoplankton survive through the process of photosynthesis. Like larger plants, they absorb light and carbon dioxide, and float near the water's surface where both are most available. Waves sometimes wash ashore billions of phytoplankton, where they remain in the wet sand.

One kind of phytoplankton—the dinoflagellate—is bioluminescent, generating light through a chemical process. With sufficient darkness, you can even see them glowing in the water. When the dinoflagellates in the sand are disturbed by an outside force—say, a foot stepping on them—they light up for a fraction of a second.

These flashes have given rise to the legend of the glowing sand.

An overabundance of phytoplankton can be evident (in the daytime) by another phenomenon they produce: brown rustlike streaks in the water. As waves crash ashore, the overly plentiful phytoplankton will often remain on the beach as large "blobs" of brown foam. They're known to confound tourists, who sometimes wonder if they are looking at an oil spill.

Both phenomena can be observed anywhere along the coast; it's really a matter of being in the right place at the right time. In recent years, however, beaches around Seaside and Lincoln City have been especially inundated with phytoplankton.

Vortex I: The Governor's Pot Party

In the 1960s, social and political upheaval and the Vietnam War brought American culture to a boiling point. Young people rejected traditional values, embraced drug use and communal lifestyles, and repeatedly confronted the stewards of what they believed was an unjust government. By 1969, seminal events like the Woodstock Music and Art Fair in upstate New York seemed to suggest that the counterculture's momentum was unstoppable.

In truth, however, the era of hippies and flower children was waning fast. That year, the Manson murders and the Rolling Stones' Altamont free concert, at which four attendees died, called attention to what many saw as the dangerous, radical side of youth culture.

In addition, the spirit of protest, or the contention that peace and justice were worth fighting for, often took a back seat to sex, drugs, and rock 'n' roll. Oregon governor Tom McCall was banking on that "front-seat triumvirate" in 1970, as Portland was preparing to host an American Legion convention in late August.

McCall knew that the People's Army Jamboree, a coalition of local antiwar groups, was planning mass protests around the city during the convention. This was due to a planned keynote speech by President Richard Nixon, as well as the convention's "Victory in Viet Nam" theme. The FBI informed Governor McCall of the potentially volatile situation, in which an estimated fifty thousand protesters and twenty-five thousand Legionnaires would likely confront one another on the streets of Portland.

In May of that same year, a protest at Portland State University had turned ugly when police in riot gear clashed with students. The last thing McCall wanted was for the summer of 1970 to be bookended by violence in Portland. Meeting with McCall, some members of the People's Army

Jamboree suggested that a free music festival might help to defuse tensions and mitigate the number of protesters. In a risky move for the Republican governor, McCall agreed to sponsor such a festival, suspecting he was sacrificing his political future in the process.

Paying tribute to Oregon's environmental sensibilities, the event was dubbed "Vortex I: A Biodegradable Festival of Life." The venue, Milo McIver State Park, was forty miles from Portland, (hopefully) a safe enough distance from which to keep the peace. Leaving nothing to chance, McCall personally—and heavily—promoted the festival on TV.

It worked. Between fifty thousand and one hundred thousand would-be war protesters made their way to "the governor's pot party" near Estacada. There, they were rewarded with laissez-faire enforcement of drug and decency laws, and lots of rock music.

In Portland, only about a thousand benign dissenters were in attendance for Nixon's last-minute cancellation.

Many local veterans of the Age of Aquarius consider Vortex I the definitive hippie event. In some ways, it was more grassroots than Woodstock, despite the irony of being the only state-sponsored music festival in U.S. history. There were no big-name performances; all the talent was strictly local. Plus, unlike Woodstock, which took place in a muddy field, Vortex I was held in a lush park.

Far from damaging his political career, Vortex I became the first of several innovative efforts credited to Governor McCall. He was easily reelected for a second term and was noted for his work in ecology. McCall later gained some notoriety by saying in a CBS News interview, "Come visit us again and again . . . but for heaven's sake, don't move here to live!"

Ancient Mysteries

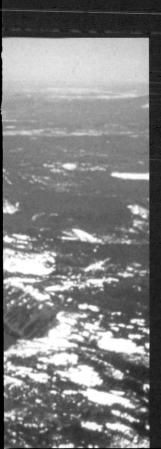

People have lived in Oregon for tens of thousands of years, and Native American traditions tell of many ancient events. The native people saw the earth change as Mount Mazama, one of their highest mountains, became Crater Lake. They camped at Fort Rock more than ten thousand years ago, leaving behind the oldest sandals in the world, and they likely explored Crack in the Ground, a two-mile-long gouge in bedrock, cut thousands of years ago. They saw avalanches block the Columbia River, as well as giant floods cut through the Columbia River Gorge, transporting boulders like the Willamette Meteorite from Montana to West Linn, Oregon.

On the Oregon coast, another mystery surrounds the fate of the disappearing multiton Port Orford Meteorite, which some people claim was a hoax. Not far away, modern tourists play along a forty-mile stretch of sand dunes where there is no desert . . . and they scale monkey-faced cliffs and meditate on balancing rocks, proving that what's old is "new" and relevant again.

rater Lake

Many years ago, before the world changed and the present age of man began, there were two gods, Skell and Lao. Skell lived above ground, on the highest mountain in the world. Lao lived in the world of darkness, below ground. One day the two began a war as Lao began digging upward through Skell's mountain, trying to reach the world of light. The war ended when Lao burst into the light, chasing Skell away. But in his triumph, Lao's last burst of energy caused the mountain to collapse, burying him under the ground again.

The above is a Native American legend explaining how Crater Lake was formed. Its true origin is based on a cataclysmic volcanic eruption around 5600 B.C., but the lake still holds within it some modern-day ancient mysteries. The Old Man of the Lake isn't a ghost or a monster lurking in the nearby woods. It is actually a famous tree stump.

The Old Man of the Lake is more than thirty feet long. He floats vertically, with his upper end sticking out of the water. Because of the lake's intense cold, the oversized stump has been preserved remarkably well—visitors first noticed it well more than a century ago. The stump is not rooted, so it floats all around Crater Lake. Boat operators often radio one another its location so as to avoid any mini-*Titanic* incidents.

In 1988, a submarine explored the depths of Crater Lake. Since a floating thirty-foot-long tree trunk could cause damage to a submerged craft, the Old Man of the Lake was tied down along the shoreline during the submarine's exploration. Soon after its binding, the tree became unthethered in intense storms, free to roam again.

Crater Lake Lodge

The construction of Crater Lake Lodge happened only seconds ago . . . in geologic terms. But it's been around more than long enough for it to accumulate its own store of ghostly lore. Crater Lake Lodge was built in 1915, and the huge log hotel was an immediate sensation because of its wild setting.

Unfortunately for the lodge, the workers took some shortcuts when they built it. They used logs instead of stone or concrete, for the foundation. During the Great Depression, the logs began rotting. Over time, the high beams of the roof began sagging under annual snow accumulations. In 1989, the lodge was condemned to close, but at the last minute, Congress provided monies to renovate the decrepit structure. After six years of work, the lodge was reopened in 1995.

A few years ago, one couple spent a few nights in the lodge and had unusual experiences. They had never stayed there before, nor had they heard anything spooky or strange about the place. All the same, when they were shown to their room on the third floor of the west wing, both husband and wife felt a strange presence. They did not see or hear anything out of the ordinary, but both felt a frightening, overwhelming presence surrounding them. After a sleepless night, they demanded a new room. But they left without complaint at the end of their stay.

The manager never admitted that there was anything strange about the hotel. At the same time, he did not seem surprised at the request for a new room, nor did he ask for an explanation.

The World's Oldest Shoes

When the first migrant pioneers settled in the Lake County area of south-central Oregon, they noticed a strange formation. There, in a wide plain, they saw what looked like a giant stone fortress. It was round, more than 350 feet high in places, and nearly a mile in diameter. The rock was worn, with many cliffs and terraces, which looked like it had been eroded by water or waves. This was amazing to them in the dry desert plain. There was an opening on the southern side of the otherwise unbroken walls. The pioneers wondered about the origin of the citadel and were told conflicting tales: It could have been a giant's fortress or a

home to gods. Geologists studied the structure, pronouncing it a natural formation, but they did not know how important the site was for many more decades.

Sometime between 50,000 and 100,000 years ago, when North America was in the middle of its last ice age, Oregon's weather patterns were vastly different. The Great Basin is now desert, but at that time it received a lot more rainfall, which created a lake of nearly nine hundred square miles in central Oregon. The area around Fort Rock is a vast bowl, and it formed a lake about 150 feet deep. A volcanic eruption shot gases, ash, and jets of lava through the lake mud. The lava settled around the volcanic vent, forming a hollow ring around it.

Eventually, the climate became drier, and about thirteen thousand years ago, Fort Rock became an island in an increasingly shallower lake. Over a period of several thousand years, wind and water from the lake wore away the volcanic rock on the southern side, eventually creating an opening in the ring. By the time the American migrants arrived, the lake had turned into a dusty desert. Collectors picked through the Fort Rock formation, finding stone tools and bits of plants used by Native Americans.

In 1938, University of Oregon archaeologist Luther Cressman heard stories of the prehistoric remains around Fort Rock. He led a group of students to a cave on a small butte near Fort Rock. He and his students found more than a hundred sandals or fragments of sandals, woven from sagebrush bark. There was no radiocarbon dating at that time, but he noted that all of the sandals were covered by a thick coating of volcanic ash. This turned out to be ash from Mount Mazama, which, geologists guessed, had erupted about 7,600 years ago and was more than fifty miles away. This meant that the sandals and the people who'd worn them had camped at Fort Rock perhaps more than 8,000 years ago.

When radiocarbon dating was developed in the 1950s, Cressman wanted to date the sandals. Unfortunately, he had treated them with a chemical preservative, which made radiocarbon dating unreliable. Eventually Cressman obtained untreated fragments of the sandals, and came up with dates indicating that they are more than 9,000 years old. This made them the oldest footwear found in the world. A private collector had a pair of sandals from the Fort Rock area that dated to between 9,600 and 10,300 years old.

The Fort Rock formation and cave are part of Oregon's Fort Rock State Natural Area, and the cave itself has been designated a National Heritage site. It is located along Oregon State Highway 5, a few miles west of the town of Christmas Valley. There is no camping, though visitors are welcome to walk around the rock formation and use the picnic areas. At times, there is a park host who takes visitors on guided tours to the cave. For more information, visit the Oregon Parks and Recreation Department Web site (www.oregonstateparks.org), where you can find a link to the Fort Rock site.

Holes, Cracks, and Lost Forests, Oh My!

Were the west-moving pioneers so busy looking at Fort Rock that they failed to see another nearby wonder? Hole in the Ground, nearly eight miles from Fort Rock, is another mystery of nature.

Hole in the Ground is a nearly perfect circular formation, and early surveyors were probably amazed to find that it was 5,250 feet in circumference, nearly a perfect mile. The rim of the hole rises 200 feet above the ground level of the plain surrounding it. From the highest point on the rim, it drops more than 150 feet below the desert outside (a 350-foot total drop) to a gently sloping basin-shaped floor. The basin is slightly off-center, as if something big plowed into the ground some time ago. Because of its size and shape, settlers and early geologists believed that it had been the site of a meteor strike. After they understood meteor strikes better, geologists looked for microscopic pieces of glass or iron but did not find any. They eventually decided that Hole in the Ground was created by a series of violent volcanic eruptions.

Between 50,000 and 100,000 years ago, a small volcano began erupting. Like the much larger Mount Mazama, this volcano threw out debris, including multiton boulders, which landed more than two miles away. When the eruptions ended a few days later, the volcano left behind an empty cone, which collapsed under its own weight. Unlike Crater Lake, this did not fill up with water, but sat empty, like a vast bowl.

Hole in the Ground is located in the Bend–Fort Rock Ranger District of the Deschutes National Forest (www.fs.fed.us/r6/centraloregon). There is a signed turnoff from Highway 31 to Hole in the Ground. The crater is only about four miles away.

Crack in the Ground is located about thirty miles away from Hole in the Ground, just north of the town of

Christmas Valley, and if you believe in ley lines (theoretical alignments of geographic places), Fort Rock is located on the line between the two places. Both Native Americans and a few of the later pioneers believed that supernatural beings or giants carved out a two-mile-long, seventy-foot-deep trench through the hard bedrock. They could not tell how long ago the crack formed, but it seemed recent to them because the stone looked barely weathered. During many hot summers, settlers held picnics in the bottom of the narrow crevasse. The temperature inside was generally twenty degrees cooler than outside of the crack, and they made ice cream, using snow at the bottom, which did not melt until the late summer.

Formations like the crack are usually formed by water erosion and go from high ground to a lower drainage. This particular crack was formed by a volcanic eruption that included several underground lava flows. The lava hollowed out a tunnel-like space, and after the eruptions ceased the ground settled, moved, and opened the crack.

It is relatively easy to find Crack in the Ground. Drive east through the town of Christmas Valley. At the outer edge of town, there is a northbound gravel road with a simple sign saying "Crack in the Ground." This road leads about seven miles north, ending at a parking lot. A short trail from the portable toilet in the parking lot leads east to the crack, which is marked by a metal stand and guest book. There used to be a two-mile-long trail through the bottom of the crack, but it was blocked by rock fall a few years ago. It is now possible to walk only partway through the crack.

About eight miles northeast of Christmas Valley, the early pioneers found a five-square-mile forest of Ponderosa pines. It is the only large stand of trees for several miles in any direction, and there are no other Ponderosa pines for more than thirty miles. With typical pioneer humor, they said the trees must have walked there and gotten lost, and called it the Lost Forest.

Again, science stepped in to solve a weird mystery. The reason Ponderosa pines do not exist in the Fort Rock basin these days is lack of water. Today it rains only about nine inches a year in the Fort Rock basin, and a Ponderosa pine needs at least seventeen inches a year to survive, much less thrive. Geologists believe that there was a large Ponderosa pine forest in the valley when there was more rain. It died out as the rainfall decreased, except for the Lost Forest stand.

Scientists examined the soils under the forest and found that the surface is a loose, sandy material. Below that is a layer of volcanic ash and other materials that is so compacted that water cannot penetrate it. Water sits on top of the compacted layer, where the pine trees' taproots can soak it up. Unfortunately, recent development in the area threatens to drain off the water, and the Lost Forest may soon be truly lost forever. The best way to see the forest—while you still can—is to head northeast of Christmas Valley, toward Sand Rock, which overlooks the basin where the forest formed.

Missing: Massive Meteorites

Long ago, the people of the sky wanted to help the people of the Earth, so one of them, Tomanowos, left the sky and fell to Earth. When he touched the ground, he became a rock—a shiny, very heavy, and honeycombed rock with many holes in which water collected. The Clackamas people recognized Tomanowos's power and sent their young men to him to wash in the rainwater that collected in his holes, to purify themselves and help them catch more game. Tomanowos turned out to be an iron-nickel meteorite—a *massive* iron-nickel meteorite.

Over time, diminished by white men's diseases, the Clackamas who remained were moved to the Grand Ronde Reservation. The settlement near Tomanowos became the town of West Linn. In 1902 Ellis Hughes was wandering around the unused lands adjoining his property. He noticed a large, rounded rock half buried in the ground. He hit it with another rock and was rewarded with a metallic ping. He recognized the rock as a meteorite, but was amazed at its size; it was ten feet high, nearly seven feet long, and more than four feet wide. He learned that it weighed more than fifteen tons.

Hughes figured that a meteorite that size would be valuable, if only as a curiosity, but it was located on land belonging to the Oregon Iron and Steel Company. Working at night, with the help of his son, Hughes levered the meteorite out of its hole and onto his land over a three-month period. He accomplished that by using a pulley system powered by a horse.

Hughes claimed to have "discovered" the meteorite and charged tourists twenty-five cents apiece to look at it. He tried selling the meteorite, but his first potential buyer was the lawyer for Oregon Iron and Steel, who offered Hughes $50 for it. Hughes refused, and the steel company sued him for ownership and won. The company put the Willamette Meteorite on display at the Lewis and Clark Exposition in Portland.

In 1905, Oregon Iron and Steel sold it for $26,000 to a private party, who then donated it to the American Museum of Natural History in New York City, where it still resides. The Willamette Meteorite is the largest meteorite of its type discovered in the United States, and the sixth largest in the world. Its rounded shape probably formed when it came through the atmosphere to Earth. That high-speed entry probably melted away softer parts of the meteor, creating the deep pits. Over time, weather and rust deepened and smoothed those pits. Geologists believe that the meteor actually fell somewhere between southern Canada and Idaho, and the Missoula floods brought it to modern-day Oregon.

At the end of the 1990s, the Confederated Tribes of the Grand Ronde, who included the descendants of the Clackamas, demanded that the American Museum of Natural History return the meteorite to them as a sacred object. The museum refused, but in 2000, the tribe and museum signed an agreement whereby the Native Americans can perform ceremonies at the meteorite every year, and if the museum no longer wants it for research or for display, they will give it to the Grand Ronde. There are two replicas of the Willamette Meteorite, one at the University of Oregon campus and the other at the Willamette Methodist Church in West Linn.

Port Orford Meteorite

In 1856, Dr. John Evans, a physician and amateur geologist, was hired by the U.S. government to take part in several survey expeditions in the Oregon Territory. On one of his journeys, Evans stopped on the slopes of Bald Mountain. While traveling along the "route from Port Orford across the Rogue River Mountains," he saw a large boulder half buried in the mountainside. About five feet of it projected out of the ground, and he estimated that the entire rock would weigh about twenty-two thousand pounds. He did not know what kind of rock it was, but it looked strange, so he took a sample and had it analyzed when he returned to the East Coast.

The analysis created quite a stir. The rock Evans collected was part of a very rare kind of meteorite known as a pallasite. A pallasite has a mix of both stone and iron, and when pallasites enter Earth's atmosphere, the forces create a semiprecious mineral called olivine within the meteorite.

For several years Evans wanted to head an expedition to relocate what would be called the Port Orford Meteorite. However, before Congress could fund the trip, the Civil War broke out. The very next day, Evans died of pneumonia. In the decades that followed, miners and geologists looked for the meteorite. The problem was that there were a lot of mountain peaks in the Oregon Coast Range that could have been called "bald." Although Evans's notebook was eventually found, it did not precisely describe the route of his journey. Some people speculate that a landslide buried or moved the Port Orford Meteorite. Others think it was all a hoax.

After two expeditions sent by the Smithsonian Institution could not relocate it, geologist Howard Plotkin suggested that Evans was deeply in debt and concocted the story as a way of earning money. Plotkin further surmised that while Evans was traveling through Panama on his way back to the East Coast, he bought a piece of a pallasite meteorite called Imilac, which was discovered in Chile in 1820. The Port Orford sample was compared with an Imilac sample, and they were similar. Even so, the search continued, fueled by dreams of wealth and fame.

In 1937, an astronomer estimated that, if found, the Port Orford Meteorite would be worth up to $100 per pound. During the Great Depression, this sum was enough to send hundreds of prospectors into the mountains above Port Orford. It has never been found.

The Bridge of the Gods

There are several Native American stories about a cata-strophic landslide that dammed the Columbia River, perhaps within the last five hundred years. This landslide created a natural rock structure known as the Bridge of the Gods. The following is one of the many legends about the Bridge of the Gods.

> Long ago, the people of the Great River (Columbia) fought for many generations. Finally they had peace, and as a symbol, the Great Spirit created a land bridge across the river, where people crossed in friend-ship. The Great Spirit appointed a beautiful woman as the guardian of the bridge, and gave her a torch to light the way across. At that time, the people did not own fire and were cold at night and in the winter. A young man visited the woman, and she gave him fire in exchange for marriage. She had another suitor from the other side of the river. The one who married her gave fire to his people. The loser and his people started a war. To punish the people for stealing fire and fighting, the Great Spirit caused the Bridge of the Gods to collapse. This formed the Cascades of the Columbia River, a set of three rapids, in and around the site of the present Bonneville Dam.

These days, the natural rock formation known as Bridge of the Gods is long gone. But a man-made bridge stands at the exact location, and it is also known as the Bridge of the Gods. The name is a tribute to the area's legends of the past. It's also a reminder of the region's geological unpredictability.

Monkey Face Rock

According to some Native American traditions, gods once walked the Earth, sometimes in human form, sometimes as animals, sometimes as something else. When their age ended, as the story goes, some of the gods died. But most were transformed into natural things, like trees, rocks, or lakes, imbued with unnatural powers that the Native people could sense. One such place was Monkey Face Rock, north of Redmond.

Skeptics have said that Monkey Face Rock is a natural formation made of multiple layers of hardened lava flows. Over time, the softer rock wore away, leaving a monolith of harder rock standing apart from the rest. But even guides know that Monkey Face Rock is different from other nearby rock formations.

There are several ways to climb the 350-foot-high rock, ranging from easy to very dangerous. The Young Pioneer route follows a bolt ladder up an overhanging face into the Monkey's mouth. It has a "panic point," where climbers step out onto the mouth.

David Potter, a certified guide for Smith Rock Climbing Guides who has led groups up Monkey Face Rock, had this to say about the climb:

Shuffling carefully over the edge at the corner of the cave, my climbing shoes found an inch-wide ledge, allowing me to move upward, my partner feeding rope as I went. Searching for more footholds, I looked down into the overhanging expanse beneath my feet. My heart pounded as tunnel vision threatened to close in, so I quickly focused back to the rock in front of my face. The rope connected me to my partner but, as it trailed across the face and into the cave, we could no longer see each other. Instead, I saw the concerned group of tourists at the Monkey Face overlook in the background, filming my every move. One of them was saying something about how crazy we were; I guess they didn't think I could hear them. The handholds were big enough, but as I pulled from one to the other my biceps wanted to cramp, reacting to the work I had put them through earlier in the 250-foot climb. "Keep moving," I told myself, "it's not that hard."

It really isn't that hard. And it's not dangerous as rock climbs go. But even after climbing Monkey Face more than a hundred times since that first ascent when I was fifteen, the experience never gets old. I may not panic anymore, but "panic point" is always a rush.

Monkey Face Rock is one of the many climbs in Oregon's Smith Rock State Park (www.oregonparks.org). Although many people go climbing alone, some hire guides like Smith Rock Climbing Guides (www.smithrockclimbingguides.com).

Don't Poo-Poo the Evidence of Ancient Man

The little city of Paisley is famous, or at least noted, for its annual Mosquito Festival. Paisley is less famous for the significant archaeological finds in some nearby caves. Finds that could push the age of human presence in North America to fourteen thousand years ago.

For decades, historians and archaeologists believed that the first humans entered North America about twelve thousand years ago. They did so by crossing a land bridge between Siberia and Alaska, created when the ancient ice sheets lowered sea levels. They then traveled south through an inland, ice-free corridor. These are known as the Clovis people, named after the large spear points they left behind, in Clovis, New Mexico, and other places. Some archaeologists suggested that people crossed even earlier by following the ancient shoreline, even though there was no evidence.

In the 1930s, several expeditions had visited the

Paisley caves, but some researchers felt that tests at the site may have been ruined by bad technique. So in 2002, archaeologists from the University of Oregon began excavating there, and found definite evidence of human existence in the form of coprolites, which is a scientific term for dried-up human feces. Yes, Virginia, we're talking about poo-poo.

Six of the coprolites were carbon dated, which showed they had been "deposited" between 13,000 and 14,300 years ago. The dry air helped preserve the little gems that were left behind, and DNA testing showed that the ancient people had some genetic ties to the modern peoples of Asia, but no close kin there. On the other hand, many of the unique DNA markers found in the ancient droppings were matched only in some modern Native Americans, and nowhere else in the world.

So *Weird Oregon* recommends you have more respect for simple biological functions. After all, you never know how valuable what you leave behind can become.

Changing Visions: The Susan Creek Indian Mounds

Among the Native peoples of the Pacific Northwest, part of the traditional process of going from boyhood to manhood involved the vision quest. Youths left their comfortable homes and journeyed to isolated places, sometimes into the deserts but usually into the mountains, where they camped and waited for their spirit guides to find them. If the youth gained a spirit guide, he led a charmed life when he came down from the mountains. The spirit guide advised and protected him while he hunted or went off to war. Men

with spirit guides became leaders of their people. Not everyone had a spirit guide.

On their vision quests, the youths first had to find a place of power. Some mountain peaks were known as places where the gods and mighty spirits lived, but they would not always speak to the youths. To encourage visions to come, the young men fasted and sat up all night without blankets or furs, trying not to sleep. During the day, vigorous exercise, such as dancing or gathering and piling rocks, was thought to attract the attention of the spirits around them. If that did not work, after several days some of them would

government turned the vision quest site into a recreation area. The Susan Creek Campground is the most popular recreation site, with a thirty-one-unit campground and small amphitheater where guides give interpretive fireside chats to campers. There is fly-fishing in the stream, and a wheelchair-accessible trail leads a mile and a half from the campground to a fifty-foot-high waterfall. Another half mile along the trail takes visitors to the highest mound of piled rocks where boys, hoping to become men, sweated and tortured their bodies to find their spirit guides.

While visitors to the site are respectful, and there is no history of vandals tumbling down the stones, the contrast between past and present visitors is interesting. The first visitors used this place to deny themselves pleasure; the present-day visitors have relative convenience and ease. Where one culture sought visions of the spirit world, the other snaps pictures of osprey and salmon.

cut themselves, or even cut off the ends of their fingers, hoping the shock would bring on visions and their guides. If no visions came, the youths returned, not shamed but merely ordinary in the eyes of their fellows.

About eight miles east of Glide, while building the road that eventually became Oregon State Highway 138, some highway workers found an abandoned vision quest site. It had been abandoned for decades, and had probably been used last by the Umpqua tribe. In 1853 the Upper Umpqua were the first Oregon tribe to sign a treaty with the U.S. government that cost them most of their lands. A few years later, during the Rogue River War, many of the Umpqua were killed when fighting spilled over into their territory. Following the war in 1856, some of the Umpqua managed to hide and live in the more remote areas of their territory. A few moved into the American towns, but most of the remaining Umpqua were forced to march more than 150 miles to the Grand Ronde Reservation, where some of their descendents still live today.

Perhaps sensing the power of the abandoned place, rather than bypassing it or cutting down all the trees, the

The Missoula Floods

In the 1840s, the Oregon Trail led settlers to the Pacific Northwest through the Columbia River Gorge. The pioneers marveled at the depth of the gorge and wondered what could have cut grooves across the hard basalt that formed its walls. Geologists knew that volcanoes erupted and spewed forth lava, which created rock. However, they explained rock erosion as a uniform process of wind and water slowly wearing away rock and depositing it somewhere else, where it gradually created new landforms. They explained the thin soils in eastern Oregon and the shape of the Columbia River Gorge as part of this process. In the 1920s, someone suggested an alternative.

Geologist Harlen Bretz compared soils and found rocks in western Oregon that came from geologic deposits in eastern Oregon. He also found evidence of a series of huge lakes around Spokane, Washington. He suggested that periodic flooding from those lakes cut through eastern Washington, into the Columbia River, into eastern Oregon, and down to the Pacific Ocean. The flood was so big that it affected many of the Columbia's tributaries in Oregon, and that is how the rocks moved from east to west. Mainstream geologists ridiculed Bretz, saying that there was not enough water in the Spokane basin to make a flood that large.

In 1925, Joseph Pardee found the remains of a larger lake in Missoula, Montana. He believed that at the end of the last ice age, between fifteen thousand and thirteen thousand years ago, the glaciers melted and natural ice dams blocked the lowlands, creating several lakes. Lake Missoula was so deep that the water pressure lowered the freezing point of water below 32°F. This water, under pressure, seeped into cracks in the ice dam. The cracks got larger as the pressure built, until the ice dam finally burst. When this happened, the flood destroyed the dams on all the other lakes downstream. Over a period of centuries, the process

repeated itself several times, as the ice dam reformed and burst again. According to some estimates, there were more than forty floods.

One of these floods may have contained five hundred cubic miles of water. The flood spread out over eastern Washington, scraping away the soils, creating the Scablands. As it headed south, it flowed into the Columbia River channel. The flood backed up as it flowed into the

Columbia River Gorge, which increased its depth and speed. The flood moved at more than fifty miles per hour, and was from eight hundred to one thousand feet high. It flowed over the top of Beacon Rock, west of Cascade Locks, Oregon. The floods probably scoured away the outer crust of Beacon Rock. It moved so fast that despite the volume of water, it took only a few days to empty into the Pacific Ocean. The flood cut deep grooves in the hard basalt walls of the gorge, which are still visible today.

As it left the gorge, the flood slowed down and spread across the landscape. It flowed up many of Oregon's rivers, such as the Sandy and Multnomah. As it did, the still powerful flood began dropping larger boulders, then rocks, and eventually soils in places like the Willamette Valley.

Balancing Rocks

One of the most bizarre and beautiful ancient sites in the entire state is located in the Deschutes National Forest in central Oregon: the Balancing Rocks.

Buried within the park are a series of tall rock columns. Atop these columns are flat, heavy stones, perched precariously. To the naked eye, it would appear that these are strange statues, designed with intent by some ancient people. Geologists see a much simpler story behind the origin of the rocks. They believe that a usual cause—erosion—has led to this very unusual site. It's believed that many millions of years ago, ash from volcanic eruptions shifted a lot of the stones in this area, pushing them around and mixing them together. At this time, and at this particular site, denser, harder stones found their way to the top of a pile of considerably softer stone. Over time, erosion has worked more quickly on the softer stone, eating away at it to the point where only the columns at the base of the balancing rocks remain. The harder stones atop have eroded at a much slower pace, and have subsequently remained closer to their former larger iterations, leading to the strange rock formations in the Deschutes National Forest today.

This is a one-of-a-kind natural landmark, deserving the respect of its visitors. Even simple winds can send the top stones hurtling from their perches from time to time.

Oregon Dunes

The western Sahara Desert has an average high temperature of 120°F, annual rainfall of 4 inches, and sand dunes. Death Valley, California, has an average high temperature of 120°F, annual rainfall of 1.7 inches, and sand dunes. Florence, near the Oregon coast, has an average high temperature of 75°F, annual rainfall of more than 156 inches, and . . . sand dunes. Lots of sand dunes.

The Oregon Dunes National Recreation Area extends from Florence to Coos Bay, nearly forty miles along the Oregon coast. These constitute the longest stretch of coastal dunes in the United States. They prove that it is not temperature and rainfall that make sand dunes; it is wind, sand, and time.

About six thousand years ago, the present Oregon coastline stabilized, more or less, as did most of the weather patterns we see today. For thousands of years, winds blew sands from the beaches upward, five hundred feet above sea level, to rest on a sandstone rock formation, where the sand began to pile up. Once there, it was contained by the mountains east of and above the sandstone bedrock. Unlike many other sand dune formations, where the winds have been steady and generally from one direction, the Oregon dunes are as ever changing as the winds.

The summer winds along that portion of the coast are from the north and average 12–16 miles per hour in summer. The winter winds come from the south, with varying force, though they can reach 100 miles per hour during storms. The winds reshape the dunes from season to season. In addition to wind action, the heavy rainfall along the coast affects the dunes in many ways. There are several lakes within the dunes; some of them silt up, and others form when rainwater fills depressions in the dunes. In some places, there are marshes and quicksand.

That changing landscape is part of the reason why some people visit the dunes. The many tour companies lining the Coast Highway give guided tours of the dunes and rent various kinds of ATVs to tourists. Yet, every year, just as sure as the tourists come to see the dunes, the tour companies and the government save many tourists and their equipment from quicksand and other natural obstacles.

Oregon Caves National Monument

In 1874, Elijah Davidson and his dog, Bruno, went hunting. The two chased a bear into a cave. Bruno followed the bear into the cave and Elijah followed, in the hopes of saving his dog. He charged into an intricate network of limestone caves taking up 480 acres of horizontal space with several vertical levels.

After the two emerged from the dark cave much later, Elijah returned to the cave with friends and stories to tell. Word spread about the cave, and almost immediately it became a tourist Mecca.

The poet Joaquin Miller called the cave the "Marble Halls of Oregon." In 1909, President Taft declared the network of caves a national monument. At first, cave tours were conducted by candlelight, then by lamplight, and later by flashlight, until electric lighting was installed in the 1930s. A space was even cleared and leveled in one of the larger chambers, and live bands would play concerts. Over the years, as more chambers have been discovered and explored, it became obvious that even though humans had not lived in the caves, other animals had. The remains of extinct jaguars and grizzly bears were found in the cave's chambers.

But the caves suffered from their popularity. In the 1920s, a paved road was laid, bringing visitors to newly built vacation cottages. In 1934, a six-story hotel, the Chateau, was built. As new caves opened, the air currents changed, which affected the water flow within the caves. The water in some chambers froze, destroying delicate formations. In other chambers, the lights caused algae to grow on the walls, and the grease and moisture from visitors' fingers blackened some of the rocks they touched. Over time, formations collapsed, and the National Park Service removed rubble and installed airlocks to restore the original climate. They even bleached the walls periodically to destroy algae growth.

Although the caves are now lighted, at times the park rangers conduct candlelight tours. The stalactite and stalagmite limestone formations within the cave resemble marble, in shapes like pipe organs, lotus flowers, and strips of bacon. There's even a "ghost room," of formations of robed figures, 250 feet long, 50 feet wide, and with a 40-foot ceiling.

In a picturesque place like this, guests who stay at the nearby Chateau hotel expect to see ghosts—and they're not disappointed. In the past, employees were sworn to keep the resident ghost, Elisabeth, a secret. According to the legend, Elisabeth was honeymooning at the lodge with her groom.

One afternoon, Elisabeth took a long walk on the trails around the lodge and her husband stayed behind. She returned early, horrified to find her husband in bed with one of the hotel's maids. That night she locked herself in the bathroom and slit her wrists. Since that time, Elisabeth has created added work for the lodge staff.

Elisabeth has a tendency to pester female staff members. Several maids have complained that they cannot keep linen folded. If they leave the room for a few minutes after folding the sheets

and towels, they find the stacks of folded linen turned into heaps of wadded cloth when they return. In the kitchen, when female cooks turn off the gas stove when they close the kitchen, they frequently hear the sounds of the gas jets on full blast as they prepare to leave for the night.

Elisabeth supposedly stayed in Room 308 (now subdivided into Rooms 309 and 310) . . . and remained there after her death. Some guests have reported an uneasy feeling when staying in that room. Guests and housekeeping staff have heard the sound of someone pacing up and down the hallway when either Rooms 309 and 310 is occupied. The pacing usually ends around sunrise.

Guests reported an uneasy feeling.

In June 1997, a couple was staying overnight in a second-floor room. The wife sensed something strange in their room, but her husband laughed at her fears . . . until he had to use the bathroom. After washing his hands, "John" turned to leave the room when suddenly the water turned itself on full blast. He quickly shut it off again, and when he turned to leave it turned itself on again. After that, the couple questioned the staff about any other strange doings. When they heard about the hallway pacing, they decided to investigate. They did not see or hear anything, but the temperature dropped nearly ten degrees as they walked from the stairway to the hallway outside of the haunted room. This is a strange coincidence, if coincidence it was, for a temperature drop like that to happen in the middle of June.

The Oregon Caves and Chateau lodge are not open for tours during the winter. Check their Web site (www.oregoncaves.com) for open dates, tour restrictions, and lodging information.

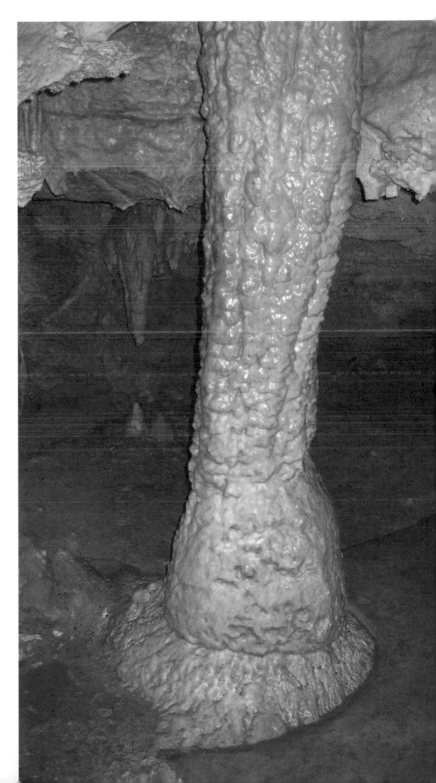

Fabled People and Places

Oregon was once a fabled land and hosted many famous explorers. Some say Sir Francis Drake was the first person to set up a European colony on the Oregon coast. Later, Lewis and Clark built Fort Clatsop, and their journals captured America's imagination. Oregon was the starting place for enterprising madam Nancy Boggsand the resting place for Howard Hughes's fondest dream. Oregon has welcomed all comers, from crooning Pat Boone to mooning sea lions. And in a sad and twisted irony, Asian immigrants settled in Oregon, while some unfortunate Oregonians were kidnapped and sent to Shanghai as captive sailors.

Hey, we're packing four hundred years of weird in here.

New England in Oregon: Francis Drake's Nova Albion

Most people credit the Spaniards with the earliest European exploration of the Oregon coast. A few historians believe that English explorer and privateer Sir Francis Drake may have been there earlier and attempted to colonize the Oregon coast in the sixteenth century.

Drake's fleet departed England on December 13, 1577. By September 1578 he was attacking Spanish towns and fleets along the South and North American Pacific, losing many men and ships along the way. Drake may have sailed north of the forty-eighth parallel, looking for the Northwest Passage, into modern British Columbia. He sailed south again and eventually beached his ship, the *Golden Hind*, for repairs.

According to the official account of his voyage, on June 17 he chose a harbor somewhere near the thirty-eighth parallel, which is in central California. Drake named the area Nova Albion, an ancient name for the British Isles, in honor of the high white cliffs that overlooked the beach.

They stayed in Nova Albion for a little over a month, built a stockade, and made contact with the local Native Americans. Their relations were peaceful, perhaps because some Native Americans believed that the English were supernatural beings. Before Drake left, he erected a monument, claiming the land for England. This monument included a written proclamation of the claim on a metal plate, an English coin, and a picture of Queen Elizabeth I, making Nova Albion the first British colony in the New World.

Many people searched for Drake's Nova Albion in California, and they selected several locations, such as Drake's Bay, Bodega Bay, and San Quentin Cove as possible sites. In 1936, an amateur historian found a brass plaque with an inscription matching Drake's claim of sovereignty near San Francisco. They called it Drake's Plate of Brass, and for many years it was considered proof that that Drake's New Albion had been there. In the 1970s, the plate was found to be a fake. Later investigations suggested that members of an amateur historical society made the plate and planted it as a practical joke. Unfortunately, the finder convinced everyone that the plate was real, and the rest became mistaken history.

The location of Nova Albion is still being debated. Drake's voyages were state secrets, and detailed maps and full journals of his voyage were not published while Drake was

Feda corporum laceratione & crebris in montibus facrificiis, hujus
Novæ Albionis portus incolæ, Draci, jain bis coronat., decessum defient.

alive. Some people suggest that what information was published was purposely falsified.

Amateur historian Bob Ward examined maps and other documents relating to Drake created after the death of Queen Elizabeth I. He found two accounts of the voyage that give New Albion's location near the forty-fourth parallel, which meant the real location of Drake's camp was somewhere in Oregon. After examining maps of the coast and reading descriptions of the geography of the shoreline, Ward believed that Drake landed at a place called Whale Cove, north of Newport, Oregon.

Years after the voyage, one of Drake's relatives wrote that the explorer left behind a small captured ship with a crew of twenty-five to continue exploring the West Coast. Other journal accounts of his voyage show that between the time they stopped in New Albion and the time they arrived in Asia, twenty or so sailors somehow disappeared. There is no record of what happened.

Drake never returned to the West Coast, and the men he left behind sailed into mystery. A handful of sixteenth-century English coins have been found along the Oregon coast, and while the money isn't proof positive, Ward believed that the wreckage of that mystery ship is located somewhere along this coast.

The address for the Drake in Oregon Society is P.O. Box 412, Depoe Bay, OR 97341. You can see Whale Cove from the Rocky Creek State Scenic Viewpoint, along Highway 101.

Finding Fort Clatsop

The expedition of Meriwether Lewis and William Clark across North America from 1804 to 1806 was the most thoroughly documented journey of exploration in North American history. Within weeks of their return to the east, the government printed maps of their trip for sale to the public. Many of their landmarks were visible to those who followed, even generations later. As part of the Lewis and Clark bicentennial in 2004, many agencies located several of Lewis and Clark's waypoints and established parks and museums dedicated to them. Nearly every place the explorers stopped in the Pacific Northwest was located. Unfortunately, no one knows the exact location where the Corps of Discovery spent the winter of 1805–1806, a place they called Fort Clatsop, named for a local tribe of Native Americans.

Fort Clatsop would never have been built if it hadn't been for President Thomas Jefferson, who in 1803 asked Congress to fund an exploratory expedition to the Pacific Ocean. In addition to commissioning a military evaluation of European threats to U.S. interests, he wanted maps; studies of American botany, geology, and wildlife; and reports about the people who lived in the vast spaces between European American settlements. Congress funded the expedition, and Jefferson picked Meriwether Lewis, an army captain and his private secretary, to lead the expedition.

Lewis contacted William Clark, who had once been his commanding officer in the army, and asked him to be co-commander of the Corps of Discovery. Technically Lewis was the commander because, as a captain, he outranked Clark, a lieutenant, but the two co-commanders never mentioned this detail to their men.

The Corps of Discovery started with two officers, thirty enlisted soldiers, and Clark's slave, an African American man named York. Lewis also brought a dog he named Seaman on the journey. It took months to gather supplies for the trip, but eventually, on May 14, 1804, they left Camp Dubois, near modern Hartford, Illinois, traveling up the Missouri River on the first leg of their journey. Lewis and Clark noted that in most places they were well received.

In late November 1805, they sighted the Pacific Ocean. The Corps marked trees with the date and their names, probably buried a coin there, and drew a map of the site. At the time, that was all they needed to do to claim the area for the United States. On November 24, the entire party, including York and Sacagawea, who had joined the party a year earlier, voted to establish a winter camp on the south side of the Columbia River. In early December, Meriwether Lewis found a spot that had wood, a spring, and plenty of game near present-day Astoria. According to their journals, they cut down trees and cleared land to construct their quarters.

Fort Clatsop was about fifty feet by fifty feet in size. Instead of a large stockade of vertical spikes, the log walls were horizontal and chinked, resembling the walls of a

mercury was frequently used as a preventative for many diseases, and every man in the expedition took regular doses. The archaeologists took soil samples, looking for traces of mercury. They believed they would find higher concentrations of the metal where an outhouse had been. Once the outhouse was found, the fort would have to be nearby. But they were never able to pin down with certainty the exact location of the original Fort Clatsop.

In the twentieth century, the National Park Service established an interpretive center near where they believed Lewis and Clark had built the abandoned fort. In 1955, using original drawings, craftsmen built a replica of Fort Clatsop on top of the place that they felt was the original fort site. Some historians compared the structure to a movie set and complained that it was too well constructed, built as it was with notched logs using modern tools. In 2005, a fire destroyed most of the buildings, so a new replica was built in a more accurate period style.

The Fort Clatsop, featuring the replica, visitor center, and interpretive trails, is located at 92343 Fort Clatsop Road, Astoria. The Web site is www.nps.gov/lewi.

log cabin. There were seven buildings, three on one side and four on the other, each with its own fireplace. These buildings were attached to the palisade walls, like sheds. There was a wide parade ground between the buildings. Inside Fort Clatsop, they repaired their equipment for the voyage home and went over their notes and maps and traded items with the local Natives.

Fort Clatsop was opened for trading with the Clatsop people for only about twenty days, between November 26, 1805, and March 22, 1806. Perhaps the Clatsop wanted a better price for their goods than the Corps of Discovery could afford. Lewis and Clark had hoped to get some goods from a European ship visiting the Columbia River that spring, but none arrived until after they left. The expedition set out on March 24, 1806, abandoning little Fort Clatsop to the Native people. The Corps of Discovery reached St. Louis on September 23, 1806. At Fort Clatsop, the log walls slowly rotted away and were forgotten.

Archaeologists tried to locate the original Fort Clatsop. Their excavations did not locate the old fort, so they tried another experiment. In Lewis and Clark's time,

Found: Nancy Boggs's Floating Bordello?

In the late 1800s, Portland struggled (on the surface, at least) to clean up vice within its city limits, particularly prostitution and gambling. Portland was much smaller then, and it was easy for madams and hustlers to move into hamlets like Fulton, south of Portland. The first paved street outside of Portland, in fact, passed through Fulton, which made it easy for city folk to travel there, where the waterfront was lined with bordellos and gambling houses. When Portland annexed Fulton, the city shut down most of those businesses as part of its new push for respectability.

Nancy Boggs was tired of having the police raid her bordello. Even when most of the local police were paid to tip her off, it still cut into her business. In 1880, she bought an old barge that used to haul sawdust, put a log deck on it, and built a house on top of that. She anchored it in the Willamette River as her own floating bar and bordello. On the first floor, Nancy set up a bar, while her prostitutes had rooms on the second floor. She had rowboats transport her customers to her whiskey scow and take them back to shore.

The whiskey scow shifted its anchorage: Sometimes it was in the middle of the channel, other times on the west or east bank of the Willamette. That was part of Nancy's defense. She paid some friendly police for word of when there would be a raid on her establishment. If the raid came from the Portland police, on the west bank, she moved her boat to the other side of the river, toward East Portland. If the East Portland police were on their way, she moved to the west bank. In the case of a true surprise raid, she could see any police coming from her vantage point on the roof. She always seemed to be one step ahead of them.

In 1882, police from both sides of the river conducted a joint raid. When they boarded her scow, Nancy welcomed them with a shower of steaming hot water from a fire hose, fed by her boiler. A night or two later, a small group of policemen rowed out to Nancy's place and cut the anchor rope. In response, Nancy paid a ship's captain to catch and tow her floating business back to its usual resting place. This went on for a few more years before Nancy moved on to drier and greener pastures. No one seemed to know what happened to her or her whiskey scow.

But then we spoke with John and Wendy Fencsak, who own the Fulton House Bed and Breakfast in southwest Portland. They bought the

house in the 1990s and recently remodeled and restored it, turning it into a bed-and-breakfast. John grew up on the East Coast, and he noticed that it was a narrow building, more like houses he grew up with rather than the wide roomy houses built on the West Coast. It had a widow's walk, a railed walkway on the roof where nineteenth-century women would stand, waiting and watching for their sailor husbands to come home.

Wendy, a member of the Oregon Historical Society, reported that there were few records on the house because a series of fires had destroyed most of the property records for the area. They spoke with their next-door neighbor Helen, who was born and raised in Fulton and whose grandfather had built many of the older houses in the neighborhood.

According to the surviving records and Helen's family history, the Fencsaks' house had been the floating bordello, and it had been moved to the current site in 1902. Helen's grandfather reported that a man named Webber bought the house and hired men (and several teams of horses) to move the house off the river to Virginia Avenue. They somehow managed to get the house centered over a dirt cellar and set up the whole thing using cinder blocks and logs as a foundation. They did a good job, too—the house did not move during two earthquakes.

Had Nancy Boggs paced the widow's walk, on the lookout for the police? Had her girls posed on the veranda, flaunting their wares to all and sundry on the passing ships? Had customers lounged on the sun porch, exhausted after a hard night of debauchery? We will probably never know.

When John and Wendy renovated and restored the home, they refinished many original fixtures like the hardwood floors but retained as much original integrity as possible. During the renovation, one of their workers, a man in his twenties, asked if a girl had been killed there. The man said, "I'm a little bit sensitive, and as I was working, I kept on feeling that there was a young girl killed in or around the house."

In the backyard, there is a thirty-foot-long water stream and koi pond. A few years ago, while working in the garden, John found a spot with lots of burned wood and nails just under the earth's surface. Helen explained that one of the former homeowners had built a garage there. He was backing into or out of the garage one day when he accidentally hit and killed his granddaughter. He was so distraught that he burned the garage down.

The Fulton House Bed and Breakfast offers two types of guest rooms, both with private baths. Their Web site is www.thefultonhouse.com.

The Pat Boone Inn

The Howard Johnson Inn in little Waldport has seen some interesting visitors over the years. Sometime in the 1960s, singer-songwriter Pat Boone and other investors built the Pat Boone Inn, with the singer appearing at the grand opening. In those times many entertainers built clubs and hotels in out-of-the-way places, hoping to start a new Las Vegas. We spoke with a current hotel staff member who said that periodically Boone returned for visits, perhaps to perform. To capitalize on Boone's celebrity, the hotel's marquee featured a giant image of Pat Boone wearing a pink leisure suit.

The Pat Boone Inn's marquee and name went the same way as the leisure suit. By the late 1970s, it was the Bayshore Inn that hosted a set of guests who would later become infamous. In September 1975, Marshall Applewhite and Bonnie Nettles reserved a meeting for a Total Overcomers Anonymous seminar. One hundred people showed up—quite a large crowd, considering the population of Waldport was only seven hundred people at the time. Applewhite and Nettles told their audience that they had been chosen for future enlightenment and would ascend to a higher spiritual level through the aid of extraterrestrials.

After Applewhite and Nettles left, twenty people followed them to Colorado. Over the next two decades, their group grew. Applewhite became Bo, Nettles became Peep, and their group became known as Heaven's Gate. The group later moved from Colorado to settle in a mansion in California, where thirty-nine of them eventually committed suicide while waiting for a spaceship trailing behind the comet Hale-Bopp to come and collect them.

Given the choice, the hotel might prefer to publicize their associations with Pat Boone instead of Heaven's Gate. The first time we visited, the manager told of plans to display some historic photos and memorabilia associated with Boone, but we were unable to confirm whether or not this ever happened. We hope they found the leisure suit, because fashions always come back around. . . .

The Waldport Howard Johnson is located at 902 NW Bayshore Drive in Waldport.

Portland's Chinatown

Shortly after gold was discovered in California in 1849, men and women from across the world left their homes in search of the mother lode. In China, many men sold themselves into virtual slavery to get to America, in the hopes of returning home rich—or at least with the financial means to send their bones back home. Like most pioneers, many of them found hardship, building railroads, digging tunnels in mines, or working in other menial jobs. They also formed vibrant ethnic neighborhoods in most of America's largest cities, including Portland, Oregon.

Portland's Chinatown was a narrow strip of West Portland, about six blocks wide, which extended from Glisan Street in North Portland south to Washington Street. Within it, the people retained many elements of their culture. Most of the people living there were businessmen, artists, herbalists, restaurant owners, and simple tradesmen, all trying to earn a living.

Some nonresidents complained about prostitution, gambling, and particularly opium abuse in Chinatown. Far more nonresidents fed their vices there, rather than dine, buy art, or visit a traditional healer. In November 1893, young Gong Fa was murdered under a streetlight near the intersection of Second Avenue and Pine Street. The police noted bystanders stepping over her body as if she was beneath their concern.

Gong Fa was an unfortunate victim of the court system of the day. A year earlier, Asian pimps had won legal control of prostitutes in the Multnomah County court. As a result, each woman, including Gong Fa, had to pick her "husband" from the assembled pimps. Some people suspected that Gong Fa had left her pimp for another, and the first pimp killed her. Of course, while white society *tsk*ed over this state of affairs,

their neighborhoods along the docks were not much better.

These days, Portland's Chinatown is a rough rectangle between Burnside Street on the south, Glisan Street on the north, First Avenue on the east, and Sixth Avenue on the west. In 2000, the Portland Classical Chinese Garden opened in a park that covers a whole city block. It was built by sixty-five workers from China using a mix of imported materials and locally grown plants. Yet despite this important attraction, the neighborhood has lost a lot of its flavor.

There are only two dozen or so Chinese-owned businesses left in Chinatown. Many near-homeless individuals live in various cheap hotels. As urban renewal has begun converting these buildings into office spaces, non-Asian businesses have moved in. Many of Portland's Chinese businesses have moved across the Willamette River, establishing a new community along SE Eighty-second Avenue. Even so, it is not too difficult to imagine some of the sights and sounds of Portland's old Chinatown, if you look at things from the right angle.

Portland's Shanghai Tunnels

When we heard that there are five miles of underground tunnels snaking through Portland's downtown and waterfront areas, we knew we had to check them out. Michael Jones, the curator of the Portland Underground, took us on a tour through these legendary subterranean passageways, where "history, folklore, and terror merge together."

Jones was quick to fill us in on the dark reason that these tunnels exist in the first place. "Shanghaiing," he told us. "Kidnapping men and selling them to sea captains, who forced them to work aboard their ships for nothing."

During the late 1800s, Portland was the second largest port on the West Coast, even bigger than Seattle. The gold rush and logging business created a flurry of shipping and trading activity that demanded able-bodied workers. Oftentimes, the demand outweighed the supply of available sailors, so unwitting parties were drugged, held against their will, and then shipped out to sea. The tunnels below Portland were built specifically to move goods from the docks to the shops and stores lining the waterfront. Because Portland was a jumping-off point for the Orient, and because Shanghai was generally the farthest destination from the city, the practice came to be known as "shanghaiing."

"We had an average of fifteen hundred men [kidnapped] a year, beginning in 1870," Jones said. "That was average. It soared to three thousand. Portland became number one in the world for shanghaiing."

The waterfront area, which most of the tunnels run below, was the perfect staging ground for this illegal activity. That seedy section of Portland was filled with saloons, boardinghouses, and brothels. The area attracted the perfect candidates for shanghaiing: transients who had come west in search of opportunity and fortune.

"They were looking for wanderers, sailors, cowboys, loggers," Jones told us as we stood in an abandoned underground holding cell, "people that didn't have any roots here . . . any families." The men who coordinated these mass kidnappings were known as crimps, and they employed muscle known as bully boys.

Monetarily, the process was straightforward and lucrative. At that time, when sailors signed up for a voyage, most received a bonus that was meant to pay for their clothing and any equipment they needed for the voyage. As part of the shanghaiing scheme, the crimp would find a drunk or unconscious man and forge the victim's signature in return for the advance money. He'd keep the sailor's advance and leave him with a bag of shoddy clothes and necessities. Sometimes the kidnapped men were sailors, other times just men off the street.

One of Portland's most infamous crimps was Joseph "Bunco" Kelly. A sailor himself, Kelly jumped ship in Portland in 1879. After that, he haunted Portland's streets, bars, and brothels, looking for unwary victims. After a few years, he bought a small warehouse, which he converted into a boardinghouse, a more convenient place from which to pluck unsuspecting transients. Kelly received the nickname Bunco when a client put in an order for a man at the last minute. It was a slow night, and Kelly could not find a victim. In a moment of inspiration, he stole a cigar store Indian and wrapped it in a tarp. He wrestled it into a bunk and collected the bounty. The captain did not discover the scam for several hours.

There were even more frauds waiting for Kelly. In 1893, the *Flying Prince*, a British ship, was ready to sail but needed twenty-two sailors. The captain promised Kelly $30 a head if he provided the sailors. Kelly was prowling the streets along Front Avenue when he saw two dozen drunkards, groaning or passed out on the basement floor. Kelly found that they were, in fact, dead or dying.

The men, all sailors, had been thrown out of the bar on the street above but still wanted to drink. Thinking the door led to the bar's basement, they had forced the trapdoor and tapped the kegs they found there. They had actually broken into the basement of the undertaker next door, and drank the barrels of formaldehyde. Kelly climbed out of the trapdoor, gathered his bully boys, and delivered fourteen dead men and ten dying men to the *Flying Prince.* He explained that the men were dead drunk.

Although Kelly was questioned, he was never charged with manslaughter or kidnapping. But the following year he was charged with murdering a man in a shanghaiing gone wrong. He spent fourteen years in prison before being pardoned.

The owners of the business establishments on the surface—especially saloon owners—were enlisted by crimps to help find easy targets for kidnapping. Patrons who came in alone, and those who got particularly drunk, were often removed from the bar and locked underground until they could be transported to a ship. Sometimes bars would even be fitted with trapdoors that would drop the drunks straight through the floor into their cells. These trapdoors were called deadfalls. "You would have a lot to drink," Jones explained, "or else they helped you along with some knockout drops. The best knockout drops were made out of opium."

He continued: "Bartender pulled a lever, and down you went. And this was instant. The door worked on a counterweight system. It would slam back, shut. The objective was not to hurt anyone—the objective was to have able-bodied men for these sea captains."

On our journey through the dismal tunnels, we were puzzled to come across piles of very old discarded shoes. "Before they were locked up in the holding cells, shanghaiers

would grab your shoes," he informed us. "They broke glass and spread it throughout the underground. If somebody escaped, they couldn't run too fast or too far."

In many instances, men were passed out, drunk, or drugged, and never even knew that they had spent time in the Portland Underground. They simply came to, hours after their kidnapping, onboard a ship already at sea. They had been sold, usually to American or British vessels, for a mere $50. And the voyages themselves were hard ones, their endings as inconsiderate as their beginnings.

"They were gone three to

six years," Jones told us. Then, "they [were] kicked off the ship . . . on their own. Didn't matter where they were—East Coast city, foreign country. They had to get on another ship, eventually maybe get back here. Some of those men never returned."

Jones took time during our underground journeys to show us rooms dedicated to other illegal activities. "Opium dens were very, very popular here," he explained as we entered a dark labyrinth. Not surprisingly, many opium patrons were easy targets for shanghaiers.

Political corruption enabled such practices. Local law enforcement was routinely paid off and a number of crimps were elected to public office, often through vote tampering. Naturally they blocked any legislation that would inhibit their ability to earn big money—some crimps made $200,000 per year in the trade of human trafficking.

By 1915, a number of laws had been passed to stop the practice of shanghaiing. It helped that steamships had become the standard, vessels without sails, which needed constant tending. In 1941, Portland sealed the entrances to these dark passageways, and, in the process, the city attempted to literally bury forever this dark aspect of its history.

Expectations Sagging for the Return of Hung Far Low

One notable landmark in Portland's Chinatown is the huge, rectangular sign marking the entrance to the Hung Far Low restaurant. Opinions vary on what the Chinese words *Hung Far Low* really mean—or what they meant in 1928 when the owners opened up the restaurant. Some people with knowledge of China's many dialects claim the words mean "a flower blossom." Another person claimed that it means "building of golden prosperity."

Regardless, Portlanders came to love it and many tourists traveled to Chinatown to have their pictures taken under the phallically funny sign. For a long time, but not anymore.

In 2005, Hung Far Low's owners moved the restaurant to Eighty-second Avenue, leaving behind their famous sign. In 2008, they hired a crew to remove the sign, in hopes of moving it to their new locale. Unfortunately, workers found that the sign had been damaged by years of Portland weather, and it was too unsafe to rehang.

They removed it to a repair shop, and assessed the damage. Local newspapers and citizens learned of the sign's removal and called for its return. Although it cost $3,000 to remove, the estimated cost to repair the sign ranged from $6,000 to $30,000.

Several organizations have tried raising money to re-erect the Hung Far Low sign. *Weird Oregon* hopes they succeed.

Mermaids on the Oregon Coast: The Sea Lion Caves

Some scientists have suggested that sailors mistook seals or sea lions sunning themselves on rocks for mermaids, the half-human, half-fish mythological creatures who could be friendly toward seamen . . . or could lure them to their watery deaths. We believe that a sailor would have to have been at sea a bit too long to mistake a barking sea lion for a singing mermaid. Still, we get it: Humans are fascinated by seals and sea lions.

According to local legend, in 1880, Capt. William Cox was sailing his ship north of Florence, Oregon. He saw a small channel between the coastal rocks and managed to sail inside, where he found a massive cavern. He returned several times, and once was trapped there by storms. He was supposed to have stayed alive by killing and eating one of the many sea lions lounging there among the coast rocks. A tall tale? Perhaps, but Cox did buy the land above the cave, and it remained in his family until 1926.

At more than 125 feet in height and more than two acres in size, Sea Lion Caves is the largest grotto in the world. It is the only known mainland place where both Steller and California sea lions breed, then return to spend the winter. Depending on the weather, about two hundred sea lions live around the cave. In addition to housing sea lions, the cave is also home to several species of coastal birds.

In 1927, R. E. Clanton bought the land to develop the cave as a tourist attraction. In 1930, as construction of Highway 101 began, Clanton and partners J. G. Houghton and J. E. Jacobson cut a 1,500-foot trail along the rock face, a wooden tower, and 135 steps leading to the cave. Clanton left the partnership to be replaced by S. A. Saubert. The families of the owners still manage the caves.

In 1958, work began on an elevator shaft connecting the clifftop with the caves. It took three years to build, because they paused during the months when the sea lions were living inside the caves. The elevator itself was an engineering marvel, taking a little bit less than one minute to go 208 feet.

When we visited the Sea Lion Caves, we received a safety briefing from one of the employees. We wondered about the joking caution "don't mind the noise and smell," until we got to the foot of the elevator. We heard something, faintly at first, that sounded like a cross between a dog barking and a car honking. It grew louder as we walked down the passageway. One of the people at the head of our group sniffed and said, "It smells like a wet dog that's been eating rotting fish."

We agreed. Even so, we spent nearly a compelling hour watching the sea lions play on the nearby rocks. But we are still trying to figure out how any sailor could mistake a sea lion for a mermaid.

The Sea Lion Caves are about eleven miles north of Florence, along Highway 101, and their Web site is http://sealioncaves.com.

Whorehouse Meadow

Just outside the small town of Frenchglen is a small, nondescript meadow that stands on the slopes of Steens Mountain. To anyone who happened to pass by this place, there would be no reason to think of it as anything more than what it appears to be.

But locals know that looks can be deceiving. For this is no ordinary meadow—this is Whorehouse Meadow.

Many decades ago, this area was the stomping grounds primarily of sheep herders and cattlemen. Most of those men had certain traits in common. For one thing, they worked in remote corners of the world. For another, they led generally solitary lives, putting in long hours isolated from other people.

Yesteryear's madams saw such lonely caretakers as a potential gold mine. But, the isolation presented a real problem. It's hard to set up a respectable whorehouse without a headquarters.

It wouldn't have been economical to erect a building out in the middle of nowhere for a rural rutfest, so the ladies of the night came up with a solution that proves that, if nothing else, those who run prostitution rings are resourceful. The section of land now known as Whorehouse Meadow regularly filled up with tents, makeshift wooden shacks, and other temporary structures. Just as the sheep herders and the cattlemen of the area were constantly mobile, so too became the ladies who profited off of servicing them.

The area is still remote and underpopulated—the population of Frenchglen hovers around a dozen people. And though there are no more makeshift rutting tents in Whorehouse Meadow, the name remains, despite a 1960s mapmaker's changing the meadow's name on a local map to Naughty Girl Meadow. Surprisingly, locals scattered in towns throughout the area went into an uproar. The legend of Whorehouse Meadow had become beloved over time, particularly during the heyday of free love in the 1960s. Indeed, battles raged between town officials, pious townsfolk, and the fun-loving for years. Eventually, in 1976, under the direction of the U.S. Board on Geographic Names, the Whorehouse Meadow name was retained—not just colloquially, but officially.

As far as we know, there are no whores in Whorehouse Meadow, but there is evidence of their former presence. Local lore suggests that bored sheep herders carved reminiscences—words and drawings—into tree trunks scattered throughout the area. If you look hard enough, you might even find verbal and visual depictions of some of the savored (and unsavory) acts that once took place there.

Suspended Flight: The Spruce Goose

Howard Hughes's lasting obsession was not a woman—he had several wives and mistresses—it was an airplane. Specifically, "her" name was the Hughes H-4 Hercules, better known as the Spruce Goose, and she resides in McMinnville.

In 1942, the United States lost over eight hundred thousand tons of ships, crew, and cargo to German U-boats in World War II. The government looked for a safer alternative, and industrialist Henry Kaiser suggested a massive cargo airplane. He approached Howard Hughes, a longtime aviation enthusiast and uber-rich eccentric, who agreed to help build three prototypes.

Kaiser and Hughes designed what was the largest airplane in the world at that time. Because of wartime shortages, they could not use steel or aluminum, so they proposed using wood in a glued lamination process, similar to plywood. As they built the airplane, a flying boat actually took shape, and people began calling it the Spruce Goose, even though it was built out of birch, balsa, and basswood. In addition to being the largest airplane in the world, it was a monument to engineering and innovation. The Spruce Goose would take off and land in the water, and could carry 750 soldiers or two Sherman tanks more than three thousand miles (enough range to cross the Atlantic Ocean) on a single load of fuel. The Spruce Goose had a wingspan of more than 319 feet, and grown men could stand up and walk inside the hollow wings. With all this, it only needed a crew of three to fly. Yet it was a dream that only barely succeeded.

Henry Kaiser pulled out of the project in 1944, blaming a shortage of materials, although there was probably some conflict with Hughes, who was a perfectionist. Hughes ran out of government money and the war ended before the Spruce Goose was finished. Hughes put several million of his own dollars into the project. Finally, on November 2, 1947, he finished the Spruce Goose. He piloted a series of trial runs at Long Beach, California, where the Spruce Goose finally took flight. Under Hughes's control, the Spruce Goose rose to a height of seventy feet for about a minute, flying about a mile. Shortly after that, the U.S. Senate killed the HK-4 Hercules "flying boat" project.

Hughes stored the Spruce Goose in a special climate-controlled hangar—remember, it was made of wood, not metal—maintained by a crew sworn to secrecy. He spent an estimated $1 million per year to keep it flight-ready until his death in 1976. He never flew the Spruce Goose again, and may have never even seen it again after it was put into the hangar, where it remained for more than twenty years.

In 1980, the Spruce Goose went on display in a glass dome, next to the *Queen Mary,* in Long Beach. In 1988, Disney bought both attractions, but a few years later decided not to keep the Spruce Goose. In 1992, the Evergreen Aviation and Space Museum in McMinnville, Oregon, gained ownership of the Spruce Goose.

In August of that year, they disassembled the flying boat

and shipped larger portions of it on a barge to Portland. All of the pieces of Spruce Goose did not arrive in McMinnville until February 1998. The Evergreen Aviation Museum then built a new display building while volunteers restored the pieces of the Spruce Goose in another building. On September 16, 2000, the larger pieces of the Spruce Goose were moved into their new home and reassembled. Although the museum opened in early 2001, the last portion, the tail, was not reassembled until December 7, 2001—Pearl Harbor Day.

The Spruce Goose resides at the museum surrounded by more than thirty other airplanes, some dating to the early twentieth century. It is so large that its wings spread over these other aircraft like a goose and her goslings. We believe that Hughes would be happy to see that his dream was taken care of, still ready to take flight.

Visit the Spruce Goose and the other displays, including some NASA artifacts at the Evergreen Aviation and Space Museum (www.sprucegoose.org).

Unexplained Phenomena

Occam's razor, a principle of logical thought, is commonly stated as, "All things being equal, the simplest solution is probably the best." In other words, don't assume what isn't evident as an explanation for any other unknown.

This is all fine and well until a "logical" explanation doesn't quite stand up to scrutiny or is rejected by those who are most in the know. This is the point at which a mystery enters the realm known as The Unexplained: that crossroads of reason where esoteric theories seem just as valid as any other solutions. Many strange events in Oregon over the years fall into this category: UFO sightings, an encounter with walking tree stumps, the sudden appearance in the desert of a quarter-mile-wide Hindu religious symbol, and more.

While some of these stories might be more dubious than others, and while some may have perfectly reasonable, nonesoteric explanations, they still contribute to Oregon's rich heritage of legends. It is in this spirit that we present them for your consideration.

And rest assured: While Occam's razor has its place, we recognize that it limits the scope of our reasoning. Until a better explanation is offered for some of the truly mysterious events herein, we reserve the right to toss aside Occam's razor and consider, if but for a moment, more fantastic possibilities!

"Turtle Ship" over the Ocean

USOs—unidentified submerged objects—are the aquatic equivalent to UFOs. They're sometimes seen diving into, emerging from, or generally hovering around the ocean. They're not often differentiated from UFOs that appear over land, despite their distinctive choice of environment.

The late naturalist and paranormal guru Dr. Ivan T. Sanderson speculated that aliens have built underwater bases in the dark, hidden depths of our oceans. It makes a weird kind of sense: Given the lack of population (save for the occasional ship), what better location is there from which to operate without being disturbed by meddling humans?

Oregon's annals of weirdness contain at least one possible USO. On April 12, 1950, a married couple were enjoying themselves on Pacific Beach. The husband, a Mr. Hermann, stood on the shore preparing to take a picture of his wife, who was in the water. Suddenly, the Hermanns spotted a silvery "turtle-shaped" craft farther out over the ocean. It was close enough that they could make out six holes, perhaps exhaust ports, on the underside. The ship was said to be trailing an orange flame and leaving a white vapor trail. The Hermanns watched it for a few moments until it flew in the direction of Tillamook Head and disappeared from sight. A few days later, Mr. Hermann showed a picture he took of the craft to the *Oregonian*. Its authenticity was unclear, and it failed to generate the kind of excitement that the McMinnville photo did just a month later. (See "McMinnville's Famous Flying Saucer Photos," later in the chapter.)

If Mr. Hermann's photo was genuine, however, the question still persists: Did the location of this flying "turtle ship" indicate that it came from underwater? Your guess is as good as ours!

OFFICIAL GOVERNMENT USE: SEIZED FROM "PACIFIC BEACH INCIDENT" (UNDEVELOPED FILM WITH ANOMALY)

Water They Doing at Eagle Point?

The late Coral Lorenzen of the Aerial Phenomena Research Organization interviewed an Eagle Point woman, identified only as "Mrs. M," regarding a UFO she saw near her property in February 1958. The craft was about three to four times bigger than Mrs. M's house and seemed to be examining some flood water. Ms. Lorenzen related the incident in her 1970 book, *Shadow of the Unknown*:

Mrs. M. walked to her kitchen window and looked out toward the road in front of her house. She saw a huge object hovering from 30 to 40 feet above a lake of backed-up rain water near the irrigation ditch there. The color of the object was amber "as if it was hot," she said, and it presented a huge and strange appearance. A funnel-like contraption extended down into the water below the object which itself was "like a disk," and appeared to be about 500–600 feet in diameter. The underside of the disk was flat except where the funnel was attached, and at the outer edges of this bottom portion were what appeared to be large round rollers "like huge marbles" spaced about 10 to 15 feet apart. Mrs. M. did not count these rollers but was certain that there were a large number of them.

She was not able to discern any configuration of the top of the object except that it was round and she got the impression that it merely sloped down to the edges; no dome was visible. She and her four-year-old son watched the object hovering there making a humming sound for a total of about 20 minutes, then the "funnel" retracted up into the object and only a huge bulge was left where it had been. After this operation was completed the whole bulk moved slowly straight up into the air until they couldn't see it anymore

because of the limiting edges of the window frame. "As it lifted up," Mrs. M. said, "it seemed to take the fog with it." Then, she said, as soon as the UFO was gone the sun came out and shone brightly until about 4 P.M. that afternoon, when the fog closed in again.

"Mrs. M" could not hazard a guess as to what the strange craft had been doing. After its departure, the water level in the ditch did not appear reduced in the least. (We're reasonably sure that the city of Eagle Point never contracted water quality tests or drainage surveys to space aliens.) In any case, that the craft supposedly affected the weather by "taking the fog with it" is a particularly uncommon element to UFO sightings.

The Flying Saucer Flap of '47

The summer of 1947 holds special significance in ufology, especially as it pertains to the Pacific Northwest. Two key UFO events in Washington State got the ball rolling for others soon to follow elsewhere.

On June 21, Harold Dahl and two acquaintances were boating in the Puget Sound near Maury Island, clearing stray logs from the water. Accompanying them were Dahl's son and his dog. Six enormous donut-shaped objects appeared directly overhead, one of them in apparent distress. As the others surrounded it, the damaged craft rained hot metal fragments down on Dahl and company, damaging their boat, burning his son's arm, and killing their dog.

Three days later, Kenneth Arnold of Idaho was piloting his airplane near the Cascade Mountains when he spotted nine crescent-shaped aircraft flying between Mount Rainier and Mount Adams. Not only did this encounter inaugurate the modern era of UFO sightings, it also, by way of a misquote in a newspaper article, inspired the term "flying saucer." (For further details on both incidents, read our companion volume, *Weird Washington.*)

Lesser known is the baffling series of aerial anomalies reported in Oregon over the next few days. Like a symphony of weirdness, it escalated from at least two smaller passages to a dazzling crescendo.

On the evening of June 29, a Mrs. Smith, along with her eight-year-old daughter, witnessed a disc-shaped object flying southward just east of Seaside. Although it was fairly high up, it was close enough that they should have heard engine noise; instead, it flew silently. Mrs. Smith was the wife of a local policeman, which (in less cynical times) lent additional credibility to her claim.

Around noon on July 1, reports of flying saucers poured into local police departments in Astoria, Madras, and Portland as about a dozen mystery craft followed the course of the Columbia River. Herb Baillet and his wife, Portlanders who up until then had been skeptical of regional UFO reports, were just two of many witnesses. Mrs. Baillet told the Portland *Daily Journal,* "I first saw three of them as we sat down to lunch and called my husband's attention to them. Later there were ten or twelve of them, flying low below the foothills . . . There was no noise and they did not appear to be flying fast."

And things were about to get quite a bit weirder.

The Original "Independence Day"

The next day, July 2, marked the famous flying saucer crash in Roswell, New Mexico, which distracted much of the nation's attention away from another spectacular incident. On the afternoon of July 4, as Portlanders celebrated Independence Day, scores of people saw numerous flying saucers over the city. (Thankfully, it was not a hostile invasion, as presented in a certain 1996 movie about ill-intentioned space aliens on the Fourth of July.)

According to the *Oregonian,* the saucers were first spotted over Oaks Amusement Park, south of downtown.

Visitors and employees were treated to the strange sight of three to six aluminum-colored or eggshell white discs "wobbling and weaving" as they flew rapidly to the southwest.

Three members of the harbor patrol also reported seeing the discs. They estimated the objects' altitude at about ten thousand feet.

Meanwhile, several people around the city called police. There was little that law enforcement could do about the odd spectacle, but an "all cars" alert was issued nonetheless. Soon, three policemen in two separate cars reported that they had spotted them. Two of the officers, Walter Lissy and Robert Ellis, were pilots. Even so, they could not judge how fast or high the discs were traveling because of their "terrific speed." The third officer, Earl Patterson, an air corps veteran, corroborated their account, adding that whatever the objects were, they were definitely not airplanes. The discs disappeared from the officers' view after roughly thirty seconds.

In addition to Portland police, Sgt. Claude Cross of the state police saw two of the objects from headquarters on Southeast McLoughlin Boulevard. He described them as resembling "toy balloons."

The *Oregonian* also reported that the flight crew of a Portland-bound airliner from Boise, Idaho, spotted the strange discs, or others like them, later that evening. Captain E. J. Smith, first officer Ralph Stevens, and flight attendant Marty Morrow reported that at 9:04 P.M., shortly after takeoff, the flying saucers were visible at least thirty miles away. They watched them for ten or fifteen minutes, noting that they appeared "very thin, very flat on the bottom, and . . . rough or irregular on top."

"They are not aircraft," they insisted. "They are bigger than aircraft."

No 'Saucers,' Army Declares

Portland, Ore., July 8 (AP)—The Oregonian said today that Maj. Gen. Nathan F. Twining, chief of the AAF materiel command, told it flatly that the "flying saucers" are not the result of experiments by the armed services.

"Neither the AAF nor any other component of the armed forces has any plane, guided missile or other aerial device under development which could possibly be mistaken for a saucer or formation of flying discs," the newspaper quoted Twining as telling it by telephone from Kirtland army airbase, Albuquerque, N. M.

Meanwhile, air national guard squadrons flying from Portland, Boise and Spokane bases patrolled Pacific northwest skies late yesterday, landing after sundown, without observing any of the objects.

Col. G. Robert Dodson, com-

The various witnesses, except for Sergeant Cross, agreed that the discs emitted flashes of light, which made it difficult to ascertain how many objects there were (accounts vary between two and twenty). At times, one or two appeared as a crescent shape, which recalled Kenneth Arnold's encounter over Washington a few days earlier. They flew erratically, with sudden changes of direction. Fourth of July fireworks were ruled out as an explanation, as the discs emitted no sound other than a subtle hum.

If there was a conventional earthly explanation for what was seen that holiday, the best suggestion came from army brass at Fort Lewis, Washington. Although they denied having any experimental disc-shaped aircraft, they pointed out that twenty-four Lockheed P-80 Shooting Stars were flying over Portland in a Fourth of July demonstration. These planes, the first fighter jets used by the army, would certainly have been perceived as state-of-the-art and unusually fast in 1947. To accept this explanation, however, one has to also accept that dozens of reliable witnesses mistook a recognizable, albeit streamlined, airplane shape for a disc or a crescent. This seems unlikely, especially given the other UFO events in the area over the previous few days.

The Start of Something Big

Washington and Oregon were by no means alone in their preponderance of UFO sightings during the summer of 1947. The phenomenon was happening all over North America. Just three days after the spectacular air show over Portland, newspapers were reporting that "flying saucers" had been seen in thirty-eight states, the District of Columbia, and Ontario, Canada. Subsequent sightings made it clear that whatever they were, they would define post–World War II America as much as the Cold War and the space race. As in 1947, the Beaver State would continue to be caught in the middle of the phenomenon. In fact, just three short years later, a farmer and his camera would attract to Oregon the widespread attention it was denied in 1947 . . . and then some. (See "McMinnville's Famous Flying Saucer Photos," later in the chapter.)

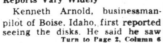

'Flying Saucers' Now Claimed Seen in 38 States, Canada And D.C.; Mystery Unsolved

San Francisco, July 7—(AP)— From one end of the country to the other, new reports of disk-like "flying saucers" skimming through the skies today added to the mystery which has baffled the nation since June 25.

There was no satisfactory explanation of the phenomenon. The saucers were first reported seen in the state of Washington on June 25. Then persons in other western states said they had seen them. The peak came over the July 4 holiday, when they first were reported seen east of the Mississippi.

The latest tabulation showed the mystery objects had been reported seen in 38 states, the District of Columbia and Canada.

Yesterday they were reported to have been seen in more than a dozen states, and in southwestern Ontario.

An aerial patrol by the Oregon national guard reported it had

Idaho, where a woman said ten persons saw eight of the disks disappear in timber on July 3.

Reports Vary Widely

Kenneth Arnold, businessman-pilot of Boise, Idaho, first reported seeing the disks. He said he saw the

Turn to Page 2, Column 6

Oddities in the

No Copping Apples

Yonkers, N. Y., July 7 (AP)—In a new edict handed down today by Deputy Public Safety Commissioner William J. Comey, this city's policemen are ordered to pay for all merchandise and drinks—including apples from fruit stands.

Hill Ice-solated

Norwich, Conn., July 7 (AP)—More

Vide(UF)o?

An anonymous videographer claims to have shot roughly sixteen seconds of video somewhere near Eagle Point and White City in March 2007. The video shows a shiny object of indeterminate shape apparently hovering beneath some dark clouds. The videographer admits that it may have just been an airplane, but the shaky video makes it hard to determine (it was shot from a moving vehicle). The video is posted on the Internet, where debate rages as to the object's true nature. (See the video here: http://www.ufocasebook.com/oregon032007.html.)

Who Are Oregon's Cattle Killers?

Finding livestock dead—blood drained and eyes, genitals, tongue, and other soft organs removed with surgical precision—has disturbed many a farmer and rancher. The phenomenon of animal mutilation is perhaps one of the most multifaceted mysteries around.

Occurring numerous times across several states, the incidents have involved farm animals like sheep, pigs, horses, and (primarily) cattle. The killings have been blamed on a variety of culprits with just as many motives: Satanists participating in some obscene ritual, government agents sowing fear to distract from more sinister conspiracies, or space aliens engaging in some kind of biological research. (While strange animal deaths in general often suggest Satanism, UFOs or black helicopters have been reported near places where mutilations occurred, accounting for suspicion of aliens or the government.)

By the 1990s, the phenomenon was so widespread that pop culture began referencing it, with heavy emphasis on cattle and aliens. The two camps were suddenly at odds in movies like *Mars Attacks!* and television programs from *The X-Files* to *South Park.* A few video games have even featured cattle mutilation as an objective. The surreality of Jack the Ripper–like aliens slaughtering unsuspecting bovines and stealing their body parts is a concept that, for some reason, many people find appealing.

The Northwest has certainly had its share of cattle-killing conundrums. Although most have occurred in Idaho and Montana, Washington and Oregon's cattle have not escaped the strange massacre. For our purposes here, of course, we submit the following incidents from Oregon.

In 1977 a cow was found dead and mutilated on a farm in the Grande Ronde Valley, Union County. Five days later, a nearby resident experienced problems with his television reception. As he got up to adjust the antenna, he looked out the window and saw a large white UFO hovering over the street..Unfortunately, it's impossible, however tempting, to definitively link the two occurrences.

In 1991 in Hood River, a farmer found one of his cows lying dead about five hundred yards from his house. Initially he assumed it was the work of Satanists, but upon closer inspection noticed that the wounds where an eye, the tongue, and the genitalia were missing were slightly cauterized. He wondered if some kind of laser cutting tool was used, and couldn't help but wonder if aliens, rather than Satanists, had anything to do with it.

These incidents were minor compared to others around Bend, which has been a hotbed of animal mutilation since the late 1970s and early 1980s. At that time, as dead, mangled cattle were being found to the southeast near Brothers, at least one rancher claimed to have regularly seen bright white flying saucers dragging, lifting, and tossing about the unfortunate bovines with beams of energy. He compared the noise from the beams to that of arc welders. As much as this sounds like campy science fiction, in 1979 two men at nearby Sand Springs discovered a dead cow mysteriously stuck high up in a ponderosa pine tree.

One of the men, Dwain Wright, got a strong sense of déjà vu when he saw this. He recalled a similar find years earlier on a property he had owned near the Tumalo Reservoir (northwest of Bend): "I had a huge pine tree in a canyon and it was hundreds of feet from either side of the canyon and yet, there was a cow . . . in the top of that pine tree. There was just no way it could have gotten up there . . . I thought . . . the only way it could have gotten there was taken up by a flying saucer and dropped out. There weren't any helicopters working in the Bend area at that time."

Evidently, Wright had a knack for finding strange cattle deaths. In 1980, he was back at Sand Springs when he discovered a bull that obviously died under bizarre circumstances. Its eyes, tongue, and anus were removed and the carcass was partially embedded in the ground. "It reminded me a lot of what they do in England with catapults," he stated in an interview. "They catapult dead animals and I've seen pictures of where they land and it makes quite an impression in the soil." Despite the removal of body parts and the apparent drop from a great height, there was no blood on the ground whatsoever. Whatever was happening, the perpetrators were not finished by any means.

On March 18, 2000, two pairs of dead calves lying about a quarter mile apart were found in the Millican Valley between Brothers and Bend. The next day, eight more calves were found dead in the area. There were no signs of blood or tracks on the ground around any of the carcasses. Kimball Lewis, executive director of the Humane Society of Central Oregon, investigated the incidents. In a later interview, he described the condition of the first four calves, and four of the eight found the next day: "these animals had their skins removed from just behind their front shoulders, if you will, in a 360 degree pattern down

to—if you can imagine what would be the equivalent of our ankles on their hind legs. The skin removed was neatly and uniformly down to that area on these animals."

The calves' hides had been removed with impressive precision; the lumen tissue—the thin membrane covering the muscle—was intact and uncut. A necropsy revealed the calves to be about two weeks old and definitely not stillborn, as evidenced by milk in their stomachs. It also revealed another anomaly: a highly reduced amount of blood in the bodies. The heart chambers were completely empty.

Dr. Trish Kentner, the veterinarian in charge of the necropsy, was unable to determine the sex of the calves, as the reproductive organs had been completely removed. Despite Kentner and Lewis's investigation, the mutilations remained as much of a mystery as ever.

X-Files episodes aside, the FBI really has looked into animal mutilations. Their investigation was undertaken in the late 1970s following one by the Bureau of Alcohol, Tobacco, and Firearms, which came up short on answers. The FBI concluded that most cases were simply caused by natural predators. The "excised" organs, which are composed of softer tissue, were the first portions eaten by parasites and other scavengers, thus accounting for the "surgically precise" wounds. "Missing" patches of outer skin can be attributed to postmortem bloating, which can stretch and tear the skin, making it appear as though pieces were cut out. What appears to be blood loss, said the FBI, is the result of blood pooling in lower parts of the body or consumption by parasites.

Still, the FBI conceded that this conclusion doesn't necessarily explain every case of animal mutilation. Anomalous circumstances in many incidents cannot be accounted for.

Given this admission, perhaps it's best that Satanists, government agents (perhaps the FBI itself), and especially aliens are not let off the hook just yet.

McMinnville's Famous Flying Saucer Photos

Fate can throw curveballs during the most ordinary moments. On occasion, unexpected events can even have life-altering effects. But what if the event is so incredible that it leaves an indelible mark on your home and community, and sparks a heated decades-long debate? Consider the modest farm couple who, on an otherwise average evening, irrevocably thrust McMinnville into the annals of ufology.

It wasn't that Paul and Evelyn Trent sought publicity. Years later, they would express regret that their actions resulted in so much disruption, and people who knew them would vouch for their sincerity. But the singular event on the evening of May 11, 1950, might have resulted in such repercussions in any case.

As the story goes, it all began on the Trents' farm nine miles west of McMinnville, at about 7:30 P.M. Evelyn was outside feeding the chickens when she noticed a metallic disc-shaped aircraft hovering in the northeast sky. It was silver and bronze colored, with a tapered shape, a flat bottom, and a protruding, antennalike structure on top. She excitedly called indoors for Paul to grab his camera. He did so, and came outside to see that the disc was moving slowly westward. He quickly snapped a photo as the craft began picking up speed. He advanced the film and snapped a second photo from a slightly different angle before the craft sped off.

Enter the Media

Although the "flying saucer" craze of the post–World War II era was growing at the time, the Trents apparently did not associate the strange object with little green men from outer space. Instead, they believed they'd witnessed an experimental military aircraft. The film was developed not quite a month later, after the remaining exposures had been used up with more everyday fare. Meanwhile, Paul told his friend, banker Frank Wortmann, about what they'd seen. Once the photos were developed, Wortmann was among the first to see them. He got copies and hung them in the front window of his bank.

That same day, Bill Powell, a reporter, saw the photos at the bank. Later that day, he interviewed the Trents for an article in the local paper. He asked to borrow the photo negatives for publication. Although they were concerned about getting in some kind of "trouble" with the military, the Trents reluctantly agreed. Powell's headline on the June 8, 1950, edition of the

McMinnville *Telephone-Register,* above large reproductions of both photos, reflected widespread public curiosity about the UFO phenomenon: AT LONG LAST—AUTHENTIC PHOTOGRAPHS OF FLYING SAUCER?

The question remains unanswered more than fifty years later, despite the intense scrutiny the photos touched off. In the weeks immediately following the *Telephone-Register* story, the photos became an international sensation. The Portland *Oregonian* published them on June 10, as did the Los Angeles *Examiner* on June 11. On June 12, the photos were shown on national television news. The following day, they appeared on international news broadcasts. They were published in the June 26 issue of *Life,* the country's best-selling magazine at the time and considered one of the most prestigious. John and Evelyn became instant celebrities; on July 10, they appeared on the New York City–based television program *We the People.* By popular demand, the June 8 edition of the *Telephone-Register* went back to press three times during this period. About ten thousand reprints were distributed throughout the United States and Canada. In the midst of this media circus, McMinnville was nicknamed Saucerville.

Official Investigation

Of course, all this attention was bound to attract certain other parties—specifically, the U.S. government. U.S. Air Force and FBI investigators called on the Trents to check their story and verify the authenticity of the photographs.

Through the years, Evelyn griped about their overbearing and somewhat threatening demeanors.

The air force confiscated the negatives from the *Telephone-Register,* presumably adding them to their collection of UFO evidence. (Some accounts, however, claim that the negatives were somehow passed along to United Press International and misplaced for seventeen years.)

At the time, the air force's formal UFO investigation was called Project Grudge. It was preceded by Project Sign and replaced by the longer-term Project Blue Book in 1952. By the 1960s, Project Blue Book was increasingly being criticized. Politicians, scientists, and others felt that it was suffering from careless research and possible cover-ups. In any case, the study had become too ponderous, and the air force wanted to scrap it altogether. Rather than ending it in the midst of all the criticism (which they feared would only encourage conspiracy theories), they asked physicist Edward Condon to chair a university-based study of Project Blue Book data. Thus, the University of Colorado UFO Project, better known as the Condon Committee, effectively took over Project Blue Book in 1966.

Soon, the Trents' negatives were rediscovered, and the Condon Committee undertook the first of two in-depth examinations of the flying saucer photos and the incident in general. As it turned out, William Hartmann, the case investigator, was duly impressed. After some consideration, he officially stated: "This is one of the few UFO reports in which all factors investigated, geometric, psychological, and physical, appear to be consistent with the assertion that an extraordinary flying object . . . evidently artificial, flew within sight of two witnesses." This is particularly significant in light of the generally skeptical tone held by the Condon Committee toward other UFO cases.

Opposition and Support

Skeptics were not convinced of the authenticity of the Trent photos, however, and "rational" explanations were suggested. Many believed that an object—an outdoor light, truck mirror, or model—was simply suspended from the power lines. They cited alleged discrepancies with the shadows on the building in the foreground in relation to the time frame in which the Trents said the pictures were taken.

These suspicions prompted a new analysis in 1975 by Dr. Bruce Maccabee, a well-known optical physicist and prominent UFO investigator. Maccabee tended to disagree with the contention that the pictures were faked. For his own analysis, he combined a slightly modified version of Hartmann's methodology with his own highly technical approach. He determined to his satisfaction that the object was not suspended from the power lines, but was indeed in the sky, some distance away. As for the shadows, subtle technical details led him to disregard the alleged discrepancies. (As of this writing, a summarized version of Maccabee's report is available on the Internet at http://brumac.8k.com/trent1.html.)

Maccabee's endorsement of the photos' authenticity did little to convince some skeptics. As part of his investigation, he interviewed Evelyn Trent several times. To some, like the late UFO debunker Philip J. Klass, excerpts from these conversations (included in Maccabee's full forty-six page report) only raised more suspicion. On different occasions, Evelyn seemed to relate slightly different details about the same aspects of the sighting. Specifics about whether her in-

laws, who lived a few hundred feet away, also saw the UFO seemed slightly contradictory across various retellings. Then there was the mysterious Mrs. Worth, an alleged neighbor of the Trents' who Evelyn said had also seen the aircraft. Efforts to track down Mrs. Worth for an interview were fruitless, as Evelyn cited new obstacles in contacting her every time Maccabee asked about it. Eventually, he dropped the subject—an incredulous action in itself, according to his critics.

"So what," the believers said. "He was asking about an incident that happened twenty-five years earlier. Maybe Mrs. Trent didn't remember every last detail."

"But it was such a momentous event in her life!" replied the skeptics. "How could she *not* remember?"

"Well," protested the believers, "Many people, including the Trents' relatives, have vouched for their integrity! They said the Trents would *never* perpetrate a hoax of this kind!"

"Of course their family vouches for them," said the skeptics. "Would you expect them *not* to?"

"But the Trents never made a dime off of the photos. . . ."

So it went, and so it continues going. More authentication and debunking followed throughout the 1980s and 1990s, each camp firmly insisting that their conclusion was correct. Meanwhile, McMinnville welcomes the controversy and celebrates the UFO sighting, genuine or hoaxed, with an annual festival. The festival embodies its own brand of weirdness, thus earning a separate entry in the Local Legends chapter.

As for the photos, the original negatives are currently archived at the offices of the McMinnville *News-Register* (successor to the *Telephone-Register*). There they wait for the next believer or debunker who will invariably come along to "prove" their opinion of them.

Maccabee's endorsement of the photos' authenticity did little to convince some skeptics.

Bend's "Dancing" Saucers

Years before flying saucers abused cattle in areas around Bend, they engaged in aerial maneuvers over the city itself. So says one report from 1949, which has a pair of disc-shaped UFOs "dancing" in the sky over Bend. Traffic stopped as motorists were either amazed by the display or blinded by the glare of the sun reflected from the shiny flyers. One witness, who had been a pilot during World War II and could presumably make an accurate guess, estimated that each was about the size of "a large bathtub," flying at a height of about ten thousand feet. Witnesses lost sight of the saucers as they moved along to the west.

The Diamond Peak "Mystery" Photo

On November 22, 1966, an anonymous biochemist was driving on the scenic Willamette Pass and pulled over to take a picture of the spectacular view. When the film was developed, he was startled to find an extra detail that he hadn't noticed. Against the backdrop of forested mountains near Diamond Peak was what appeared to be a flying saucer!

It seemed to be rising from beyond the road's edge. The object was clearly trailing a vertical column of vapor and appeared to be "stacked on top of itself" in triplicate. The photo was submitted to the National Investigations Committee on Aerial Phenomena (NICAP), under whose auspices it was analyzed. Famed ufologist Dr. J. Allen Hynek and photo analyst Adrian Vance declared it authentic. According to their calculations, the saucer was about three hundred feet away from the observer and measured twenty-two feet across. They speculated that the "stacking" effect was an indication of advanced "quantum propulsion" technology. That is, the craft was quickly "phasing in and out" of our reality. This may explain why the photographer hadn't noticed the saucer while taking the picture; according to Hynek and Vance, it might have been rendered invisible to the naked eye.

That's one explanation for what was captured on film, anyway.

The other, proposed in 1981 by biotechnologist Dr. Irwin Wieder, is far more mundane. He disregarded the contention that the photographer pulled over, declaring that it was just a drive-by photo of a road sign. Because of the parallax effect—visual perspective while in motion—closer objects appear to pass by faster. Since the sign was the object closest to the passing camera, it appeared as a horizontal blur. The sign post is thus distorted into a "vapor trail," while the stacking effect was caused by the blurring of light-and-dark contrasts on the sign, which probably read DIAMOND PEAK. Meanwhile, the background is less blurred because of its distance. In the picture, there is no middle ground between the blurry foreground and slightly sharper background, which further enhances the illusion.

A similar picture from Belgium was proven to be exactly this, and the effect has been easily reproduced elsewhere. Accordingly, NICAP seems to have accepted the explanation, since the incident doesn't currently appear on their UFO chronology (www.nicap.org/chrono.htm).

The "unexplained" issue here may not be the image on the photograph, but rather the reason Hynek and Vance were so convinced of its authenticity. It seems they overlooked the parallax effect.

The Blue Mountains Ghost Light

State Road 204, commonly known as Weston-Elgin Road for the two towns it connects, traverses about forty miles of scenic forest over the Blue Mountains. Along this road, the Blue Mountain ghost light, a floating luminescent orb of unknown origin, sometimes appears. Motorists who are not startled by the shimmering blue apparition might instead be unnerved by the humming sound that sometimes accompanies it.

Ghost lights, sometimes also known as will-o'-the-wisps, are usually explained as gas from decaying vegetation that is ignited through a natural chemical reaction. They are known to occur mostly in wetlands. Even if the ground on the mountain duplicates wetland conditions enough for a ghost light to appear, what's with the humming? Admittedly, we at *Weird Oregon* had only a few slim leads about this phenomenon. Please contact us if you know more about it, especially if any legends are connected to it.

Let Weirdness Rain!

Editor Mark Moran once remarked, "Charles Fort must have walked around with an umbrella all the time!" Fort, the first and most famous collector of weird-but-true stories, is widely known for his writings about anomalous rains.

He catalogued many accounts of unusual objects, animals, or substances falling from the sky, and popularized theories that such odd "precipitation" was launched by distant waterspouts or tornadoes. Whether these twisters were ever verified is another question entirely.

Here are some anomalous rains that fell in Oregon, as collected by Charles Fort.

The Portland Weather Bureau reported a tornado on June 4, 1894, followed by a downpour of ice fragments. No mere hailstones, these chunks were about three or four inches square, and about an inch thick. One contemporary writer stated that they "gave the impression of a vast field of ice suspended in the atmosphere," which broke into pieces and fell to Earth.

In June of 1911, young Arlene Meyer was walking along the Sandy River near Boring when it suddenly began raining dark, rubbery objects. She looked around and saw countless salamanders "literally covering the ground and wriggling and crawling all over."

Then, in 1920, during another squall, "glistening, white fragments" resembling china or porcelain are said to have pummeled Portland. Fort disputes the standard theory on this one, doubting that a tornado could be so selective. "One supposes," he writes, "that a storm brought to this earth fragments of a manufactured object . . . from some other world."

Perhaps, but it's completely appropriate that they fell on the world we affectionately call Weird Oregon!

Gravitation Vexation at the Oregon Vortex

One Oregon tourist trap has left a new slant on thousands of visitors' perception of reality. The area in Gold Hill known as the Oregon Vortex has always been a bit off-kilter. Native Americans are said to have avoided the area, calling it "forbidden ground." Clearly, the laws of nature are a bit lopsided here.

When the Old Grey Eagle Mining Company built an assay office on the grounds in 1904, they quickly became aware of the phenomenon. The building slid off its foundation and came to rest at an odd angle. No longer fit to conduct business in, it was converted into a tool shed. The property was later acquired by John Litster, geologist, mining engineer, and physicist. He grew

fascinated with the localized magnetic disturbance here, which results in an erratic gravitational pull and other strange occurrences. Litster recognized the educational value of the "forbidden ground" and opened it to the public in 1930.

The old office and tool shed, now called the House of Mystery, became the main attraction, but the Vortex in general has since made the grade as one of the state's most intriguing destinations.

The disturbance that causes the anomalous phenomena is described as "a spherical field of force, half above the ground and half below the ground." It has been likened to a gravitational tornado that tends to exert force toward magnetic north. Outdoors and in, objects roll uphill, people and objects lean at odd angles, and visitors grow and shrink while walking across a level plane.

Litster spent forty years studying the Vortex in detail and appears to have uncovered some disturbing information. Announcing that "the world isn't ready for what goes on here," he specified in his will that his family was to destroy his notes upon his passing. Although they did not immediately honor his wishes, a leaky roof soon did. Fortunately, copies of Litster's self-published 1940 booklet, "Notes and Data," featuring thirty-odd pages of scientific diagrams pertaining to the Vortex, are still available in the gift shop.

Many dubious vortices and "mystery spots" cropped up across the country around the same time as the Oregon Vortex. Although staff members have always stood by its authenticity, some skeptics are unconvinced. Ultimately, experiencing the strange phenomenon for yourself may be the only way to decide if the Oregon Vortex is on the level.

Light-Headed at the Vortex

I live in Washington, but I have family down in Oregon. In a small town called Gold Hill, there is a place that claims to be home to the original uneven house, where golf balls roll up hills. I've been there several times myself and they not only prove the house is level, but the ground itself. Complete with ruler, level, and simple stick. And trust me, you *will* get light-headed! —*Michelle Henderson*

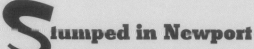tumped in Newport

In one memorable scene of the classic 1939 film version of *The Wizard of Oz,* Dorothy and her friends are chased by enchanted walking trees. We wonder if one Kathy Reeves had ever seen this movie prior to April 5, 1966, and, in regards to this particular scene, thought to herself, "Thank goodness this is only a movie! Those walking trees sure look surreal and creepy!"

If so, the sixteen-year-old's experience that evening must have been especially distressing.

Kathy and a friend (who seems to remain anonymous in all accounts of this incident) were walking to Kathy's house on Pioneer Mountain in Newport. Partway there, they noticed a faint glow a short distance away. They would later describe it as resembling "a flashlight with a cover over the end."

Assuming it was coming from pranksters who were trying to spook them, Kathy picked up a rock and threw it at the light. In response, several larger lights lit up around it. Suddenly not so confrontational, the girls nervously and more briskly continued along their way.

A few moments later, they saw something even weirder: Waddling across a pasture toward the lights were three short, squat beings with no discernible head or arms. According to the girls, they looked like garishly colored tree stumps, down to the rootlike tentacles they hobbled on. Had these "tree stumps" come from somewhere over the (planetary) rainbow, somewhere far?

The girls didn't stop to ask. Now completely frightened, they ran the rest of the way to the Reeves home, and some time later recounted their startling experience to reporters. Luckily, the tree stumps hadn't followed them—or had they?

Soon after, the Reeves family experienced an outbreak of seemingly paranormal activity at home. Orbs of light appeared around the house, inside and out. Some darted from room to room. These phenomena were witnessed by several others, including police officers. Deputy sheriff Thomas Price reported seeing an orange light, "bigger than any star," flying over the house. "I know it wasn't a meteor or a satellite because it was maneuvering," he insisted. "There was a noise like a giant spinning top." Max Taylor, a chemist who volunteered to investigate the incidents, camped overnight on the family's front lawn and witnessed two blue lights atop the roof.

The Reeves family, weary of the strange goings-on, eventually moved away. The household light show reportedly ceased with their departure. Subsequent owners of the house did not report any similar incidents.

The surrounding area, however, was a different story. There were no further sightings of walking tree stumps, but within six months of Kathy's encounter, more than two dozen other locals claimed to have seen similar unexplained lights, as well as UFOs and giant one-eyed humanoids.

All of them, no doubt, courtesy of the cosmic Wizard of Odd.

The Sri Yantra Mystery of Mickey Basin

Weirdness permeates Oregon so thoroughly that even the state's remote southeast corner—the Alvord Desert—can't escape it. The population here is sparse. The landscape is rocky and barren, pocked with small mountains and dry lake beds, including one known as Mickey Basin. It's the last place anyone would expect to come across a mystery—which, of course, makes it the perfect place to find one.

On August 10, 1990, Bill Miller, a pilot in the Air National Guard, was flying near Mickey Basin when he spotted something amazing. Within the lake bed was a quarter-mile-wide pictograph etched into the ground, a desert equivalent of a crop circle. It consisted of several overlapping triangles surrounded by concentric circles and arch patterns, all enclosed within a stylized array of lines bending at right angles.

Miller took photographs and reported his find via radio. On September 14, the news media broke the story on the unlikely artwork. It was quickly identified as a Sri Yantra: a Tantric Hindu meditation symbol. This ancient emblem is highly revered for its representation of divinity and admired for its complexity and its mathematical relation to phi, the "golden ratio."

Measurements showed the Sri Yantra to contain 13.3 miles of lines, ten inches wide and three inches deep. Ufologists Don Newman and Alan Decker examined the area and noted that there were no footprints or tire tracks around the pictograph. This was rather odd, given that as they drove to the spot, their truck left quarter-inch indentations in the terrain. Further examination by a group of architects called attention to the precision with which the lines were dug. Although they were not perfectly straight when measured on the ground, they appeared so from the air (which, after all, was the intended vantage point). Even

the dirt dug out to form the image was equally distributed on either side of the lines. It was estimated that it could have cost up to $100,000 just to survey the area for the symbol's creation.

A religiously symbolic image of this scale, in such a remote region and created with this high a degree of precision, could be expected to generate a lot of speculation. Deities were credited for its creation by proponents of a holy or mystical origin. Many New Agers believed it was created by UFOs and/or space aliens. Agnostics, atheists, and skeptics insisted it was put there by good old-fashioned human ingenuity.

As the factions of belief debated, Bill Witherspoon, an Iowa artist, came forward claiming credit for himself and a team of assistants. According to Witherspoon, the design was surveyed, laid out with shallow "sketch" lines on the terrain, and then dug out with a garden plow. He was even able to provide video of the effort. It appeared that the mystery was solved; the "human ingenuity" camp seemed vindicated.

Witherspoon's explanation was almost immediately met with skepticism, however, from those who believed the Sri Yantra had more ethereal origins. Beyond the lack of tracks and the assumed cost of such a project, they questioned the feasibility of a group of four men dragging a plow around the desert—in August, no less—for more than thirteen miles.

Witherspoon explained that they did it in the cooler morning and evening hours from July 31 to August 9. He ascribed the lack of footprints to a "sudden rainstorm" that smoothed them out on the last day. As for tire tracks, he said, there were none because they simply never drove up to the site. Instead, they camped a mile or two away and lugged their equipment to the site daily.

This did not quiet his detractors, who felt that his

explanations were too perfect. Witherspoon, they felt, had a convenient answer for everything, particularly the bit about the rainstorm. Plus, they questioned why the Sri Yantra was never spotted as it was being created. Surely, if it took ten days to complete, the Air National Guard, which regularly flew over the area, would have noticed it sooner. Instead, it was noticed all at once, as if it had appeared overnight.

To the naysayers, even Witherspoon's most compelling evidence—his video—was suspect. They claimed that he and his associates simply filled in portions of the design with the loose dirt around it, and then re-enacted the purported plowing. This was evidenced in the video by dark swaths on the ground being traced with the plow, and the obvious ease with which it was being done. The dirt appeared to dislodge easily from the hard terrain, and none of the men showed any sign of fatigue after what surely would have been very hard work.

This skepticism notwithstanding, the government certainly believed Bill Witherspoon: They fined him for unauthorized use of public land. Interestingly, he and his associates went on to create (undisputed) land art in the desert and on farms as a commercial venture. Eventually they turned their attention upward, forming Sky Factory, a manufacturer of simulated sky views for ceilings and walls.

Did Witherspoon's later efforts quell the suspicions of his critics? Not entirely. His claims to the Mickey

Many New Agers believed it was created by UFOs.

Basin Sri Yantra are still hotly debated on Internet message boards. Since the Alvord Desert is also known for sporadic UFO sightings, including some around the time the pictograph appeared, the debate as to its true creators will probably continue for quite some time.

The Sri Yantra is long gone, worn away by the weather. The Mickey Basin is once again a blank canvas, waiting for the next inspired artist—human or otherwise.

Beaver State Beasts

Oregon's catalog of mysterious critters is relatively straightforward. Sure, there's at least one modern-day sighting of what may have been a flock of legendary Thunderbirds, but by and large, the Beaver State's cryptids almost always fall into one of two categories. One category is water dwellers. Oregon's rivers, lakes, and shores have reportedly hosted some of the strangest animals this side of Loch Ness. The other category is the undocumented North American primate (most often referred to as Bigfoot). The Pacific Northwest seems to teem with these ape men, and Oregon boasts some of the most compelling encounters on record.

Of course, the jury is still officially out on the existence of these creatures. Mainstream science may still consider them more bunk than biology, but we encourage skeptics to keep an open mind. After all, even in recent years, new and rare animal species have been discovered. Multiple reports of similar mystery creatures throughout the state may indicate that there may be more to these stories than simple folklore.

Also presented are some tales of culture shock experienced by a few out-of-town fish and reptiles who opted, or were forced, to visit Oregon. It just goes to show: Even in a state as civilized as Oregon, it's a jungle out there!

Bigfoot

Bigfoot is known globally by many names: Yeti, Swamp Ape, Sasquatch, Yowie, Alma, Wild Man, and others. These names conjure images of large, smelly, apelike bipeds who inhabit the wilderness and leave behind footprints as large as the legends they've inspired. Here is a sampling of local encounters.

Deer Bigfoot . . .

Larry Martin got the scare of his life in 1961. While out cruising the back roads of Alpine, he and some friends engaged in a spur-of-the-moment hunt, shooting a deer and skinning it on the spot. So as not to bloody up the car they were riding in, the group left the carcass behind as they went to get a pickup truck belonging to one of the men.

They returned to the spot at about 9 P.M. to retrieve the deer. It was gone, but whatever had taken it left a trail as it dragged it into the nearby woods. Flashlights in hand, the men followed the trail and soon stumbled upon a violent ruckus coming from behind some brush. It sounded like whatever had taken their prize was agitated. Martin briefly turned his back to the noise, shining his flashlight around the area. When he turned back around, he found that he was five feet away from a creature lunging at him!

The beast towered over Martin, who was nearly six feet tall. He said it had "human-like features . . . an ape or gorilla, or something like that . . ." with a hairy face, broad shoulders, and a weight of four hundred to five hundred pounds.

It was enough to convince the group to get the hell out of there, which they did with considerable haste. They jumped back into the pickup truck and sped off. Although Larry Martin and friends lost their deer, they got away with something far more precious: their lives.

The Bigfoot Trap at Rogue River National Forest

During the Bigfoot craze of the 1970s, the North American Wildlife Research (NAWR) team was determined to get to the bottom of the mystery. Proof of the now defunct group's perseverence resided in the Rogue River National Forest, on the Collings Mountain Trail just west of Applegate Lake. That is where NAWR placed what is likely the world's only Bigfoot trap.

The trap consisted of a ten-by-ten-foot wooden shed, with a rabbit carcass suspended from a hook in the ceiling as bait. A rope was tied to the hook; the other end was tied to a release mechanism. This secured a vertically sliding metal grate over the shed's entrance. Ostensibly, a wandering Sasquatch would enter the shed to get at the yummy morsel, yank the carcass from the hook, and unlatch the release mechanism. This would drop the grate and trap the Sasquatch inside. Simultaneously, an electronic alarm would alert a watchman in a shelter a few hundred feet away. The watchman would alert authorities, and NAWR would reap publicity and recognition.

NAWR was headed by filmmaker Ron Olson, director of the documentary *Sasquatch: The Legend of Bigfoot.* Olson was partly inspired by the late Perry Lovell, an elderly miner who had lived nearby. Lovell claimed to have observed Sasquatch groups passing through the area every fall and had once discovered eighteen-inch footprints in his garden. Olson found that many of Lovell's neighbors believed him.

But all the trap caught over six years were a couple of bears, proving at least that the trap worked. By 1980, the Bigfoot trap had become more of a tourist attraction than anything else, so the U.S. Forest Service bolted the grate open and in 2006 allowed volunteers to repair it.

Flix: The Conser Lake Monster

"I am called Flix. There are many like me, but I am the one called Flix."

This is what reporter Betty Westby and her friend, a psychic who remains anonymous in Westby's account, were supposedly told while trudging through the woods near Conser Lake, in the rural town of Millersburg, during the wee hours of a summer morning in 1960.

The message was delivered telepathically by a creature that might be described as a semiaquatic albino Bigfoot. Various witnesses described it as being seven feet or more in height, white-furred, cat-eared, and—despite having flipperlike, webbed feet—able to run extremely fast. Westby and friend were the only humans privy to his name—everyone else called him the Conser Lake Monster, which (according to Westby) offended him.

Millersburg, located just west of I-5 between Salem and Eugene, had been known mostly for its odd smell. The notorious stench from a paper mill to the south mingled with the fresh scent of area mint farms, creating an aroma that many locals were at a loss to describe. Encounters with Flix would temporarily suspend the smell's status as Millersburg's signature and increase the town's "weird quotient" considerably.

In the 1950s, Conser Lake was a popular nighttime hangout for area teens. Around the time of the creature's first sighting, a rumor circulated that a flying saucer had crashed into the lake and lay submerged at its murky bottom. In 1959, a truck driver was scared out of his wits by a tall white-furred primate that ran alongside the truck, peering into the cab as it kept pace at up to thirty-five miles an hour.

About a year later, on Sunday, July 31, 1960, seven teenagers from nearby Albany were out for an evening stroll on footpaths near the lake. Two of them walked ahead and hid behind some brush, intending to jump out and scare the others. The tables were turned, however, when they heard a huge crash behind them, followed by "squishing" footsteps that sounded like someone with "water in his overshoes" (according to Westby's account in *Greater Oregon*). Abandoning their prank, the two startled teens ran back toward their friends. To the astonishment of all, a tall white-furred biped emerged from the woods and ran past them at an incredible speed, emitting a high-pitched cry.

The teens excitedly told police and relatives about their encounter. As a larger group of people investigated the area later that same night, Flix was briefly spotted again, standing by a tree before disappearing into the woods. Witnesses described it as "something like a gorilla" (or a polar bear), weighing approximately four hundred pounds.

When Albany radio station KGAL reported on the incident two days later, posses of teenagers from far and wide converged on Conser Lake with hunting rifles. As Westby wrote, they "rendered the woods horrible as they fired at random at every bush." This lasted for several days; that Saturday night, about two hundred people patrolled the area.

Westby and five friends investigated the woods around Conser Lake in the wee hours one morning. They found gigantic webbed footprints, six or seven feet apart. Westby says she returned a few days later with her psychic friend, who then engaged in her brief rapport with Flix. Their "conversation" was cut short when more would-be monster hunters appeared on the scene, resulting in their quarry's hasty exit.

Later that month, Flix turned up in Stayton, eighteen miles northeast of Millersburg. Police, volunteers, and even the mayor responded to a reported sighting but succeeded only in finding and turning back another bloodthirsty group of teens.

Was Flix, the Conser Lake Monster, real? Was he the product of mass hysteria or, perhaps, Betty Westby's fiction-writing skills?

Sasquatch in the Blue Mountains

The Umatilla National Forest, in the Blue Mountains of eastern Oregon, is a Bigfoot hot spot. The general store at the Tollgate Resort on Highway 204 in Weston is decorated with Sasquatch foot- and handprint casts. If you're lucky, you might run into an old-timer there with stories like these to tell.

The McKay Creek Creature

According to a 2007 article by Phil Wright in the *East Oregonian,* four friends decided to go camping near McKay Creek in Meacham. They set up camp on a small island in the creek to scout for the upcoming deer hunting season.

The quartet observed with disappointment that there weren't as many deer around as in previous years. While scouting, they found a cave, its mouth littered with animal bones. The four concluded that they'd found a bear den and that perhaps this was the reason for the low number of deer.

That evening one of the men saw "something" moving in the campers' direction. As the men hastily vacated the campsite with a few supplies and some beer, the creature began shrieking, resulting in a frantic, every-man-for-himself scramble.

Later that night, two of the men slept in the back seat of their truck while the other two sat in the front, talking and drinking. Wide awake with alcohol-fueled courage, the two stepped into the eerie night and walked to a small grove of trees about two hundred yards from the truck. Almost immediately, they heard the sounds of branches breaking somewhere in the nearby dark, approaching them.

One of the men was quoted in the *East Oregonian* article: "I said, 'We got to go.' And at that moment I heard a blood-curdling scream. . . . It was louder than a cougar or a bear or anything like that. It was the loudest thing I ever heard."

The two men made their way back to the truck, one of them running into a tree along the way. The creature seemed content to scare them off.

The next morning, as the four men walked back to their camp, they found more evidence that a Bigfoot had been following them. Their camp was completely ransacked and twelve-to-fifteen-foot logs had been moved. The creature had left footprints twice as large as adult human feet and coarse brown hair, five to eight inches long, around their damaged supplies.

The quartet never got a close-up look at their stalker, although the brown hair and high-pitched cries jibe with other Bigfoot encounters in the area, such as those reported by late U.S. Forest Service patrolman Paul Freeman.

Tracker or Trickster?

To Bigfoot enthusiasts, Paul Freeman is a name that evokes either admiration or disdain: admiration because of the seemingly solid Sasquatch evidence he found over the years; disdain for his uncanny (i.e., suspicious) success at finding so much of it.

In June 1982, Freeman claimed to have seen a Sasquatch while making his morning rounds on the Washington side of the Umatilla National Forest. He took several photos of its footprints and made a plaster cast of one. The next day, a search-and-rescue team also happened upon the footprints while on an unrelated assignment. They, too, took photos and a made a cast.

A week later, Freeman and some colleagues found similar tracks a few miles away in the Mill Creek watershed. These tracks showed that a pair of creatures had passed through; one set seemed to match the Sasquatch from a week earlier. The prints were about fifteen inches long, seven inches wide at the ball, and four inches wide at the heel. Three more footprints were cast from the two sets.

Owing to the extremely fine soil in the area, these casts are highly detailed, clearly showing ridges and pores from the creature's skin. Extensive examination by biologists, latent print examiners, and even footwear specialists concluded that the tracks were either real or exceptionally accurate hoaxes. On the other hand, an official U.S. Forest Service investigation declared the tracks to be a hoax.

Over the next few years, Freeman continued amassing casts of similar footprints as well as knuckle prints. He insisted that they were all real, despite his confession that he'd fabricated previous Bigfoot prints. Ironically, a set of tracks he found in 1987 were thought to be a hoax because they lacked the dermal ridges of his previous casts—the very same ones whose authenticity was being called into question.

In 1994, Freeman unveiled what would become his most controversial evidence of all: video of a purported Sasquatch. The video, readily available on the Internet, begins as Freeman is videotaping Sasquatch footprints on a Umatilla forest trail. As the camera follows the tracks, Freeman comments that he hears the brush beyond

"popping." Raising the camera toward the forest, a gorilla-like biped is seen walking from right to left behind some foliage. "Oh, there he goes!" exclaims Freeman. He repositions himself where he believes he'll get a better look but is unable to find the creature again. While narrating, he comments that he saw two of them.

Freeman's video generated heated debates and brought renewed scrutiny of the famous 1966 Patterson-Gimlin film shot in northern California. Freeman maintained, up to his death in 2003, that his 1982 print casts and his 1994 video were absolutely genuine.

Sasquatch activity in Umatilla National Forest continues to be reported to this day. To many locals, it's not a question of whether these primates exist, but rather of when the rest of the world will be convinced.

Stan Johnson, Sasquatch Ambassador

Stan Johnson of Oakland, Oregon, is more than your typical Bigfoot enthusiast. He is a self-professed "friend of the Sasquatch people," whom he's visited and (telepathically) communicated with since the 1980s.

His first contact was in late October 1983, at age seventy, while deer hunting on a nearby mountain. He came across a Sasquatch leaning on a tall tree stump. The creature was intimidated by Johnson's rifle, but relaxed when Johnson laid it down to demonstrate that he meant no harm. The creature, whom Johnson described as nine feet tall, four hundred fifty to five hundred pounds, and possessing very human facial features, turned around and walked away without incident. Still, the encounter unnerved Johnson, who avoided the area until mid-1985.

He returned at the behest of friends who encouraged Johnson to face his fears. It was then, he claims, that he began his telepathic rapport with the Sasquatch people. Initially, he met a male named Allone ("awl-own"); his mate, Nate ("nah-tay"); and Lockel ("lock-el"), possibly a daughter. They referred to themselves as the Rrowe family, who hailed from the fifth dimension. Johnson went on to meet other groups he refers to as the Crystal family, the Beverly family, and others.

According to Johnson, his Sasquatch friends are psychic beings who work as scouts for a planet called Sitka, presided over by Queen La Tara, who explained their mission and convinced Johnson to be an ambassador of goodwill. Their eventual goal, Johnson reported, is to guide humanity away from its dangerous habits of warfare and environmental destruction. For the time being, however, Sasquatches are discouraged from interacting with humans to avoid confrontation and injury.

Johnson, in his nineties as of this writing, has become familiar in the more fringe circles of Bigfoot research. He wrote a book, *Bigfoot Memoirs: My Life with the Sasquatch* (http://users.sdccu.net/alahoy/johnson.htm) and he was featured in *On Bigfoot's Mountain,* a documentary directed by paranormal journalist Dick Criswell.

Don't Mess with Bigfoot

Bigfoot scored a major civil rights victory in 1977.

Introduced by State Representative Ted Kulongoski —who eventually became governor—the Oregon state legislature passed a measure that prohibits harassing, annoying, or intimidating "the wildlife species known as Sasquatch or Bigfoot."

So far, nobody has faced a charge, which carries a punishment of two days of highway litter pickup.

Curiously, the North American Wildlife Research team was never cited for their Bigfoot trap.

Over the Fence in Wilsonville

Despite the hundreds of reported run-ins with Bigfoot, incidents of physical contact are rare. Sasquatches tend to stay hidden, their concern leaning more toward scaring away intrusive humans. One notable exception occurred on August 29, 1970.

A woman from Wilsonville heard shooting from the woods next to her farm. She grabbed her shotgun and headed off to look for the culprits and inform the shooters that they were trespassing.

As she was crouching through a barbed-wire fence, something "big and hairy" grabbed and threw her some fifteen yards back over the fence. Her husband found her an hour later, scratched up and covered in burrs, but otherwise unhurt.

Watery Whatsits

According to our research, 2.4 percent of Oregon's 98,466 square miles is water. That may not sound like a lot, but do the math: It amounts to more than 2,363 square miles of rivers, lakes, reservoirs, and tributaries. And that's not counting Oregon's 260-mile coast.

Oregon has plenty of water to sustain a healthy amount of aquatic life. Which begs the question we're floating here: Does all this water contain only familiar fish and reptiles, or does some of it hide . . . other things? Are there giant eels, prehistoric plesiosaurs, as-yet unknown creatures, or are rumors to that effect merely local folklore? Dive right in and decide for yourself.

The Annual Sea Serpent

As trade developed along the west coast in the 1800s, sightings of sea serpents were not unheard of. In fact, one such creature even seemed to exhibit a migratory pattern, as it would be spotted every year in roughly the same locations at specific intervals. After the creature made an unexpected appearance off the coast of Oregon, the following article, which originated in San Francisco, was published in newspapers nationwide on October 18, 1888.

A Sea Serpent Sighted Off the Coast of Oregon

Capt. Edgar Avery, of the bark Estella, *while traveling from Tacoma to San Francisco with coal, described the monster when the boat was wpassing the Umpqua River. The serpent was swimming on the surface of the water in a southerly direction.*

As it was ten o'clock in the morning, and the sun was shining brightly, the startled captain had a good view. When he was satisfied that he beheld a real live serpent, the captain sprang below and got his rifle, calling to his wife and crew to come on deck and view the wonder, about 80 feet long and as big around as a barrel. He rode over the waves with his head and about 10 feet of his body elevated above water, every now and then dipping his immense head into the water, the body making gigantic convolutions while gliding caterpillar-like over the waves. The head was flat, or "dished," as the captain described it, and the body appeared to be covered with scales. About 10 feet of what might properly be called the neck, was covered with coarse hair, resembling a mane.

The Captain fired several shots at it but the bullets fell short. The sea serpent seemingly paid no attention to the shooting, but kept on in the even tenor of his way. The excited spectators kept it in view for fully a half hour, when, without any apparent flurry, it sank out of sight in the sea, and was not seen after.

Amhuluk, the Water Dragon

The Kalapuya Indians of western Oregon tell of a formidable "water dragon" called Amhuluk that once inhabited Forked Mountain Lake. Although the creature seems to be long gone (its last sighting was in the 1890s), its infamous cruelty is cemented in tribal lore. Described as a four-legged serpent with long, spotted horns, its trademark was a passion for drowning whatever and whomever it could.

One Kalapuya story is said to definitively illustrate Amhuluk's brutality. The creature came upon three Native children—siblings, two brothers and a sister—digging for roots. When the children approached it, the Amhuluk impaled the two youngest on its horns and disappeared into the muddy ground. The older boy ran home, told his parents what happened, then fell unconscious as a disease overtook him and spots appeared all over his body.

The father ran down to the lake to search for the other two children. Amhuluk taunted him, emerging at five different spots in the mud and water with the children still impaled on its horns. The father camped in the area for five days, and every day the Amhuluk taunted him with the sight of his children, who, in an "undead state," cried out for him. After the fifth day, Amhuluk no longer appeared and the father left for home with a heavy heart. When he got there, he learned that while he was trying to save his two children at the lake, his oldest son had died from the mystery illness.

Its trademark was a passion for drowning whatever and whomever it could.

Colossal Claude

Oregon's arguably most famous sea monster, Colossal Claude, has appeared in or near the Columbia River for decades.

The crew of the Columbia River lightship saw Claude in 1934. A few of them wanted to lower a rowboat to get a closer look. The ship's officers nixed the idea for fear that it would attack the boat. L. A. Larson, the lightship's mate, described Claude as having "a mean looking tail and an evil, snaky look to its head."

The lightship's crew saw Claude many times over the years. In fact, it's widely believed that it was they who named the creature.

In 1937, Claude was spotted by the crew of the trawler *Viv.* Capt. Charles Graham described it as a "long, hairy, tan colored creature, with the head of an overgrown horse, about 40 feet long, and with a 4-foot waist measure."

Capt. Chris Anderson of the fishing schooner *Arpo* reported an encounter with Claude at the mouth of the Columbia. As Anderson told it, Claude was covered with grey fur, and had a camel-like head with "glassy eyes and a bent snout," which it used to remove a twenty-pound halibut off the *Arpo*'s fishing line.

For some reason, Claude disappeared sometime in the 1950s. Many Columbia River regulars assumed the animal had either died or moved on. After a strange incident in September 1989, however,

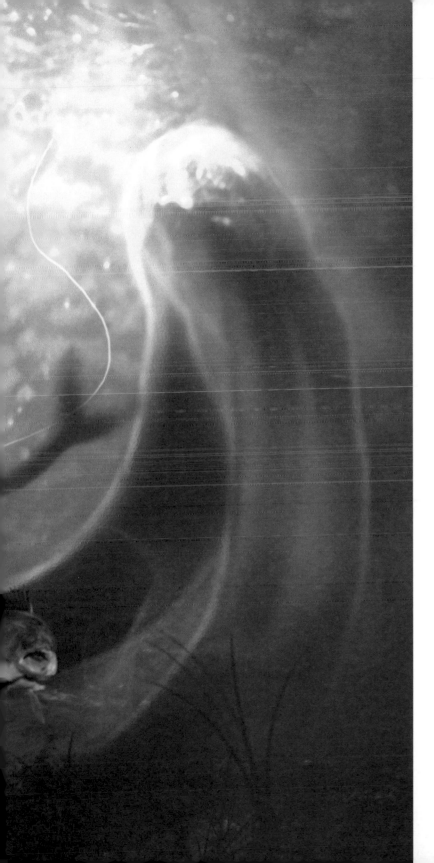

some local old timers began to wonder if Claude hadn't returned.

One Donald Riswick, joined by a friend, took his twenty-eight-foot fishing boat to the Shoo Fly drift, just east of Astoria, for some gillnetting.

After an hour and a half of trailing a net several hundred feet in length, they began reeling it in with a motorized winch. Suddenly, the net caught on something that was either stationary or pulling against the winch. This was exceptionally odd since the water here was eighty feet deep, and the net was only about thirty-four feet underwater. Theoretically, there shouldn't have been anything there for it to snag onto or to pull it with such force. Try as they might, they couldn't get it unstuck, and as the winch continued reeling, the bow began sinking.

L.A. Larson, the lightship's mate, described Claude as having "a mean looking tail and an evil, snaky look to its head."

Riswick quickly ran to the controls and opened up the boat's throttle. It's 225-horsepower engine roared to life, finally pulling the net free. Riswick and his assistant finished reeling in the net and found that a large hole had been ripped in it.

This incident surely has a logical explanation, whatever it may be. Given the circumstances, however, a tug-of-war between fishermen and sea monster may be as reasonable a possibility as any!

Marvin the Monster

In 1963, after Claude's mid-1950s disappearance, divers for the Shell Oil Company spotted a strange animal off the Oregon coast. Although a few folks from around Astoria believed that this marked the return of Claude, the majority acknowledged it as a whole new critter, which they nicknamed Marvin.

Fortunately, the oil workers managed to videotape the creature as it swam around in a spiral pattern. It looked to be about fifteen feet long with barnacled ridges along its body.

Marine biologists at the Universities of Washington, Texas, and California, as well as the Scripps Institute of Oceanography, examined the video, but their range of conclusions hardly identified Marvin. It was declared to be two kinds of jellyfish, a chain of salps (a species of invertebrate that group together in coiled patterns), or a plesiosaur or other prehistoric creature.

Whatever it really was, this seems to be its only recorded sighting.

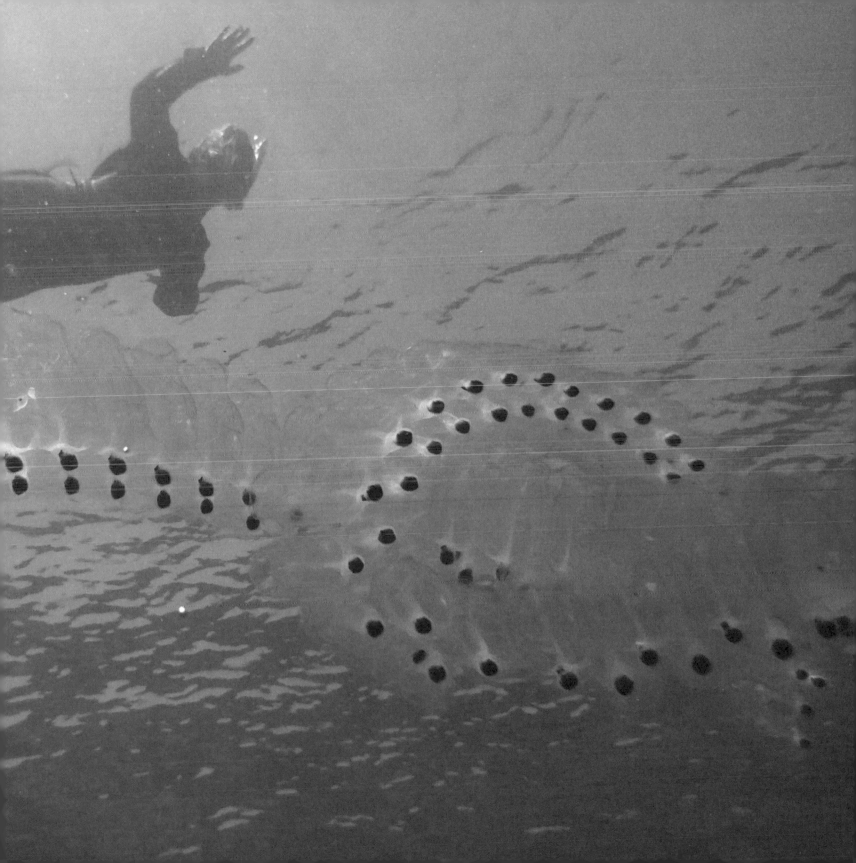

Wally of Wallowa Lake

Located just south of Joseph, Wallowa Lake is about five miles long and a mile wide. It's also 283 feet deep. Essentially a tear in the earth from the last ice age, the lake and the surrounding wilderness inspire the imagination and possibly conceal some undiscovered secrets of nature.

Legends about Wally, the lake's seven-humped, horn-headed monster, date as far back as the 1600s, when local Indians considered him not a cutely named local mascot, but a dangerous beast.

In one such legend, Nez Perce and Blackfeet Indians, who inhabited opposite shores of Wallowa Lake, negotiated peace after years of war. As part of their conciliation, Tlescaoe, son of the Blackfeet chief, and Wahluna, daughter of the Nez Perce chief, were married. After their wedding ceremony, the newlyweds went canoeing on the lake, taking in an especially impressive sunset. Without warning, a great serpent lunged at them under water, capsizing their canoe and killing them. The Blackfeet worried that, by ending hostilities between their people, the chiefs defied their warriors' preordained destiny and angered the Great Spirit. The giant serpent may have simply acted as an emissary of punishment.

Another legend states that Wally originally lived high up in the mountains surrounding the lake. An Indian brave who was exploring startled it and caused it to flee. The adventurous young man chased it over the mountains and, eventually, the serpent came to Wallowa Lake and dove in, quickly followed by his pursuer. After a few moments, the brave gave up, turned around, and began swimming toward shore. As his friends approached, they saw him jerk and scream as he was pulled under.

Stories like these have caused generations of Native Americans to approach Wallowa Lake with caution. Though

the newlyweds and the Indian brave are said to never have been seen again, the monster has since been spotted from time to time.

In 1885, shortly after settlers began using the lake for recreation, the first known sighting of the monster by a white man was reported in a local newspaper. A prospector was roughly halfway across the lake when he saw a ten-foot-long neck with a flat, cowlike head rise out of the water fifty yards to his right. It called out in a few low bellows, submerged, and soon reappeared to his left. This time, the serpent's entire body rose to the surface. The prospector estimated it to be about one hundred feet long. It glided along the water surface for a few hundred yards before submerging again.

In 1932, a couple in a boat saw what they described as a "monster fish" about three hundred feet from the west shore.

Irene Wiggins, who owned a lakeside lodge, claimed to have seen the monster several times, from 1945 onward.

She may have been among the first to refer to the creature as Wally. Her description of Wally was consistent with previous sightings.

In 1950, three witnesses saw two sleekly shaped creatures with heads resembling those of buffalo. The creatures were approximately sixteen and eight feet long. Previous descriptions of a larger lake monster therefore suggest that these two were youngsters. It follows, then, that what is commonly thought of as a single animal may instead be a group of some sort.

In his book *Oregon's Ghosts and Monsters,* author Mike Helm claims that his father once saw Wally while fishing.

He writes that, based on his father's description, he's "always pictured it as a huge snake with a head like a Chinese dragon, a regular medieval sea serpent, rippling across the surface of the lake."

He also touches on other legends of Wallowa Lake, such as speculation that it's connected to the Great Lakes by a vast underground river. (As Helm heard it, some time ago the body of a man who drowned in Wallowa Lake was supposedly recovered in Lake Erie).

This concept raises another interesting question: Could Wally be the same creature as, or a relative of, South Bay Bessie, the Lake Erie Monster?

The Devil's Lake Monster and "Old Hairy"

According to Native American legend, something big and hungry lives (or used to live) in Devil's Lake, north of Lincoln City. The story goes that Chief Fleetfoot, crossing the lake in a canoe one night, was grabbed by gigantic tentacles (or fingers) and pulled under.

Beyond the terror of seeing the chief killed this way, his tribe was also greatly worried, because their survival largely depended on use of the lake. They held a ceremonial feast in the creature's honor to (hopefully) appease him. As the tribe beat its drums on the lakeshore, the creature raised its large head out of the water. A sacrifice was offered—accounts are vague on whether it was human or animal—and the creature submerged, never to bother them again.

Sightings of (presumably) the same monster are occasionally reported by locals. But no plausible theory has explained what could have grabbed the unsuspecting Indian chief all those years ago, if something indeed pulled him under.

Harder still to rationalize was a dead creature that washed ashore on the ocean beach just west of Devil's Lake. The local marshal's teenage daughter, Marybell Allum, came upon the bizarre monstrosity on March 4, 1950. One description had it at about a thousand pounds and twenty-two feet long with "the body of a cow, approximately nine tails, and . . . hair all over the body and legs." (Some accounts assign feathers to it, as well.) There were plenty of ideas as to what it could possibly be, such as a tiger shark or a lump of whale blubber.

Confounded, locals dubbed it "Old Hairy."

Oregon's Other H₂Oddities

Many of Oregon's watery whatsits date back to centuries-old Native American lore, and their descriptions are often similar. We cast a statewide net researching this topic; here's a summary of what else we pulled up.

The coastal town of Bandon, twenty-five miles south of Coos Bay, claims a relatively small, twelve-and-a-half-foot-long sea monster known to some as the Bandon Beast. It's said to (again) somewhat resemble a cow, complete with brown fur and a bulbous nose.

The Bandon Beast might tie into another local legend. Bandon Face Rock, located just beyond the shoreline in the water, is a natural rock formation that vaguely resembles a facial profile. Native American lore claims it to be the remains of a tribal princess turned to stone through a fearsome sea monster's curse. Could the inclusion of a sea monster in this legend be an indication of long-ago sightings of Bandon Beast?

In Empire, off of Coos Bay, Capt. Ben Tanner and crew came across a rather clumsy mystery creature. Apparently, it wasn't watching where it was swimming as it approached their troller, the *Gold Coast*. Explained Tanner: "It smacked its mouth [on the boat], rolled its long-lashed eyes at the crew, then pointed its tail in the air and dived straight down."

In 1937, a possible cousin of Claude was spotted south of Yachats, off the stretch of rocky shore known as Devil's Churn. Once more, witnesses described a "horse's head" on a fifteen-foot neck, a six-foot body, and a long tail. Some people believe that it was Caddy, a mysterious sea creature usually seen considerably north of Oregon, around Vancouver Island, Canada.

The Devil's Lake Monster, catalogued previously herein, is said to have a neighbor about two miles south, off the coast of Nelscott. A sea serpent has been spotted here on several occasions. Typically, it's said to have a snakelike head and a "fan-shaped" tail. Is it merely a giant eel? While anything is possible, we tend to doubt it, given its reported thirty-foot length.

A large-headed animal from the depths of Crescent Lake was seen by several witnesses over the years. A century-old floating log in Crater Lake (see the Ancient Mysteries chapter) may be the basis for "monster" sightings that loosely inspired a 1977 low-budget movie, *The Crater Lake Monster*.

Last, but not least, we come to Cape Kiwanda. Rumors of a "sea monster" living in and around the cliffs just west of Pacific City have persisted for years. Details tend to be sketchy; little more is cited than a dark form seen just under the water's surface from the tops of the cliffs. At least one online columnist dismisses the story as a cautionary tale resulting from the area's treacherous currents, which have pulled people out to sea. So is the Creature of Cape Kiwanda real? Short of investigating at the base of the cliffs, where one would risk certain death, there may be no way of knowing.

Aquatic Anamolies

Some conventional but very out-of-place water critters have appeared in Oregon.

The Tragedy of Tommy Turtle

In times of war, mistakes are sometimes made. Individuals, especially outsiders, can be misidentified. Inevitably, innocents can be killed. Alas, it's a sad truth that such a fate befell one large and luckless leatherback turtle during World War II.

Tommy Turtle, as he was named postmortem, was a prodigious specimen: more than six feet long, three feet wide, and weighing about one thousand pounds. He was more than likely lost as he swam through the Columbia River one late summer day in 1942. Leatherbacks, the only sea turtles lacking a shell, are concentrated mostly in the Atlantic Ocean off of Florida and equatorial America. They exist in the Pacific Ocean in lesser numbers, but usually nowhere near the western United States. A stranger in a strange land, Tommy was confronted by a boatload of fishermen, who mistook him for a small Japanese submarine as he swam just below the water's surface.

The patriotic fishermen, intent on defending the Northwest from Emperor Hirohito's navy, grabbed their guns and opened fire on unfortunate Tommy. Realizing their error as blood gushed from his dark, ridged back, they did the only thing they could: hoisted him aboard, took him into port, and cut him into turtle steaks.

A newsletter from the Tongue Point Naval Air Station in Astoria aptly concluded: "This is the unromantic end of Tommy Turtle, whose first visit to the Pacific Northwest ended so disastrously for him."

Of Pacu and Piranha

The pacu is a South American freshwater fish, a herbivore cousin to the piranha. The two look similar—flat and oval-shaped, with prominent teeth—although pacu are considerably larger (they can grow up to about a yard long). Pacu teeth are not pointed, like those of piranha, but they can be just as sharp; they can break open seeds and nuts that fall into the water and chew hard vegetation. When confronted with an unfamiliar, potentially edible morsel, pacu harbor no aversion to an experimental nibble. In other words, while they're not as dangerous as piranha, they may still bite flesh, should they be curious as to whether it suits their diet.

Given the pacu's South American origins, it's surprising and a bit alarming that at least two have been caught in Oregon waters.

In September 1998, Greg Asplund reeled one in while pond fishing at Jackson County's Expo Park. He'd noticed it in the pond beforehand and thought it to be a bass or a crappie. But there was

something—if you'll pardon the pun—fishy about the way it chased smaller fish. It seemed overly aggressive.

Upon closer inspection after catching it, Asplund was sure he'd caught a piranha. It was only after taking it to the Oregon State Police, who then turned it over to the Oregon Department of Fish and Wildlife, that this piscine puzzler was properly pegged as a pacu.

A similar catch was made by fourteen-year-old Nicole Wells in August 2004 at Round Lake in Camas. She was taken aback by the mean-looking teeth on a foot-long fish she caught. Her mother strongly suspected it was a piranha, but a manager at a tropical fish store later identified it as a pacu.

Pacu can grow up to about a yard long. They may bite flesh, should they be curious as to whether it suits their diet.

In August 2003, another young fisherman, Jason McGinnis, caught a piranha in Milwaukie's Johnson Creek. He's got the scar to prove it, as the pacu's carnivorous cousin bit him on the finger while he was removing the hook. Nevertheless, the fourteen-year-old kept the fish, hoping to sell it.

It isn't hard to figure out how these out-of-towners got into Oregon's waters. Both pacu and piranha are readily available in some pet shops. When their owners get bored with them, or pacu grow too big to keep in a fish tank, they're sometimes dumped into the wild. Cold water in the fall and winter will eventually kill either fish. In warm summer water, however, they'll gladly try out the local cuisine!

The Willamina Gator

If you're nervous about the prospect of encountering nonnative predatory fish, we suggest you avoid Willamina Pond altogether. Located at the west end of the town of Willamina, the pond is as popular with fishermen as it is with the frogs and ducks that make it their home. If rumor is to be believed, however, it hosted a far more dangerous denizen during the summer of 2001.

Witnesses claimed to have seen an alligator swimming lazily in the water and gobbling up unsuspecting ducks. Authorities indeed noted a decrease in the pond's duck population but never verified whether a gator was the cause.

When the sightings eventually died down, some local fishermen, loath to miss a good opportunity for reputation building, began bragging about how they captured or killed the Willamina Gator.

Thunderbirds over Hillsboro

Impossibly large birds are a mainstay of cryptozoology and almost always inspire comparisons to the Thunderbird of Native American legend. If there really is a connection, sightings around the world, including one in Oregon, suggest that the Thunderbird may be more than a myth.

A woman named Gladie Bills, in a letter to *Fate* magazine, reported that on February 27, 1954, she and her teenage daughter saw what they initially thought were six fighter planes in the sky over Hillsboro. They assumed the planes were engaging in a training exercise, although the pilots' maneuvers seemed random and erratic. After a better look through a telescope, they realized that they weren't planes at all, but giant birds with "glossy white wings." The birds apparently flew off after a few minutes, leaving mother and daughter in baffled awe.

The Melrose Creep

I live in Melrose, a little township outside of Roseburg, Oregon. It's the proud home of the Melrose Creep.

I am a bit nocturnal and used to go for walks in the woods at night. One night, I was up on a clear cut behind my house when I heard soft, padded footfalls behind me. I looked all around before I saw it: the Melrose Creep.

Now, I've always lived in the sticks and am used to bears and cats and coyotes but this was like nothing I had ever seen before. I could see it perfectly in the full moon: It was about three to four feet tall and hunched over, had no hair, long arms with six-fingered hands, and stubby clawed feet. It also had a very humanlike head and bulging, glowing red eyes.

The Melrose Creep seemed unafraid of me, but I was scared of it. It approached me. I freaked out, ran back home, and didn't go out again for weeks.

A few months later I was walking down the Docrner Cutoff. About a half mile from the end of the road, I heard the eerie pitter-patter of those damn little feet again. I ran again to the end of the road, but my friend was late in meeting me, so I had to wait another five minutes in the dark—alone with that little creep. —*Captain Morgan*

Local Heroes and Villains

The flavor of a geographic area is largely defined by the character of its inhabitants. However you slice it, Oregonians have been a hearty bunch. Local Native American tribes met natural challenges, surviving and thriving in a rugged wilderness. Later, settlers of many races toiled in logging camps and coal mines to forge a modern state. Today, this legacy of resilience manifests itself in many ways. Though we focus here on a few of the more unusual personalities to have cropped up over the years, their claim to this legacy is just as legitimate.

From a man who dares to journey across the state suspended from helium-filled balloons to a child prodigy with a magical connection to Oregon's very life force; from communities at incredible odds with religious cults to Les U. Knight, who faces an uphill battle encouraging voluntary human extinction, this small sampling of Beaver State heroes and villains will illustrate that Oregonian moxie makes for some great stories.

With a track record like this, it's inevitable that many more such individuals will rise in years to come—or not, if Les U. Knight gets his way.

Over the Falls with Al Faussett

Between the MTV show Jackass *and a number of rowdy Japanese game shows, many people are shocked that sense-less and inevitably injurious stunts are "suddenly" being pre-sented as entertainment. In fact, dangerous recklessness has long vied for an audience, and many of today's mass media lunatics owe a lot to the daredevils of yesteryear.*

Take, for example, Alfred "Al" Faussett, the owner of a small logging business in Monroe, Washington. Struggling against competition from the Weyerhauser Company, Faussett was always open to making an extra buck. In 1926, a movie crew came to town to shoot a Western. They offered what was then a whopping $1,500 to anyone willing to work as an extra, portraying an Indian. There was only one catch: They'd have to ride in a canoe through Sunset Falls, an incline of treacherously churning water on the Skykomish River. The stunt was doubly dangerous: A whirlpool at the bottom had killed at least twenty people in recent years.

Faussett was the only person to step forward to accept the challenge, but he didn't trust his safety to the filmmakers. Eschewing the inadequate canoe they provided, he carved one of his own from a thirty-four-foot spruce log. He reinforced it with sheet metal, canvas, and "bumpers" made of vine maple branches. He even added a safety harness of sorts. The result was a watercraft that looked very little like a canoe. The filmmakers rejected it outright; the stunt was canceled, and Faussett wasn't paid.

Still, he was undaunted. Since he'd already built the boat, and since he'd already resigned himself to going over the falls, Faussett decided to do it anyway.

The stunt was advertised for a few weeks, and a one-dollar admission was charged. On May 30, 1926, in front of a crowd of more than three thousand, Faussett rode the falls at more than eighty miles per hour, hitting a rock halfway down and deflecting, nearly airborne, to the bottom. Luckily, he overshot the whirlpool. He splashed down into heavily churning water and reemerged a few nervous seconds later. Faussett waved to the cheering throng as he paddled toward calmer water ahead. He was aching, but he'd survived.

Between the rush of adrenaline and the recognition that followed, Faussett was hooked. He began touring the Northwest to ride over other waterfalls.

That Labor Day, he dropped down Eagle Falls, four miles away, inside two hollowed-out log halves. The following June, he went over Spokane Falls in a similar vessel. He hit a rocky ledge part way down the seventy-five-foot drop and somersaulted straight into a whirlpool. Twenty minutes later, when assistants were finally able to pull him free, Faussett was found dazed and bleeding from several cuts to the head.

The experience dissuaded him from further exploits for several months, but the call of danger proved too strong to resist. On March 30, 1928, he appeared at Oregon City Falls, this time inside a thirty-foot-long wooden cylinder, essentially a "limousine barrel." He intended to point the bow forward as he approached the drop, duck inside, and close the hatch.

It didn't quite pan out that way. The vessel dropped over the falls sideways as Faussett was still trying to straighten it, landed upside-down, and disappeared into the rushing water for more than a minute. Faussett's helpers caught up to him a little farther downstream. Despite the wild ride, he was in much better shape than after the previous year's drop. As he later explained to the *Oregonian* newspaper: "We hit the middle of the falls just right, but the strong wind and current simply made me powerless to shoot the rapids as I had planned. I had no time to close the trap door above me so I just hung on. Air under the upturned boat made it possible for me to breathe."

Three months later, Faussett's penultimate drop solidified his status as an Oregon legend. So determined was he to ride Silver Creek Falls near Salem that when its landowners refused him access, he purchased the land from them, as well as one hundred surrounding acres.

He built his strangest boat yet for the occasion: an oddity consisting of thirty-six inner tubes held together with a wooden frame and covered with orange canvas. The inner tubes would theoretically cushion the bumpy ride and the splashdown, as well as keep Faussett from being submerged for too long. Additionally, he built a ramp extending twelve feet beyond the precipice, so as to launch himself past some jutting rocks below. Five thousand people showed up on July 1, 1928, to see the big show.

Again, Faussett hoped to land nose-first in the water, but instead the boat rushed over the ramp, dropped one hundred and eighty-six feet, and splashed down hard on its bottom. The fall and Faussett's resulting injuries were spectacular. He broke a few ribs, sprained his ankles, and cracked a wrist. Somehow, he also contracted a four-day bout of constipation. A six-week hospitalization wasn't enough to dissuade him from considering further wild rides, including his ultimate goal: Niagara Falls.

Though in the end logistics prevented him from riding the world's most famous waterfall, he went over an even higher one in July 1929: Shoshone Falls on Idaho's Snake River.

Using the same inner tube boat from the previous year, this time he suffered only a broken hand. On the plus side, he set a record for the highest waterfall ever ridden (212 feet). It was a fitting end to his career as a daredevil, though he didn't specifically plan it as such. He continued toying with the idea of a drop over Niagara Falls until his death in 1948.

Meanwhile, back in Oregon, locals who had witnessed the Silver Falls drop were impressed enough to eventually begin celebrating an annual Al Faussett Days festival in the town of Sublimity, twenty-six miles southeast of Salem. Among the more popular events are speeches by members of Faussett's family and the screening of a newsreel showing his drop over Silver Creek Falls.

We at *Weird Oregon* can't help but wonder if someday, somewhere, people will celebrate "Jackass Days" in a similar fashion!

Les U. Knight for Human Extinction

"Live long and prosper," goes the old Vulcan salutation, countered by an unlikely one from Earth: "May we live long and die out."

Such is the motto of Portland-based Les U. Knight's Voluntary Human Extinction Movement (VHEMT). Many supporters tend to be outspoken, validating the pronunciation of the acronym as "vehement." The premise here is simple: Humans have never been good for Earth's natural state, and we should each contribute to a gradual and orderly phasing out of our species.

Let's be perfectly clear: Neither Les nor VHEMT advocate suicide or murder. According to their website (www.vhemt.org), abortion is also beyond the scope of their focus. And VHEMT certainly isn't a cult, at least in the traditional sense. Rather, they're a loosely organized cadre of like-minded people. Their only goal is to convince us, as supporters put it, that the "desperation to breed" is just social programming. Ideally, they would like us to do something about it: namely, pledge not to reproduce.

Knight began pondering the concept of voluntary human extinction in the early 1970s, during a postmilitary enrollment in college. He became interested in the environmental movement and joined a campus group called Zero Population Growth. As the name implies, they espoused the idea of maintaining a set number of human beings on Earth. However, Knight came to feel that this group's answer to ecological imbalance was not radical enough. As he told the *Economist* in 1998, "It took a very short time to see that all of the environmental solutions were linked to the number of people on the planet. That's when I realized that the best thing for the planet would be for us to phase ourselves out completely."

He organized the Human Extinction Movement on the basis of this realization, later adding "Voluntary" to the name for clarification. Knight refuses to call himself its "founder" for reasons explained on the website: "No one person is the founder of VHEMT. *Les U. Knight* gave the name . . . to a philosophy or worldview which has existed for as long as humans have been sapient."

Indeed, the idea of voluntarily abstinence from reproduction is not new. In a somewhat famous example, four brothers living on New York's Long Island followed through on a vow to that effect. Their reason: As nephews of Adolf Hitler, they felt it best to end their bloodline. Of course, others have come to the same decision for personal or environmental reasons with neither prior knowledge of VHEMT nor an aim toward human extinction.

Yet, the concept's promotion by Knight and other volunteers makes it seem radical, controversial, and strange. It was even included in a 2005 *Ripley's Believe It or Not!* cartoon panel.

Knight has published a few issues of a newsletter, *These EXIT Times,* to introduce and better explain the group's core beliefs.

It's to be expected that most people dismiss out of hand the concept of voluntary human extinction. But pause for a second and consider the current crop of politicians, pundits, and celebrities. Now ask yourself: Is it really that bad an idea?

Big Trouble in Rajneeshpuram

The early to mid-1980s became a time of chaos in Wasco County when a religious group moved onto a ranch and rampantly disrupted the community.

The group was led by Bhagwan Shree Rajneesh (roughly translated, "Holy Master Rajneesh"), a philosophy professor turned spiritual leader. Born Chandra Mohan Jain, by 1981 he had sufficiently run afoul of tax and land-use laws to warrant a hasty exit from his native India.

His assistant, Ma Anand Sheela, sought an overseas haven for Rajneesh and his group. Initially, she procured an estate in Montclair, New Jersey, as their new ashram, or religious retreat. Rajneesh relocated to the United States on a possibly fraudulent medical visa.

In Montclair, the guru guided his *sannyasins*, or students, in much the same way as he had in India. He preached an odd, contradictory combination of Hinduism, Zen, Western philosophy, and psychotherapy. He became best known, however, as a proponent of free love.

Before too long, Montclair residents were up in arms about the "sex cult" and the strain their ever-increasing numbers put on the community. (See *Weird N.J.*, vol. 2.) Luckily for them, Rajneesh had his heart set on a more open space. To this end, Ma Anand Sheela purchased the Big Muddy Ranch, south of Antelope in Wasco County. The Rajneeshees paid nearly $6 million for 64,229 acres—about thirty times the assessed value. This was a fraction of the fortune Rajneesh had amassed by convincing many affluent *sannyasins* to part with their personal wealth.

The ashram began relocating in August 1981. Antelope's 136 residents were perplexed, but were told not to worry; the ranch was to be a farming commune of about fifty people.

But by November, when the newly renamed Rancho Rajneesh hosted nearly two hundred and was incorporated as the town of Rajneeshpuram, folks in Antelope were more than a bit chagrined. Ignoring local laws that restricted land use to agriculture, the Rajneeshees issued themselves building permits and proceeded to set up housing, commerce, and infrastructure. Concerned Wasco County residents filed suit, challenging the legality of the ranch's status as a town. Rajneesh's attorneys successfully beat back these lawsuits, or at least obfuscated the underlying issues as a stalling tactic.

Gonzo Guru

The Rajneeshees quickly came to be perceived as arrogant religious nuts. The only consolation for better-humored

locals was that Bhagwan Shree Rajneesh was at least an interesting character. He had a collection of ninety Rolls-Royces—suitable for daily drive-by "inspections" of his red-robed flock lining the main road through Rancho Rajneesh. (A similar line of curious tourists was never very far away.) The Rolls-Royces worked equally well for driving to Antelope for his favorite treat: ice cream sodas.

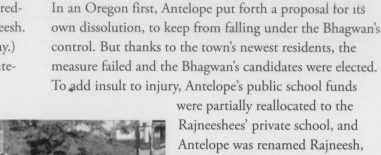

He followed a vow of public silence, talking only in private to Ma Anand Sheela and other direct subordinates. His teachings were delivered strictly via prerecorded lectures, even when he joined his gathered followers.

Among the Bhagwan's teachings: He was so holy that his presence near plants would cause them to be reincarnated as human beings. He had supernatural abilities such as telekinesis and the power to generate matter through the force of will (though he "chose not to show off" such powers). On matters of love and sexuality, he was a veritable fount of "advice," instructing his *sannyasins* to wash their hands with alcohol and wear rubber gloves during sex to avoid contracting AIDS.

Putting in the Fix

By late 1982 the population of Rajneeshpuram climbed to more than six hundred. By now, it had its own airport, artificial lake, post office, shopping mall, and police department. Finding themselves outnumbered six to one by Rajneeshees, Antelope's residents grew ever more apprehensive. Wasco County rejected the next batch of building and water-usage permits Rajneeshpuram applied for.

In retaliation, the Rajneeshees began a systematic effort to take over local government. Taking advantage of lax municipal laws, Rajneesh had several followers relocate to Antelope to help elect four of them to the town council. In an Oregon first, Antelope put forth a proposal for its own dissolution, to keep from falling under the Bhagwan's control. But thanks to the town's newest residents, the measure failed and the Bhagwan's candidates were elected. To add insult to injury, Antelope's public school funds were partially reallocated to the Rajneeshees' private school, and Antelope was renamed Rajneesh, effectively absorbing it into Rajneeshpuram.

But life was not all good for the Bhagwan. A Portland hotel he owned was bombed by a disgruntled ex-*sannyasin*. Security at Rajneeshpuram increased drastically. His application for U.S. citizenship was rejected, and other high-ranking Rajneeshees were under investigation for violating immigration laws. This only encouraged the Bhagwan to increase his control of local politics, from municipal to county level.

In late 1984, two thousand transients from around the United States became *sannyasins* thanks to a membership drive targeting the nation's homeless. They were persuaded to register to vote as a "residency requirement." (Alleged methods of "persuasion" included physical threats and the withholding of food.)

Plan B, for Bioterrorism

Anticipating that a county election would be much more difficult to rig, high-ranking Rajneeshees began devising intimidation tactics.

In September, about 750 people in The Dalles (the county seat) contracted salmonella poisoning from salad bars at restaurants. A majority of locals suspected the Rajneeshees were behind the contamination but did not have evidence at the time to prove it. Luckily, nobody died; in fact, the incident provoked a higher turnout of voters and delivered a stinging electoral defeat for the Rajneeshees.

In mid-1985, a devastating twenty-part exposé in the *Oregonian* marked the beginning of the end for Rajneeshpuram. As a result of these articles, several disgruntled Rajneeshees offered a slew of new and disturbing information to authorities. The salmonella outbreak had indeed been caused by the Rajneeshees, but it was just the tip of the iceberg. It turned out that Rancho Rajneesh had two biowarfare labs and they had considered, attempted, or carried through other attacks. They sickened two visiting county commissioners with glasses of salmonella-laced water. They infected door handles and restrooms at the Wasco County Courthouse. They attempted to affect The Dalles's water supply and a supermarket produce section. And they were actively researching viruses, including AIDS, for further attacks. In addition, they firebombed a county permit office and poisoned a federal attorney.

Bhagwan Shree Rajneesh denied all knowledge of these plots. Instead, he put the full blame on Ma Anand Sheela and his organization's vice president, Ma Anand Puja. Few believed him. With his arrest imminent, he attempted to flee to the Bahamas, only to be foiled by U.S. Customs officials. He stood trial in Portland and was deported back to India. Meanwhile, Sheela hastily fled to Germany, but was soon extradited to face charges, along with five other Rajneesh organization executives. Though the trials dragged on for a decade, all were eventually convicted and sent to prison.

Bhagwan Shree Rajneesh changed his name to Osho and returned to teaching at his original commune in India, long since upgraded to an impressive "spiritual center." He died of a heart attack in July 1990.

Rancho Rajneesh was eventually converted to a Young Life Christian youth camp.

Paul Karason's Oregon Blues

A certain celebrity frog has been known to lament, "It's not easy being green." Maybe so, but one former Oregonian might argue that it's even harder being blue.

This is because Paul Karason's skin turned dark blue after years of using colloidal silver to cure his ailments. Created by electrically dissolving silver into water, the solution has been used as an antibiotic since at least the 1880s. Though its use is much less prevalent today, some people still swear by it as a cure-all.

Karason, who suffered from arthritis, acid reflux disease, and sinusitis, read about the concoction's medicinal properties. He ordered a colloidal silver generator in 1993, began drinking silver-laced water, and has credited it with curing him of these ailments ever since.

When it was less successful in curing him of stress-induced dermatitis several years later, Karason began rubbing it on his skin. This, he insists, is when his Caucasian skin tone began to darken toward an azure hue. The change was subtle enough to not be noticed from day to day. It wasn't until a friend whom Karason hadn't seen in months paid a visit and commented on his appearance that Karason himself noticed what was happening.

The condition is known as argyria; it's caused by the gradual buildup of microscopic silver particles beneath the skin, perhaps combined with exposure to sunlight. Although the discoloration is permanent, mainstream medicine considers it the least harmful side effect of ingesting silver. More serious results can include kidney damage, seizures, and neurological problems potentially leading to death.

Paul Karason doesn't seem too concerned. That much became apparent when, seemingly on a whim, his unusual condition got worldwide media coverage in December 2007. He and his lady friend, Jackie Northup, participated in a few interviews in which Karason dismissed suggestions to seek mainstream medical treatment. He did not plan to stop drinking the solution, although he said he cut down on the quantity he drinks.

Northup explained that she's so used to his discoloration that the only times she notices it are when they're out in public and people stare. However, this is probably not a major annoyance, as Karason says he mostly avoids public places and has always been "sort of reclusive," anyway.

What apparently *was* a major annoyance was the reaction he got from some of his Oregonian neighbors. Karason endured plenty of teasing and general negativity. Feeling unwelcome, he moved to Madera, California, seeking a more accepting neighborhood, and then to Bellingham, Washington, to seek treatment for other, unrelated health issues.

Karason became a minor celebrity after his media coverage. His blue skin and white beard drew comparisons to cartoon character Papa Smurf and performance artists Blue Man Group.

The Odyssey of Bobbie the Wonder Dog

The bond between human and canine has generated many stories, from the ancient legend of Romulus and Remus's wolf foster mother to accounts of heroism by modern-day rescue dogs. Among these tales, the epic journey of Bobbie, known in his day as "the Wonder Dog of Oregon," remains one of the most incredible dog stories of all.

Originally from Indiana, Frank Brazier rented a farm on Abiqua Creek in Silverton with his wife, Elizabeth, and stepdaughters Nova and Leona Baumgarten. In 1921 Frank bought Bobbie, a collie mix, as a six-week-old puppy. Bobbie and the other family dog, a fox terrier named Toodles, became fast friends.

From the get-go, Bobbie proved to be intelligent and a natural herder. He settled into a comfortable routine: Keep the grazing sheep together, get the cow and horse into the barn in the evening, and, above all, have fun!

A Family Values Fido

Poor Toodles died from a stroke in 1922. The little dog, impressive in his own right, was buried behind the barn. Shortly after Toodles's death, the Braziers purchased a café in downtown Silverton. They moved into town and a family friend arranged to rent the same farm they were leaving. The Braziers felt that Bobbie would be better off staying behind, accustomed as he was to the farm's wide open spaces. They sold him to their friend and went on about their business. Soon after, the first hint of Bobbie's exceptional homing instinct came to light.

Like any working stiff, Bobbie seemingly knew that weekends were meant for relaxation and family time. So it was that one Saturday he walked from the farm to downtown Silverton and located the Braziers. This became his routine: Walk to town on Saturday, spend the weekend with his human family (usually greeting customers at the café), and on Monday morning trot back to the farm for another week of herding the riff-raff.

Realizing that his family was as attached to Bobbie as he was to them, Frank promptly repurchased him from the farm's new tenant—for three times what he'd sold him for! It was worth it: He and Elizabeth were about to drive back to Indiana on vacation and thought it would be fun to bring their canine companion along.

Bobbie certainly agreed. Sitting on the running board or atop the luggage in back of the car, he had the time of his life on the open road. When Frank would stop somewhere along the way, Bobbie would take the opportunity to go exploring or rabbit chasing. He always stuck relatively close and returned at the sound of the car horn, eager to continue the trip.

Where, Oh Where, Has Bobbie Gone?

The trio arrived in Wolcott, Indiana, on August 15, 1923. Frank dropped off the missus with some friends and went back out with Bobbie to gas up the car. While inside the service station, he heard the pooch yelp, looked outside, and saw him being chased by three or four other dogs. Frank would later write:

Thinking he would take care of himself as usual, I went back to the car, expecting to find him at the

*house when I returned. When after an hour or so he
had not appeared, we began to get anxious, and . . .
I drove slowly all around town, honking at frequent
intervals, never doubting but that presently I would
see him bounding toward me. It was midnight before
I gave up, very much depressed, as you may imagine.*

The next morning, the editor of the local paper, himself a dog lover, donated space for a "lost dog" ad that ran every day the Braziers were in the area. In addition, the local telephone operator rang every phone in town, asking folks to keep an eye out for the collie. The Braziers traveled around Indiana for three weeks, searching for Bobbie as they visited other friends and family. They briefly stopped in Ohio and then back in Wolcott. Sadly, there still was no word of Bobbie's whereabouts. Anyone who's ever lost a pet can surely sympathize with the Braziers when, with heavy hearts, they resigned themselves to returning home—2,551 miles away—without Bobbie.

The Comeback Canine

Back in Silverton, life went on. Frank, Elizabeth, and the girls kept busy with the café, their thoughts doubtlessly drifting to their missing dog on occasion. It's impossible to know whether, or for how long, any of them privately entertained hope of ever seeing him again, but as weeks turned to months, it's safe to assume they thought the chances were nil.

It's also difficult to say whether any of them started February 15, 1924, realizing that it was the six-month anniversary of Bobbie's disappearance. Regardless, they were about to get a reminder.

That afternoon, Nova Baumgarten, the younger daughter, was walking down the street with a friend when a pitiful creature appeared a few feet in front of them. Its shaggy, matted fur and weary gait betrayed the hard life of a stray dog. Except . . . this one seemed oddly familiar. Recognition clicked in an instant. "Oh, look!" exclaimed Nova, "Isn't that Bobbie?"

The ragged animal abruptly stopped, turned his head, and (in the words of Frank Brazier) "fairly flew at Nova, leaping up again and again to cover her face with kisses and making half-strangled, sobbing sounds of relief and delight as if he could hardly voice his wordless joy." Sure enough, Bobbie was back! This was soon confirmed by examining his markings and a few scars. Locals, who'd been well aware of his disappearance in Indiana, followed Bobbie, Nova, and friend to the café in an impromptu procession. Frank was woken from a nap and joyously reunited with his lost pal.

The Long Way Home

The happiness of the moment was tempered by Bobbie's physical condition. Whatever he'd been through, it had obviously taken a toll on his health. His first order of business after thoroughly greeting his family was a three-day nap, interrupted only by meal and bathroom breaks. Afterward, and for the rest of his life, his pace was markedly slower than it had been.

The obvious question was on everyone's mind: How the heck did he backtrack more than 2,500 miles, across all kinds of terrain, for six months to the day? Some answers came as print media and radio spread Bobbie's story across the nation.

The Braziers got dozens of letters from inquisitive strangers, all wondering the same thing: Could the stray dog

they'd briefly cared for some weeks earlier have been Bobbie? Snapshots were enclosed with some of the letters, which verified that more often than not, it was Bobbie! As it turned out, the intrepid pooch had trekked on foot, hitched rides, and stopped at numerous campgrounds, service stations, and residences along the way. He crossed the states of Illinois, Iowa, Nebraska, Colorado, Wyoming, and Idaho. A trusting soul, he simply depended on (and perhaps inspired) the kindness of strangers. Usually, an evening meal and a place to sleep would be all he'd ask, then he'd be off again at first light. His most physically demanding feat was crossing the Rocky Mountains in the dead of winter!

All of this led Bobbie to become a bona fide (bone-a Fido?) local hero. He was featured in the *Ripley's Believe It or Not!* newspaper feature, as well as the *Guinness Book of World Records.* The Oregon Humane Society gave him a silver medal. He portrayed himself in a silent movie dramatization of his adventure. He was the guest of honor at a home expo in Portland, where he was presented with a windowed suburban-style doghouse. In addition, gifts from far and wide arrived for him almost daily at the Brazier residence.

None of this changed Bobbie. He visited Toodles's grave of his own volition. He produced a litter of a whopping sixteen puppies—all boys—with another collie named Tippy. He reunited with some of the people who helped him on the long road back to Silverton. His heart was as big as his inner compass; he clearly valued friends and family over fame.

Bobbie passed away in 1927 from an illness that was probably exacerbated by the physical hardship of his six-month trek. He was just six years old, but the example he set of loyalty and perseverance is ageless. You can pay your respects to Bobbie at the Oregon Humane Society pet cemetery in Portland, where he's buried in a well-tended enclosure, beneath his doghouse.

A statue, mural, and replica doghouse honor Bobbie on Water Street in Silverton.

Silverton's Politics Are a Drag

In recent years, a history-making luminary of another kind has emerged in Silverton—with high heels, makeup, and breast implants. Meet the Honorable Stu Rasmussen, who holds the distinction of being the first—and so far only—openly transgender mayor in the United States.

After running the local theater and building the area's first cable television service, Rasmussen, a lifelong Silverton resident, served three terms as a city councillor and twice as mayor. He became known as an affable and effective leader.

But after two failed campaigns to the state legislature in the mid-1990s, Rasmussen left politics to attend to a midlife identity crisis. As he explained to *Weird Oregon,* "I evaluated my situation. Nothing so mundane as a sports car, motorcycle, or trophy wife would suffice" to fix his problem.

Feeling like "a lesbian trapped in a body with male plumbing," Rasmussen found a local cross-dressing support group and finally embraced the secret he'd shared only with his longtime girlfriend. Rasmussen began wearing women's clothing in public (but only while out of town) as "Carla Fong," a leggy redhead in a short dress and killer heels. Then, before coming out to his fellow Silvertonians, he traded in prosthetic breasts for a bona fide breast augmentation. Over time, Silverton accepted Stu's lifestyle.

Stu reentered local politics as a city councillor, then in 2008 led a successful campaign to unseat incumbent mayor Ken Hector on a "limited residential growth" platform. With a transgender mayor, sleepy little Silverton was suddenly thrust in the national media spotlight.

Says Rasmussen, "This is an amazing community and only through their acceptance and support have I been able to accomplish what I have. Maybe this will be contagious to other towns with issues about 'differences': It's not the package, it's the contents that matter."

Rasmussen is focused on the here and now, seemingly unconcerned that he may someday rival Bobbie the Wonder Dog as Silverton's icon.

"Give it twenty years and we'll see," says Rasmussen. "Bobbie is much cuter, but I have better legs."

"It's not the package; it's the contents that matter."

Edmund Creffield and His Pulpit of Perversion

On May 7, 1906, a recently arrived couple, thirty-five-year-old Franz Edmund Creffield and his wife, Maud, walked down Seattle's First Avenue. They were destitute refugees dressed in the only clothing they owned. At the corner of First Avenue and Cherry Street, among a throng of witnesses, a man snuck up and shot the man in the back of the head. He died instantly. The assassin stood calmly, smoking a cigar, and nonchalantly surrendered his gun to a pair of policemen.

The assassin, twenty-three-year-old George Mitchell, was brought to trial on June 25. The proceedings were a sensation; attendees spilled from the courtroom into the hall. A number of well-wishers, including a large group of elderly ladies, thanked Mitchell for the murder.

A sordid saga was revealed during the trial, unfolded through witness testimony.

Genesis

A German immigrant, Creffield had appeared in the Portland area in the late 1890s as a Salvation Army preacher. Although persuasive and confident in his faith, he resigned from the organization in 1901 after becoming convinced that he'd been annointed "Joshua the Second," or God's official spokesman.

In this capacity he went to Corvallis in 1903 to set up his own ministry, amassing a group of "apostles" made up mostly of prominent and respected local women. Before long, Corvallis was buzzing with rumors about "Joshua's" prayer meetings, which were held in congregants' homes. His flock would inevitably end up rolling on the floor, praying in overwrought hysterics, sometimes for more than twelve hours at a stretch. Though Creffield named his group the Church of the Bride of Christ, they were referred to more often in jest as the Holy Rollers.

Commandments

Creffield claimed that God told him to hold the prayer meetings in the afternoon, rather than at night as he had been doing. (The night air hindered the transmission of prayers, he claimed.) Most of his followers' husbands would be at work then, but that was just a coincidence. They weren't to question God's will.

Creffield preached against worldliness. Furniture was an unnecessary comfort; anything more than a simple meal was gluttony. Clothing, as per the sins of Adam and Eve, was the ultimate vanity. And, most important, Creffield was to choose, from among the women, the mother from whom the new Jesus Christ would be reborn. Naturally, God would work through his prophet to "test" each of them and impregnate only the "New Mary."

Exodus

As the Holy Rollers grew in number, decibels, and infamy, so too did their need for discretion. To this end, Creffield moved the bunch to uninhabited Kiger Island, in the Willamette River just east of town. There they built a makeshift cabin in which to live and worship.

Charles Brooks, a Salvation Army captain, visited the island on the heels of scandalous rumors about the group. But he, too, fell under Creffield's spell, joining the Holy Rollers as Creffield's right-hand man.

Despite many sermons about the virtues of personal suffering, the Holy Rollers couldn't tough out the colder months on the island. A mother and daughter among them, Sarah and Maud Hurt, invited Creffield, Brooks, and others to live at their home in Corvallis. The put-upon man of the house, O. V. Hurt, begrudgingly agreed, but only so he'd have his family back home again. Soon enough, Corvallis was abuzz with gossip about a big bonfire at the residence in which the Holy Rollers burned all the furniture and clothing, along with the Hurts' cat and dog.

Soon after, a photo was shown around town of Creffield's followers on Kiger Island, "praying" in the buff.

Exile

A few wives, sisters, and daughters were sent away to rethink their religious affiliations. Most wound up in the Oregon State Insane Asylum in Salem. One, sixteen-year-old Esther Mitchell, went to a children's home in Portland. Her removal in particular must have stung Creffield, as he would later conclude that she was the "apostle" destined to become the "New Mary."

In January 1904, Creffield, Brooks, and two (male) cult members were forcibly marched by a group of twenty men from the Hurt residence to the outskirts of town, where they were given an old-fashioned tarring and feathering. Creffield was warned in no uncertain terms to leave for good.

A few days later, Creffield hastily married Maud Hurt, but after a few weeks it dawned on him that in "testing" his female consorts for worthiness, he'd overlooked somebody: Donna Mitchell Starr, Maud's aunt by marriage and Esther Mitchell's sister. Creffield, now contending that God had promoted him to "Second Savior," decided to pay Donna a visit.

By mid-March the "Second Savior" had found and "tested" Donna Starr, then conveniently disappeared after Burgess Starr filed a criminal complaint of adultery, which carried a penalty of up to two years in prison.

But even a statewide manhunt with a reward netted zero results. The locals were hopeful; maybe this meant that Creffield had left for good.

Eden

On July 29, Creffield was found hiding—dirty, emaciated, nude, and whiskered—beneath the porch of the Hurt residence. Lying in dirt for four months with only a blanket and a few scraps of food (smuggled to him by Maud) may have been his ultimate act of righteous suffering, but it took a serious toll on his health. Luckily for him, fifteen months in the penitentiary allowed him plenty of time to recuperate.

Shortly after his parole, he announced to his followers (some had been released from the asylum, or hadn't been committed) that God was pleased; all their previous troubles were a test of faith. They'd passed with flying colors, and now God had a "New Eden" prepared for them in the coastal town of Waldport, sixty-five miles southwest of Corvallis. Here they would be safe, he said, as God's wrath destroyed Corvallis, Portland, Seattle, and San Francisco. As fate would have it, on the morning after Creffield's announcement, San Francisco was leveled by its infamous April 18, 1906, earthquake. This only gave Creffield more clout among his supporters.

For the next few weeks, impressionable women evacuated Corvallis by rail, leaving behind husbands, fathers, brothers, and fiancés. Motivated by the fear that Corvallis was doomed, they gathered at a campsite near the beach at Waldport, the new Promised Land.

One pistol-wielding man caught up to Creffield in Newport as he was departing on a ferry crossing Yaquina Bay. The would-be assassin fired, but the gun clicked harmlessly. Creffield immediately claimed this as evidence of his divine invincibility yet he also fled to Seattle with Maud. Meanwhile, George Mitchell, brother to Esther and Donna,

had had enough. He believed he was the only one who could kill Creffield, and he set about doing just that.

Judgment

Attorneys argued that when Mitchell caught up to Creffield and put his exclusive power to the test, he had done so in a fit of temporary insanity. George Mitchell was acquitted on July 10, 1906. But even though Creffield was dead, his legacy would have tragic consequences for Mitchell, almost immediately.

On July 12, Mitchell and his two brothers were set to board a train back to Corvallis. Esther Mitchell, now eighteen and released from the children's home, had been in town for the trial and accompanied her brothers to Seattle's Union Depot to see them off. Her supposed destiny as the New Mary in ruins, she gave her brother George the same treatment he'd given Creffield: a bullet to the back of the head.

Apparently Esther and Maud had planned the revenge killing together. Both women were arrested, but Maud never made it to trial. While in jail, she committed suicide by taking strychnine. Esther was declared not guilty by reason of insanity and sent to the state asylum at Steilacoom, Washington, until 1909. In 1914 she was newly married and living in Waldport when she, too, poisoned herself with strychnine.

Many of the remaining Holy Rollers settled in Waldport. Some of their descendants still live there today, and generally prefer not to discuss their ancestors' embarrassing association with Edmund Creffield's love cult. Still, as many chroniclers of this saga like to point out, one final irony remains.

In September 1975, a new and eccentric religious group held a recruitment meeting at a Waldport hotel (see "The Pat Boone Inn" in the Fabled People and Places chapter). It eventually became the Heaven's Gate cult, infamous for its mass suicide in a San Diego mansion in 1997.

Mondo Extremo

If laughter is the best medicine, Scot Campbell is either the healthiest man alive or the most over-medicated. His frequent high-decibel laughing jags are as infectious to some as they're disturbing to others. Accordingly, the fifty-something visual and performance artist is familiar around Portland as his maniacally jovial alter ego, Extremo the Clown. Whether he's driving his intricate art car, putting on creepy musical puppet shows, or painting surprisingly cute window splashes, Extremo is always bound to leave a big impression. He has enjoyed a cult following since 1996, when Campbell first donned bright garb and greasepaint.

Ladies and gentlemen, readers of all ages, *Weird Oregon* has spared no effort to bring you quality literature. It is in this spirit that we caught up to this hyperactive harlequin, and now present, for your reading pleasure, an exclusive interview with Extremo the Clown.

Tell us about your background. How did Extremo first appear on the scene?

In 1996, I decided to participate in a KNRK [Portland radio station] contest. I won $10,000 by driving around for six weeks, promoting them voraciously. One day I built a box with suspenders and painted the radio station's logo on it. I wore that with a funny hat and red Converse sneakers . . . and that was all. It caught the attention of people coming into Portland. Some guy called the radio station during the morning commute and said, "There's a half-naked clown on the Morrison Bridge!"

Their slogan at the time was "94.7 KNRK: Extreme radio!" My wife, Audrey, dubbed me "Extremo" based on that.

What makes you so extreme?

My need for recognition and creativity. My "extremosity" was born out of anxiety and panic. I arrived in Portland from

Nevada in 1986. Having been diagnosed as bipolar, I chose to avoid drug therapy and instead began journaling, reading, and exploring my inner child. Today I have the ability to become

quite manic when and where I choose, for any duration, without the depression that typically follows euphoric bouts. I can control it and use it for my benefit without any drugs whatsoever. If you ever see me driving by in my car, you will quickly realize something unusual is taking place.

Where'd you get that phat ride?
I made it! Well, I created the artwork on it. It's the world's tallest Mazda; hell, it's the world's strangest vehicle! It took about ten years, I would say about four thousand hours. I create all the original art in water- or oil-based clay. Then I produce molds from which I cast the pieces in either polyurethane resin or latex rubber. I then adhere them to the car with various adhesives. Then I paint them, and stain them individually. It has a working waterfall and a pond in back. It's name is MSV—Mirabilis Statuarius Vehiculum—which means Extraordinary Sculpted Vehicle in Latin.

You're also known for your window paintings . . .
I love painting window splashes and I actually produced three DVDs on the subject. I have been painting windows for some thirty years now and would estimate I have done well over forty thousand panes of glass.

Can you specify some "extreme" things you've done?
Pre-Extremo, in Nevada, I was a "Top Secret Cartoonist" for the navy. I was hired to work at a naval base, producing art for slides used to train certain navy personnel. It's kind of funny: A naval station in the middle of the desert!

To get on base, I had to show my security clearance at the front gate. They must have known me after a while, because one day I showed up wearing a "Coneheads" mask, driving my car with a big fried egg painted on the hood, and they let me right in!

More recently, I did a nine-hour puppet show at the Fremont Solstice Celebration in Seattle. It was pretty much a nonstop manic puppet theater experience.

I also ran for mayor of Portland and came in eighth out of thirty-three candidates. I ended up with 1,247 votes. Two of my more popular slogans were "This time elect a real clown!" and "I don't want to raise taxes, I want to raise hell!"

How would Portland be different today if you'd won the election?
We'd become the laugh capital of the world! I think it would be a safer, funner place if I'd been able to implement my programs. I had a lot of plans to entertain and create more jobs by building the world's largest year-round indoor theme park. It would've really put Portland on the map as an extreme tourist destination. Like Las Vegas is a tourist draw for Nevada and Mardi Gras for Louisiana, Portland would've had Extremoland! "Where the laughter never ends!" More jobs, more fun, more revenue for a better, well-trained police force, more education dollars; all this would add up to less poverty and less crime.

Is enough getting done to "keep Portland weird," as the bumper stickers say?
I don't know, whenever I see those bumper stickers, I wonder what that means. What does one actually need to do to keep it weird?

Will you send your kids to clown college?
Not if they have any say in it! I have three, all pretty talented and interesting in their own right. They're all grown now. When they tell people that Extremo the Clown is their father, they get mixed reactions. And my son-in-law confessed after he married my daughter that he did it partly so he could say his dad-in-law was Extremo the Clown!

So your family is okay with Extremo, then?
Sometimes, when people bring up Extremo, they will let them go on about me, then they'll simply say, "Yeah, I know, that's my dad," or "Yeah, I married the clown!" It's pretty funny!

Opal Whiteley: An Understanding Heart

As Oz has Dorothy and Wonderland has Alice, so Cottage Grove, Oregon, has Opal Whiteley. Opal foreshadowed such character types as the flower child, the New Ager, and even the down-on-her-luck Disney princess with forest critters at her side. Her childhood diary was first published commercially in 1920. *The Story of Opal: The Journal of an Understanding Heart* presents a look at life and nature in 1903 rural Oregon. Evoking a soulful innocence that's part Laura Ingalls Wilder and part Winnie-the-Pooh, it quickly became a best-seller.

But Opal Whiteley's literary success was fleeting. While many considered the diary to be a work of precocious genius, others denounced it as a fraud. This controversy, coupled with mental illness, overwhelmed her fragile spirit and propelled her life into a downward spiral.

A Magical Childhood, on Paper
The official record states that Opal was born on December 11, 1897, in Colton, Washington, to Ed and Lizzie Whiteley. The couple worked itinerantly at logging camps, so it was only natural that she developed a deeply ingrained love of flora and fauna. A child prodigy, she is said to have learned to read and write by the age of three, and did both voraciously.

In December 1903, the Whiteleys moved to Warren, Oregon, near Cottage Grove, to live on a farm owned by Lizzie's parents. Opal's diary covers about sixty-four days of adventures with fancifully named animal and plant friends, among them Lars Porsena of Clusium, a thimble-stealing crow; Brave Horatius, a faithful shepherd dog; and Michael Angelo Sanzio Raphael, an old, wizened fir tree behind the barn. She shares a seemingly psychic bond with these companions.

She describes "going on explores" in what she calls "the near woods," a patch of forest just beyond the farmhouse. Here she befriends fairies, wades in singing creeks, and prays in a woodland "cathedral" of poetry-reciting trees. Her reverential attitude toward the world around her is peppered with bits of French and praise of God.

Youthful misunderstanding results in the diary's darker episodes, where her mother spanks Opal for seemingly minor misbehavior. (Her family would later bristle at this characterization, calling it completely inaccurate.) Ed and Lizzie Whiteley are referred to by the somewhat detached monikers of "the pappa" and "the mamma," owing to Opal's lifelong belief that she was adopted.

She insisted her birth father was the deposed Prince Henri d'Orleans of France. She inconsistently identified her birth mother as various figures from European royalty. As Opal told it, she was kidnapped at an early age following the death of both her parents (the intrepid Prince Henri had died in 1901 while traveling; the mother—whoever Opal claimed her to be—supposedly drowned). Opal was then substituted and named for a recently deceased child of the Whiteleys'. She claimed that her own real name was Françoise Marie de Bourbon-Orleans and referred to her alleged birth parents as Angel Father and Angel Mother. Despite a lack of records to even suggest this scenario may be true, not to mention the Whiteley family's annoyed denials, Opal spent a lifetime working to prove her claims. She insisted that much intrigue went into hiding her true identity.

Flunking into Fairyland

Her intense study of insects, animals, and plants resulted in a self-taught expertise that amazed everyone around her. She joined a youth group called Junior Christian Endeavor in her early teens, which sponsored her in lecturing about nature throughout Oregon. Hundreds, and eventually thousands, gathered to hear her. She was admitted to the University of Oregon in 1916 on a partial scholarship after astounding several professors with her knowledge of the natural world. While at college, she retained her unusual

rapport with nature: One time, she was even spotted singing to an earthworm! The following year, both her mother—that is, Lizzie Whiteley—and her great-grandfather died a few days apart. Stretched thin by grief, lecture commitments, and a book project, Opal's grades soon dropped. Consequently, she lost her scholarship and left college.

She moved to Los Angeles to seek work in the burgeoning film industry, intending to finance her book through an acting career. After several unsuccessful auditions, she resumed work on the lecture circuit and solicited funds from wealthy—usually eccentric—investors to self-publish her book.

After a disagreement with its intended printer, Opal worked herself to exhaustion to finish roughly two hundred copies by hand, using sets of pages that had already been printed. These volumes—which included more than fifty copyright-volatile illustrations cut from other materials and pasted in, scrapbook-style—appeared in 1918 and was titled *The Fairyland Around Us.* She sent copies of this children's nature guide to several publishing houses in an attempt to secure a commercial release.

Soon after, she traveled to Boston to meet with Ellery Sedgwick, editor of the *Atlantic Monthly*. Though he was uninterested in publishing *Fairyland,* Opal's background intrigued him. Sedgwick suggested the possibility of publishing her childhood diary instead.

A Puzzling Diary

Easier said than done: The diary, written in large unbroken rows of capital letters, in crayon and colored pencil, on a wild assortment of loose scrap paper, had, according to Opal, been torn to shreds by her younger sister. Opal told Sedgwick that she'd saved the thousands of scraps, but they were divided between her LA residence (a boardinghouse) and a friend's house in Oregon. Sedgwick sent for both sets of shredded pages, and Opal spent eight months in Boston meticulously reconstructing and transcribing them.

The Story of Opal was first serialized in the *Atlantic Monthly* starting in March 1920. It struck a chord with readers and resulted in a surge of new subscriptions to the magazine. Its publication as a book a few months later continued this success, quickly becoming a runaway hit.

But not everyone was convinced that the diary was entirely authentic. The loudest voice in this camp came from Cottage Grove: Elbert Bede, editor of the *Cottage Grove Sentinel* newspaper. He argued that the diary, with its odd grammatical structure and occasional phonetic spelling, was too elaborate in several ways for a child of six to have written.

He interviewed various Cottage Grove residents who knew Opal, including members of her family, and wrote article after article chronicling his investigation into her diary. According to him, the diary—including the "original" shredded pages written in crayon—was created by Opal while living in Los Angeles. The national press, fascinated by Bede's alleged debunking of a best-seller, descended on Cottage Grove. The whole affair quickly got out of hand; allegations and rumors supporting

every angle of the debate were published. The locals were perturbed by the excessive unwanted attention. The frustrated Whiteley family, who by then were mostly estranged from Opal, disowned her completely, left town, and changed their names.

Sedgwick, who initially defended the diary as authentic, was dealing with flack from all sides. Hounded both by reporters and by an attorney representing Opal in a contract dispute, he decided that the diary, however popular, was just not worth the trouble. He pulled it off the market a mere ten months after it was released and sold its publishing rights.

Further attempts by Opal to republish it in the United States, ahead of compiling a sequel, were thwarted by various developments, although a British edition sold moderately well. She released one more book in 1923, a self-published volume of poetry titled *The Flower of Stars.*

Intrepid Adventures

Opal never returned to Oregon. For a time, she remained on the East Coast, living with a series of wealthy patrons in Boston, New York, and Washington, DC. Some of these associates took notice of her increasingly quirky behavior. She often told others about her allegedly royal heritage, sometimes changing details in her adoption story. She spoke of being followed by mysterious "agents" connected to her supposed childhood kidnapping. At times, she was withdrawn and sullen, but would perk up when she became the center of attention. When one of her hosts suddenly died, she found herself homeless for a short while, seemingly confused about how to help herself. After resettling with another patron, she began losing creative focus, allowing new manuscripts to languish unfinished.

Around March 1924, she decided to retrace her Angel Father's travels around the world. She traveled throughout Europe and India, where she struck many more unlikely friendships with aristocrats, stirred up more controversy through odd behavior, and even found romance—and, some say, matrimony—with an Indian con man who posed as a swami. This particular development so scandalized India's British government of the time (who largely accepted her claim to French royalty) that Opal was encouraged to leave. She departed for England in early 1926.

A Princess in Purgatory

Here, Opal wrote romantic letters to American publisher George Putnam, who eventually married aviator Amelia Earhart. Opal also wrote magazine articles about her experiences in India. Those who knew her noted further personality changes. Her writing got more muddled and repetitive. She no longer enjoyed the company of children, whom she had regularly taught about nature. In addition to her claims of hailing from French royalty, she began asserting that she was intended for a prearranged marriage to the Duke of Windsor. She read more voraciously than ever, but now, in the squalor of a tiny London flat, she rarely ate. Friends would find her blissfully oblivious to her malnutrition, completely enthralled in reading or writing. After the Nazi bombing of London in 1940, she wandered through the rubble, rescuing books.

In 1948, after years of increasing signs of mental illness, Opal was committed to Napsbury Hospital, a sanitarium north of London. She would remain there for the rest of her life. Her claimed royalty, if not necessarily believed by the hospital staff, was at least humored by their referring to her as "the princess." Some accounts have her undergoing electroshock therapy and a frontal lobotomy during her years of hospitalization.

Opal died in 1992 at the age of 94, by then a frail, faint shadow of her former self. Buried in London's Highgate Cemetery, she is acknowledged as both Francoise Marie de Bourbon-Orleans and Opal Whiteley on her headstone. Her epitaph reads, "I spake as a child." Perhaps the thick ivy on her grave is nature's way of thanking Opal for having done so.

Redemption

Opal's story has found renewed life over the years, and much of the debate it initially stirred is still unresolved. Her diary was eventually republished in several formats, including Benjamin Hoff's annotated *The Singing Creek Where the Willows Grow* and Jane Boulton's readapted poetry version. Opal is remembered in plays, an independent feature film, and at least one music CD using passages from her diary as lyrics. The University of Oregon has made the full text of the diary available on the Internet. Perhaps best of all, the town of Cottage Grove, once bitter toward her because of the media circus she inadvertently created, has found its own understanding heart. Opal is now accepted as part of its heritage and is honored with a small park and a mural. Two blocks away, the local library displays an Opal Whiteley statue and other memorabilia. Her family's opinion of her has also softened; descendants of her relatives find her fascinating and have openly contributed to biographies.

But even with acceptance and renewed admiration, it's still hard to understand her completely. Even in the most reasoned analyses, there remains a subtle underlying magic about her. We can't speak with certainty as to whether she was truly adopted, really wrote her diary as a child, or genuinely had a miraculous rapport with nature. Opal Whiteley is best contemplated just as she lived her life: with extraordinary wonder and unwavering faith.

Kent Couch, Balloonatic

Aviation buffs usually cite the efforts of such pioneers as the Wright Brothers and Charles Lindbergh as a source of inspiration—but not Bend resident Kent Couch! The gas station owner is instead fascinated by California's "Lawnchair" Larry Walters, who, in 1982, famously flew about ten miles on a patio chair harnessed to forty-five weather balloons.

When Kent saw a documentary about him several years ago, the experience, as well as the notoriety, seemed particularly enticing. He made it a personal goal to fly his own balloon-chair.

To this end, Kent thoroughly researched Walters's flight: how exactly he did it, what went right, what went wrong, and what could have been done differently. Eventually, his loved ones began suspecting he might actually go through with it, so they contributed to the preparations.

On the morning of September 18, 2006, Kent's plan came together in his gas station parking lot. Instead of weather balloons, large helium-filled latex balloons—sixty-seven in all—were fastened to a lawn chair using nylon cords. A cylindrical banner advertising his Stop-and-Go Mini Mart was hung from the bottom. The local airport was consulted to determine wind speed, elevation, and direction—an essential step in helping his ground crew of family and friends follow him by car. Finally, Kent donned a parachute, grabbed his BB gun, and lifted off the ground on his homemade dirigible.

Air currents carried him through the "wild balloon yonder" for six hours and about ninety-seven miles. The trip became a sometimes distressing science lesson. Helium density, lower air pressure at higher altitudes, and the sun's heat combined with unforeseen results.

As Kent explained to *Weird Oregon:* "Once I got to fifteen thousand–plus feet, the balloons started popping, The chair jerked, my stomach sank, and I had a bit of a fright. I lost six balloons, descended to three thousand feet, and stabilized. Then the sun came up and heated the ground. I ascended back to fifteen thousand feet and lost about five more balloons."

After the flight, he noticed that the remaining balloons had not been as filled to capacity as the ones that popped. This resulted in more elasticity and helped them better resist the heat and air pressure. Also, darker-colored balloons, which collected heat faster, tended to pop first.

So was there any controlling this unusual aircraft?

"There was no steering involved; I simply went where the winds took me," says Kent. "I adjusted my elevation by popping balloons [with the BB gun] to descend—usually two or three at a time."

As Kent floated over the Brothers area, he noticed a big cloud fast approaching. Worried that he and the balloons would get wet, possibly weighing them down and causing more problems, he dropped from the chair. He would later realize how risky this move had been:

"What I didn't know was that the ground had risen 1,100 feet, so while my altimeter said 3,200, I was really only 2,100 feet from the ground! I didn't figure this out until after my parachute landing. Luckily, I'd bought an oversize chute, which gave me more wind resistance."

Regardless of the rough spots, accomplishing his dream was extremely satisfying. But after his maiden voyage, Kent thought of a few ideas that might have improved the experience. Would they work? There was only one way to find out: Apply them to a second balloon-chair flight.

The slightly retooled second flight happened on July 7, 2007:

"On the second trip, I launched with 105 balloons . . . We filled the balloons to only four foot diameter instead of the five foot max that they were designed for, giving them space to expand at high elevations."

Additionally, the balloons were placed within arms' reach, so that Kent could control his altitude by gradually releasing helium. This would cut down on the jerkiness from popping balloons with a BB gun. Four five-gallon bags of water were attached to the chair as ballast. To achieve higher altitudes, he would simply release some of the water.

As it turned out, these changes worked surprisingly well. This time, he stayed aloft for almost nine hours, travelling 193 miles northeast to La Grande. Initially he'd hoped to reach Idaho, but he noticed rough terrain ahead, including Hells Canyon. Instead of continuing on, he descended to about two feet over a wheat field and tucked-and-rolled to the ground. As his chair continued on its way, Kent realized with alarm that he'd left behind his video camera.

For nearly a year, Kent offered a $500 reward for any information leading to the retrieval of his missing equipment. A rumor circulated that a United Airlines pilot spotted the chair floating over Michigan at an altitude of more than thirty thousand feet. This was found to be untrue, however, when the lawn chair and camera were found on a ranch thirteen miles northeast of Baker City in mid-May 2008.

Shortly thereafter, on July 5, 2008, Kent once again cast himself adrift over Oregon. This was his most successful flight to date. He traveled about 235 miles in nine hours. He finally reached Idaho and actually landed his chair. Locals in the small town of Cambridge, where he alighted, greeted him as a hero.

So what's the bottom line? When you get past all the science and a few glitches and oversights, what is this form of travel really like?

"Moving through the air is so pure, maybe like a child dreaming of floating on a magic carpet." reflects Kent. "One of the great things about flying in this fashion is not knowing where mother nature may take you.

"It's unique in that you're moving with the wind, so there's no noise. I could hear kids playing, dogs barking, and cows mooing at fifteen thousand feet! And I saw a butterfly at fourteen thousand feet, flying around my balloons with interest."

Curiously, this kind of aeronautic effort may be losing its "weird factor" because of a gradual change into mainstream recreation. Now known as cluster ballooning, it seems to be catching on as a "semi-extreme" sport. Much of it started after Kent's attempts garnered national news coverage. Several prospective cluster balloonists have contacted him, seeking advice. Most don't rise to the occasion after learning of the expense involved.

As of this writing, Kent is contemplating more balloon flights, perhaps overseas, possibly across Australia. It is probably safe to assume that his high-flying adventures, wherever they may happen, will continue to be annual events. His Web site, www.couchballoons.com, offers more details and presents an inside look at the life of a self-professed "balloonatic."

Peculiar Properties

We find that Oregonians tend to be quite hospitable. We were graciously welcomed into various homes and businesses in the course of researching this book, whether we were seeking local legends, historical oddities, or other weirdness. In some cases, of course, the properties we visited were what we sought to catalog. If there's one factor we did not underestimate when we embarked on this project, it was the penchant of many Oregonians to add a humorous and/or creative twist to their homes, businesses, and public spaces.

As you will see in this chapter, that kind of proclivity can take different forms. For example, city parks rarely, if ever, get as small as two we visited. Elsewhere, two private parks are significantly bigger, but one is inhabited by dinosaurs, the other by fairy-tale creatures. One business is known for a golden giant; another is known for an underwater-themed bathroom. A classic and beloved site spurs our curiosity for geology; a much newer site either offends, amuses, or vindicates our political sensibilities.

Just as there is a variety of such properties, there are different reasons why they have been created. Some are strictly decorative; others are practical. Sometimes they serve to make a point; other times, a profit. But there doesn't always have to be a motive behind them; it's valid to simply want to bring a fun idea to fruition.

In any case, we salute the visionaries who created the examples presented on the following pages. Through their hard work and creativity, Oregon earns yet another feather in its cap as a haven of offbeat Americana.

Puny Parks

From the coast in the west to the high desert in the east, from the Portland area to the California border, some of the most scenically diverse parks in the country are located within Oregon. In addition to hiking, picnicking, and other typical diversions, the *Weird Oregon* reader will be aware of such park-based activities as exploring a "witch's castle," walking on glowing sand, and contemplating treacherous drops over waterfalls, just like old-time daredevil Al Faussett. (Note: We assume no responsibility for misguided individuals who try to emulate that last one.)

Curiously, however, at least two parks in the state are known not because of what *can* be done within them, but rather what *cannot* be done within them for lack of space. Despite this commonality, each piece of land is a significantly different take on the concept of a puny park, in both scope and history.

An Inconvenient Tree

Waldo Park is located on the corner of Union and Summer Streets in Salem, on property that once belonged to a prominent local, Judge William Waldo. It seems that the jurist was rather fond of the sequoia tree he bought from a traveling salesman and planted in 1872. As Salem expanded and traffic increased on the roads near his home, Judge Waldo was forced to sell his land to the city. Concerned about his beloved sequoia, he entered a stipulation to the land sale that the tree would not be cut down. Remarkably, the city agreed.

The tree grew to impressive proportions over the next few decades. It became a landmark in addition to lending a bit of color to local history. In the 1930s, some of Salem's leading citizens joined the American War Mothers in a campaign to recognize the tree's significance to the community. Thus in 1936, a twenty-by-twelve-foot patch of land around the tree was declared as Waldo Park.

The land today is really just a big patch of ivy alongside some office buildings. The sequoia, on the other hand, is as attention-grabbing as ever. Rising eighty-two feet and measuring six feet in diameter at the base, it's hard to imagine Judge Waldo planting it as a sapling.

It's also hard to imagine Salem's nineteenth-century stewards not reconsidering the removal of the tree had they foreseen the difficulties it would present in maintaining Summer Street. To put it bluntly, the sequoia, its status notwithstanding, has long been a "pine in the ash." The road shrinks from four lanes to three (and expands back to four) because of the space taken up by Waldo Park. It's a frustrating choke point during rush hour, and many Salemites have openly proposed decommissioning Waldo Park to remove the tree. If nothing else, however, it has seniority, so it's unlikely that anything will happen to Waldo Park or its arboreal giant anytime soon.

Park in the Middle of the Street

The Rose City tries hard to adhere to its unofficial slogan, "Keep Portland Weird." In this regard, Mill Ends Park is certainly a credit to locals who contribute to the effort. It takes a healthy sense of absurdity to lay claim to the world's smallest park, located inside a two-foot dirt patch in the middle of a crosswalk.

Credit columnist Dick Fagen, of the long-defunct *Oregon Journal,* for founding the odd little property. In 1948, Fagen's office overlooked the corner of Front Avenue and Taylor Street. He had the perfect view of a small concrete median in the road, intended to (someday) be used as base for a streetlight. At that time, the only thing it held was dirt and weeds.

Fagen soon discovered a leprechaun named Patrick O'Toole frolicking inside the median. He befriended the diminutive Irishman and was promptly offered a wish.

No sooner had Fagen wished for a park in his own honor than the leprechaun cast a magic spell. The weed-choked hole was suddenly filled with beautiful flowers.

Or so claimed Fagen. On the other hand, there are those who insist that O'Toole never really existed and that Fagen planted the flowers on his own to improve the view from his window. We leave it up to our readers to decide which story to believe. What *is* certain is that Fagen named the 452.16 square inches of greenery Mill Ends Park. Over the years, he devoted many of his newspaper columns to stories about O'Toole, his leprechaun family, and their activities at the park. Again: Were the stories true? We honestly don't know.

What ultimately matters is the verifiable fact that Portlanders took Mill Ends Park to heart. On St. Patrick's Day 1976, a dedication ceremony formally recognized the humble makeshift planter as a city park. This attracted the attention of the *Guinness Book of World Records,* which officially confirmed it to be the world's smallest.

The Behemoth of Brawn

Take a good look, guys. With plenty of veggies, exercise, and clean living, you too can look like this fine specimen of studliness! Analyze those abs! Ponder those pecs! Inspect those biceps! And how about that *vastus medialis*?

Obviously, very few of us will ever reach such heights of physical perfection. Nevertheless, the sinewy statue that towers over smaller hardbodies at the aptly named Giants Gym in Portland gives us something to strive for.

This giant is made of fiberglass over a metal frame (with concrete feet). He stands twenty-two feet tall and weighs about a ton.

His keepers don't seem very intimidated by Portland's other famous giant. Says gym manager George Comalli of his golden boy: "We feel he would win a competition with the Paul Bunyan in North Portland. . . . Paul has an ax, but our guy is in better shape!"

He certainly has the background of a champion. The giant statue is a transplant from California, where he served as a backdrop to the World's Strongest Man competitions in the 1970s. Like at the Colossus of Rhodes in ancient Greece, spectators entering the venue would pass between his legs.

The legendary Zuver's Gym in Costa Mesa, Calfornia, was also his home for a while. Zuver's Gym is long gone, but many powerlifters remember or know of the club's unique touches: large decorative props and some of the world's largest, heaviest, and most innovative bodybuilding equipment. Much of it was devised and built by owner Bob Zuver, whose philosophy was to have fun while working out. (Among many outrageous stories about Zuver's Gym is that it had a wall made of boulders—which Bob Zuver stacked by hand.)

Zuver's Gym closed in the 1980s after a failed attempt at expansion. Its assets were sold off, and Casey's Gym of Portland purchased the giant along with several pieces of equipment. He was hauled up to Portland on a flatbed truck and mounted on the roof of the building. The club was soon renamed Giants Gym in honor of the sizable statue.

He was a hit with the public, but Portland officials were concerned. Citing weight and signage regulations, they insisted that the statue be removed from the roof. With considerable effort he was placed among the exercise machines, rising partway into the drop ceiling. He remains there today, providing inspiration and incentive to the club's strongmen.

Giants Gym is at 5223 NE Sandy Boulevard, and if you ask nicely, you might be allowed a quick glance at the behemoth of brawn. You'll have to crane your neck a bit to take him all in, but hey . . . no pain, no gain!

Rockin' at Rasmus Petersen's

There is rock music, rock candy, rock salt . . . and then, as a recurring theme in personalized properties, there are rock gardens. A great example, and probably one of the best known, is Petersen's Rock Garden and Museum in Redmond, in central Oregon. For a very reasonable admission fee (collected with a pay box on the honor system), you can stroll through a most majestic petrologic paradise. What wonders you'll see!

Miniature churches, palaces, towers, and even a whole mountain village, all made of countless stones, line the walking trails. Large rocks of vibrant but natural colors are stacked together upright around the grounds, resembling dense model cities. The amazing displays extend into a pond, where miniature suspension bridges allow access to a couple of small islands with a rock model of a lighthouse and other decorative elements.

Patriotic displays are also present, including an American flag of natural red, white, and blue stones. A Statue of Liberty, sculpted in oddly dwarfish proportions, stands atop a rock-covered pedestal. Below it is a sign with a good piece of advice: ENJOY YOURSELF—IT IS LATER THAN YOU THINK.

In this part of the state, a man-made miniature city of stone seems, if not inevitable, at least not all that far-fetched. Substantial volcanic activity a few thousand years ago, which created the Cascade Mountains, resulted in a great variety of rocks strewn about: obsidian, agate, malachite, thunder eggs, and more, in countless shapes and sizes, and in multiple colors. All that was needed was a visionary, someone to use those leftovers of nature's fury as the building blocks of an awe-inspiring environment.

That someone was Rasmus Petersen (1883–1952), a Danish immigrant who settled near the Cascade Mountains in 1906. A humble farmer, Petersen made a habit of collecting unusual and interesting rocks from around his land. He took trowel in hand to create his first rock structures in 1935. Thus began a creative streak comparable to the proverbial rolling stone: It gathered no moss for seventeen years, ending only with Petersen's death in 1952. By then, Petersen's stony scenery covered most of four acres and attracted visitors from far and wide.

Today, Petersen's Rock Garden and Museum is as popular and peculiar as ever. Should you decide to drop by, allow yourself a couple of hours to wander leisurely around the grounds, check out the rock collection in the museum building, and enjoy a picnic among the resident peacocks, cats, and other animals. If you're not moved and inspired by Rasmus Petersen's legacy, you must have a heart of . . .

Well, you know.

The Da Vinci of Highway 20

In August 2006, using stencil-cut tarps and a paint sprayer, Samuel Clemens created a sixty-by-forty-foot reproduction of the *Mona Lisa* on a grassy slope at the edge of his farm in Toledo. The attention it attracted was unlike anything ever seen in the area.

Traffic began jamming on State Highway 20, a 55 mph zone that runs directly past Clemens's property. Several accidents were blamed on the painting. Blocking the shoulder of the road did little to discourage admirers from pulling over.

Local, regional, and national media took notice. Coverage snowballed, and Clemens's *Mona Lisa* quickly became a phenomenon around the globe. The public clamored for more, and Clemens's delivered.

In 2007, he painted a 144-foot-long nude portrait of his wife on the hillside. It caused more traffic jams and a heated debate about the painting's appropriateness. Although some local officials disapproved of the painting, one of them ironically asked Clemens to paint a campaign advertisement for his re-election on the property. Clemens declined.

Clemens told *Weird Oregon* that he intended to produce a coffee table book documenting ten years' worth of lawn paintings. The controversy sidetracked those plans.

He remains bemused by the whole experience. As he explained to us, "I consider myself a good artist, better than many, and for years I've had a hard time getting my work noticed. Then

one day I decide to paint my lawn, almost as a joke, and suddenly everyone wants to talk to me!"

While Clemens has no plans to paint his hillside again, we hold out hope that one day, he will think back to his brief, unusual hobby and, with a gleam, walk off to the barn to get some tarps and a paint sprayer. . . .

It's been 10 crazy days for local artist Samuel Clemens after he painting the Mona Lisa on his Toledo hillside last weekend. Although he at first found the attention overwhelming, he realized he actually enjoyed it, although his wife keeps him from getting too cocky, he said. From the local newspapers to international media, Clemens has found himself featured in the News-Times, the Oregonian, and a South Korean newspaper. On television, he's been seen everywhere from Portland's KGW to the Today Show to CNN. (Photos by Barton Grover Howe)

Artist gets accustomed to 15 minutes - or more - of fame

By Barton Grover Howe
Of the News-Times

After Leonardo da Vinci finished the Mona Lisa in 1507, it was nearly 350 years before people realized just what the artist had accomplished.

Samuel Clemens got famous within a matter of days.

"When I did this I thought maybe the Oregonian (would call). That would be so cool," he says with a smile. "But I've gotten calls from Arizona, Oklahoma City, New York" - and the Oregonian. All were calls prompted by his painting appearing on Portland's KGW-TV, the Today Show, and CNN. He even heard a South Korean news agency called for a photo.

"A couple of days ago, right before the JonBenet thing, I was the top story for a day. I felt really good that I pre-empted Madonna and Brittany," he says, laughing. "I tell you when it really struck me strange is when they did the channel 8 NBC thing. They showed a map of the coast, with a big arrow pointing towards my house," he said. "Oh my Gosh, I thought, I superceded Keiko for a moment." And he laughs again.

Clemens has admitted he's not very good at self-promotion, which can be a detriment to an artist's career. This experience may have changed that. "Now I know why people want to be in the news all the

time: it's really addictive," to which he quickly adds: "My wife's going, 'All right, all right, get your head back in here.'

"That's her job," he adds with an even broader smile.

It doesn't help - from his wife's standpoint - that all kinds of people keep calling, not just reporters. And those are the people he's enjoyed hearing from the most. "I had some lady call me and just wanted to say thank you and, 'What's your address?' Evidently she wanted to send a donation for next year."

He hasn't gotten any negative calls, although a few people have asked, "How come you didn't do Jesus or a cross or the Last Supper or something?" He tells them what he tells everyone: the Mona Lisa is the most famous face in the world, and since she means something to everyone, so does his creation.

"This was a good choice the first time out," he said. "I'm trying to think what would work better."

When he created the 60-foot tall Mona Lisa on his hillside, Clemens was hoping it might lead to some art jobs. He admits that hasn't happened yet, but he figures it still might. He has an interview with the Associated Press coming up, and as of Thursday he was still seeing his creation on CNN. With all the press attention, he figures there will be a lot of people stopping on Highway 20

the next few weekends.

But even if he never makes a dime from his creation, Clemens said it was all worth it, even if at first all the attention was a little unnerving. Earlier this week he had to leave work, he said, because the whole thing was "weird," and he was unable to focus. Then, he says with the big smile returning, he learned to relax.

"What else am I going to do (but enjoy it)? How can I segue this into what I really do, my art? I haven't really figured it out yet, but it's nice exposure." Da Vinci himself should have been so lucky.

But, he admits, it was another artist that inspired him to enjoy his time in the sun rather than run from it.

"My daughter was home and she kept calling me and saying I gave your cell phone number out to some radio guys," while he was working a job at the Olalla Golf Course. "And then I started realizing, what am I doing here? This is my Warholian 15 minutes!

"I'm pounding nails in a project, and I realized, I'm the boss. I'll just take the day off to deal with this. Luckily I did that."

And he smiles again, maybe the second biggest in Lincoln County.

Barton Grover Howe covers north Lincoln County for the News-Times. He can be contacted at 921-0408 or barton.howe@gmail.com.

Weird Way to Clean a Home

Perhaps the best way to describe Frances Gabe is to say she's a cross between Martha Stewart and Thomas Edison.

It seems that Gabe, following her divorce in the 1960s, sought something—anything—to distract her from a prolonged bout of depression. Long resenting that so much time and effort was needed to clean her home, the Newberg resident found herself inventing a new house with several unorthodox cleaning innovations.

Wash, Rinse, Reside, Repeat

The core parts of her self-cleaning house are the spinning soap and water nozzles on the ceiling of each room. Wash and rinse cycles are activated via a control panel. The walls, ceilings, and floors are covered with waterproof resin. Household items that are safe to wash are stored on wire mesh shelves so that they, too, get a good cleaning. Other items, such as books, are stored in cabinets or drawers protected with rubber molding. Furniture is kept safe by either waterproof coating or plastic

covers. Afterward, hot air blowers take care of the drying. The house's construction was necessarily unusual to work with such a system. Its size was kept deliberately modest to increase the effectiveness of the cleaning features. The walls are made of cinder blocks rather than drywall, for

obvious reasons. The ceilings are made of resin-coated wood, as are the floors, which tilt ever so slightly toward a drain. The kitchen dish cabinet also functions as a dishwasher. A closet contains its own dedicated cleaning system, so that clothes can be washed as they hang inside.

Gabe patented every innovation in her self-cleaning house. Over the years, a few real estate developers purportedly expressed interest in licensing her concepts, but no deals were ever finalized.

A House in Transition?

The self-cleaning house is tucked back in the woods along NE Stevenson Road, a dead-end gravel turnoff. Unfortunately we saw no clear means of approaching it. We then drove to a nearby market to ask a few locals for any pertinent information.

Strangely, relatively few of them seemed to know about the self-cleaning house. It was as if it were washed from the memories of those most likely to know about it.

A little more research finally yielded some answers. It seems that the self-cleaning house was damaged several years back in an earthquake, leaving only the dish cabinet-washer operational. As of this writing, Frances Gabe is well into her nineties and has supposedly moved to a retirement home. This does not spell the end of the self-cleaning house, as it may ultimately be donated to the Chehalem Parks and Recreation District.

Korsakoffee Kulture

While networking with other chroniclers of the offbeat, I was honored to meet Portland author and actress Athena (yes, genuinely of single name). In one small way, her personal journey as a published author was the inverse of my own. Whereas I frequently traveled from Washington to Oregon to research *Weird Oregon,* she traveled from Oregon to Washington to research her own book on paranormal phenomena in Seattle. During one of my trips to the Rose City, we agreed to meet for coffee at a place I'd heard a little about: the Rimsky-Korsakoffee House, 707 SE Twelfth Avenue (at the corner of Alder Street).

Don't expect a sleek glass-walled Starbucks-type establishment; from the outside, this desserts-only café looks rather like an unassuming Victorian home. As well it should, since that is exactly what the building once was. Marxist writer Louise Bryant is said to have lived here while married to a Portland dentist. For movie buffs, Bryant's subsequent extramarital affair, travels to the Soviet Union, and efforts at promoting communism in America are the subject of the 1981 film *Reds.* The exterior of the house, which is painted a deep red, thus lends a historic symbolism, whether intended or not.

Further implicating Russian culture, the café's name is a play on the moniker of Russian composer Nicolai Rimsky-Korsakov. In fact, each table inside the coffeehouse is named after a famous composer. Placed within adjoining rooms on the first floor, each has a glass overlay under which customers are welcome to leave notes, clippings, or other mementos of their visit.

There are whispered rumors that some tables are haunted, possibly by the spirits of their namesakes. Startled patrons often report strange activity such as tables shaking or rising. One table has supposedly been known to disappear through a wall and reappear moments later. Some patrons

drop by to experience these phenomena as much as to pleasure their palates.

But while the tables might briefly interrupt your dessert, it's the restroom that takes the cake. "Don't be scared," advised owner Goody Cable somewhat unreassuringly, as she directed me to a door in the upstairs hallway. Cable, an artist, opened the Rimsky-Korsakoffee House in 1980, envisioning it as a tribal business. That is, she does not consider herself the manager so much as a collaborator in day-to-day operations among others who wish to work there. It is this same organic thinking that produced the startling vision before me as I opened the door.

Inside, a kayak sat on the floor. A goatee-sporting intellectual reclined in it, tangled in a fishing net, staring blankly. Was he real, or was he a mannequin? For a moment I wasn't sure. Gradually his eerie stillness convinced me that he was the latter. Then, another nibble of unease: Was he really a mannequin, or a drowning victim? Why would I even wonder that? Of course: the paint job. The entire room was painted to appear as if it were underwater. Behind a foreground of coral and seaweed, the blue-green walls seemed to extend into a hazy distance. In the corner, next to the commode, a mermaid's hands emerged from the wall, holding the toilet paper. A school of fish hung from the rippling ceiling. Nearby, a foot stepped downward, near the underside of a dock.

I snapped some pictures and went back downstairs, my mind trying to parse the meaning of what I had just seen. It didn't help that I was still recovering from the myriad wild sights I'd seen in the neighborhood.

Athena had arrived and was waiting for me. We sat at a table and I listened intently as she explained how, for her and many other Portlanders, "Rimsky's" symbolizes the city as a whole. Both are unapologetically carefree and bohemian. Both encourage an atmosphere of intellectualism and quirkiness as an art form. I had to admit, I could see where she was coming from.

We discussed the specifics over coffee and a delicious raspberry sundae.

A little later, as we were leaving, the people at the table behind us—the low one surrounded by couches—were a bit perplexed. It seems that while they were lost in conversation, an unseen hand had shifted around their food and drinks.

—*Al Eufrasio*

Ziggurat's Zallright!

On a drive along the central Oregon coast (Highway 101), it's worth stopping in Yachats to admire the architecture of this unusual building, known as the Ziggurat, after the ancient similarly shaped structures in the Middle East. Up until a few years ago, the four-story modern-day pyramid was operated as a seaside bed-and-breakfast. It was for sale when we stopped by in early 2008. The asking price: about $1.25 million. Zounds!

Prehistoric Gardens

Steven Spielberg hasn't filmed it, Richard Attenborough doesn't own it, and as far as we know, Jeff Goldblum hasn't warned people away from it. Still, Prehistoric Gardens along Highway 101 in Port Orford is as close to *Jurassic Park* as you're likely get on the Oregon coast.

As one of a diminishing breed of tourist traps across the United States, this dinosaur park seeks to promote knowledge of long-extinct prehistoric beasts through colorful life-size sculptures. (By life-size, we mean "very large"—at least one is forty feet tall or more.)

Prehistoric Gardens' brochure touts the "scientifically correct restorations, authentic in detail and restored in as life-like a manner as possible." Well, as lifelike a manner as steel frameworks, wire mesh, and concrete will allow for, anyway. The dinosaurs look a tad more cartoony than realistic, but that's part of their appeal. Their look, especially the bright color schemes, provides a certain charm that might otherwise have been missed.

The park is located in a temperate rain forest, hence the name Prehistoric Gardens. Heavy rainfall and highly enriched soil result in abundant vegetation. Rare plants, giant ferns, moss-covered trees, and other botanical wonders are all found around the park. It makes for an appropriately primeval atmosphere in which to display the sculptures.

Prehistoric Gardens opened in 1953 with just two dinos created by the late owner, Ernie Nelson. A lifelong dinosaur buff and amateur paleontologist, Nelson took his work very seriously. He thoroughly researched the animals he sculpted, referencing fossils and skeletons in numerous museums and vetting his data with several natural history experts. In subsequent years, he added twenty-one more creatures to his menagerie.

Rumor has it that he also designed the dinosaurs at the former Thunderbeast Park in Chiloquin, but did not build them and was less than impressed with the final result. (See "The Last of the Thunderbeasts" in the Roadside Oddities chapter.)

Nelson went extinct in 1999.

Incidentally, during an early-evening midwinter visit to Prehistoric Gardens, *Weird Oregon* author Jeff Davis says he witnessed two young ladies taking, shall we say, racy and revealing gag photos near one of the dinosaurs. In deference to marital bliss, he did not investigate further.

If you would like to see Ernie Nelson's dinosaurs (alas, there is probably little chance of Jeff Davis's lewd beauties returning), Prehistoric Gardens is open every day from March through November. Phone 541-332-4463 for more information.

A Sanctuary of Make-Believe

Once upon a time, in a world between fantasy and reality, one family risked everything to make their dreams come true.

We apologize profusely for beginning a *Weird Oregon* entry with combined clichés from fairy tales and movie trailers. We think you'll agree, however, that in this case it's completely appropriate.

The family in question is named Tofte—more on them momentarily—and the fruits of their time, money, and labor are located alongside I-5 just south of Salem. Spread out over twenty acres of wooded hills is the Enchanted Forest theme park, a magically weird place if ever there was one.

A glance from the highway or from adjacent Enchanted Way offers a tantalizing glimpse of Old World architecture with a cartoon bent. This seems to be enough to entice most visitors, and it's gratifying to discover that what you see from the outside does not do justice to all you'll find inside.

You're surrounded by a mix of tangible interactive childhood fantasies, a world of castles, forts, and the kind of footwear that old women live inside of. Winding paths weave through the forest, leading you to scenes straight out of books, nursery rhymes, and popular folklore. The park is roughly broken up into three sections: Storybook Lane, the frontier town of Tofteville, and the European Village. Each section, of course, corresponds to a different genre of escapism for the young and the young at heart.

An Enchanting Stroll

The first attraction beyond the entrance is a pastel-colored castle with a "moat" of ivy and (inside) dioramas of scenes from *Sleeping Beauty.* From here, you can take Storybook Lane to visit such wonders as the candy-coated home of the witch from *Hansel and Gretel* and the rabbit hole from *Alice in Wonderland.* An egg-ceptionally jovial Humpty Dumpty

sits high up on a wall. By his red cheeks and nose, it's easy to imagine why he's destined to fall off!

Further along is a walk-in witch's head that doubles as a slide, the Crooked Man's crooked house, the Old Woman's Shoe, and more.

Tofteville hams up the Western motif with a ramshackle boomtown. The wooden buildings are slightly askew for humor's sake, and the saloon cleverly simulates the effects of a few drinks with a tilted floor. A dentist's office, a barber, and other businesses are tended by humorous animatronics.

To the north of Tofteville, the path rises uphill to an ominous Victorian house. Its peeling paint and broken windows indicate that it's abandoned. Visitors are allowed, even encouraged, to walk through and investigate rumors that it's haunted. (Let us know what you find!)

If you're not up to the task, to the south of Tofteville is Fort Fearless, containing much to explore. Nearby is the Challenge of Mondor, a popular newer attraction that combines a tunnel of love with laser tag. A log flume, bobsled ride, and outdoor theater—renowned for its humorous takes on fairy tales—fill the back of the park.

The European Village emulates a city street from the Middle Ages with similar charm and humor. Look for animatronic maidens watching from second-story windows, and take in one of Enchanted Forest's most popular features: the indoor water fountain show.

Putting aside the fantasy elements and examining the Enchanted Forest from a strictly pragmatic angle, the park hearkens back to a more innocent time in America, when dozens of storybook-based mom-and-pop theme parks dotted the landscape. Many, if not most, of those properties still in existence are in perpetual states of disrepair. This is often due to competition from bigger, corporate-owned theme parks. Happily, this is not the case with the Enchanted Forest, thanks to its local popularity and its

isolation from any similar attractions. It is profitable enough to fund its maintenance and expansion, but it exudes a down-home grassroots feel without the commercial glitz of a Disney or Six Flags park.

Diligent or Daft?

The Enchanted Forest is the brainchild of Roger Tofte, an Oregon Department of Transportation draftsman and watch repairman. In the late 1950s and early 1960s Roger, his wife, Mavis, and their six children regularly took family road trips to other states. They enjoyed stopping at local attractions whenever possible, especially small fun parks. Roger lamented the fact that there were no similar parks near their home in Salem. Long possessing a creative streak and considerable artistic talent, he decided to take on the seemingly futile task of building his own. In 1964 he purchased twenty

acres of wooded land along the highway and got to work.

Roger cleared brush from the property and laid down the beginnings of the footpath. His free time was also dedicated to building scenes from classic children's fare. At first, he designed and built the displays at home. The Tofte residence became known for the mannequins, fairy-tale houses, and large concrete mushrooms in the backyard. When they proved too impractical to haul uphill to the park, Roger began building these elements on site. Aiming for minimal environmental impact, he avoided cutting down trees, developing the park along the forest's natural layout.

Given the storybook theme he was working with, it was ironic that Roger was briefly considered a local Don Quixote: dedicated, but a bit insane. His coworkers at ODOT jokingly referred to his project as Idiot Hill. Roger's daughter Susan Vaslev (who runs the park today with her sister, Mary) recalls overhearing some local youths' take on her dad while she worked a summer job: "I was picking beans in the fields one day (before child labor laws) and heard several teenagers in the row next to mine talking about this crazy man who crashed his airplane in the forest and started building witches' heads and caves up in the hills south of Salem."

Roger, by all accounts the underdog, did his best to ignore the naysayers and focus on the task at hand. The Toftes were working-class people with a tight budget. "I always believed in my father's dream," says Susan, "but we really struggled financially when I was growing up. Every extra dollar went into buying bags of cement for Enchanted Forest."

While the expense and constant ribbing could well have become a source of domestic conflict (perhaps rightfully so), it instead made the Toftes all the more determined to see the project through. Everyone in the family pitched in with the park's design and construction. They kept an eye toward frugality, improvising to meet their needs while keeping costs down. Materials were often donated or salvaged from junk piles. Their first picnic tables were made from large discarded cable spools.

It was initially estimated that the park would take two years to build; in actuality it took seven as Roger kept tweaking, adding, and experimenting. With considerable last-minute efforts by family and friends, the Enchanted Forest finally opened to the public on August 8, 1971. The timing was a bit off: They'd missed nearly two months of the tourist season. The Toftes chalked it up as the first of many lessons learned in the Enchanted Forest's crucial early years.

In subsequent years, the park expanded and evolved, and it continues to do so today, nearly forty years after it first opened. Without a

doubt, Roger Tofte's crazy dream has been vindicated many times over. Approaching eighty years of age, he still does his daily rounds at Enchanted Forest, although Mavis, long the force behind daily operations, has retired. Why not pay a visit to experience the wonderment for yourself? Surf over to www.enchantedforest.com for seasonal schedules and other information.

This sanctuary of make-believe seems to hold much enchantment yet to be discovered. We at *Weird Oregon* hope that, following in its own tradition, the Enchanted Forest lives happily ever after!

Over the Rainbow at the Funny Farm

From alpacas to zucchinis, many farms specialize in raising specific kinds of livestock or crops. Growing weirdness, however, takes a special kind of eye for detail, and a special kind of property. Such a place exists in Bend. At 64990 Deschutes Market Road is the one and only Funny Farm.

Its proprietors claim it to be the "off-center of the universe" and the "far-out park and playground of reuse and recycling." A comparison to a mental institution is suggested by its very name. None of these descriptions are very far off. Simultaneously existing as an antique store, costume shop, folk art gallery, animal shelter, and mind trip, this place exudes a happy, homespun schizophrenia.

The Funny Farm was established in 1977 by Gene Carsey and Mike Craven, who initially intended only to start a secondhand store. The pair quickly realized that they needed something to draw in customers from among the motorists zipping by on nearby Highway 97. This is when they decided that an art yard was right up their alley—their bowling alley, that is. The first attention grabber set up at the Funny Farm was its bowling ball garden. That's right: The fertile soil of the Funny Farm is said to support the growth of whole trees of the heavy, pin-knocking spheres. You can even buy your own bowling ball seeds and roll out a striking harvest at home. If you think this notion is strange, wait until you see the statue of a pair of three-legged conjoined bowlers.

Gene and Mike's whimsical decorations worked. Curious guests poured in from the highway. The business began expanding. When they began selling flamboyant vintage clothing, many customers wanted to rent the garb instead. Thus began the costume rental side of the business.

When some neighbors moved and had to leave their donkey and sheep behind, the pair stepped up to care for the critters. This, too, snowballed and established the Funny Farm as a sanctuary for abandoned animals. Although they host a varied menagerie, the Funny Farm goats seem to be most visitors' favorites. One reason is the Goat Feeding Wall, a hole-pocked barrier through which they stick their heads as guests feed them, with rather funny results. The "fainting" goats they have cared for every now and then have also received high marks from visitors. Goats of this breed, which originated in Tennessee, stiffen and tip over when startled.

While not admiring totem poles made of found objects, an Agitator Wall, and the heart-shaped Love Pond, you'll want to devote some time to the Funny Farm's extensive celebration of the Wizard of Oz. Over the rainbow mural

on the barn, scenes from the story play out along a yellow-brick road, depicted with folk art. Have a look at the Oz Electric Kaleidescope. The Funny Farm's tribute feels like a collaboration between L. Frank Baum and Timothy Leary.

Here's our own idea for potentially enhancing your Funny Farm/Oz experience: Bring along a personal audio player and put on Pink Floyd's *Dark Side of the Moon.* Some folks contend that the music in the 1973 album syncs up to the visuals in the 1939 Wizard of Oz movie. You can test this theory for yourself. Go in the store and stand next to the dollhouse. Cue your Pink Floyd and watch the doll family's tiny television: It repeats the movie all day long.

Locals, luck, and the law have not always been kind to the Funny Farm, especially in recent years. Early on the business was threatened by a land use dispute. Although it was eventually settled by moving across the street, it became clear that some locals considered the activities on the property a nuisance. To this day, a few of them hold a contemptible opinion of it.

In 2002, Carsey and Craven were busted for selling marijuana (they contended they sold only to the terminally ill). Mike Craven died suddenly in 2005, causing brief but unwarranted worry that the Funny Farm would shut down. Two more drug busts plagued the property in 2007, resulting in a seizure of marijuana, hallucinogenic mushrooms, and a small amount of methamphetamine. Gene Carsey, his son, and his brother were arrested. This time the Funny Farm closed for a while, then reopened sometime later.

We hate to conclude on a pessimistic note, but it behooves all weird-seekers to pay a visit sooner rather than later. At this rate there may soon be very little to laugh about at the Funny Farm.

Brouhaha at Brahalla

The first impression you're likely to get of Jim Skinner is that he's not exactly happy with politics-as-usual. Engage him in a conversation—it doesn't take much to get him started—and you're sure to get an earful.

As a veteran of the Vietnam war, Skinner has had plenty of time to form his opinions. As a homeowner, he has happily transferred his sentiments into incendiary art on his property at 1815 N. Sumner Street in Portland. We're not sure if the neighborhood is more enlightened by his efforts (in Portland, he's preaching to a largely liberal choir), but it's certainly weirder!

When *Weird Oregon* visited, most of his contempt was directed at the political right, and he expressed it in no uncertain terms. A Bush–Cheney "Wall of Death" (a garden border of cement skulls), a gravestone for habeas corpus (1776–2006), and one of his most ambitious pieces, a Tree of Shame ("flowering" with the heads of George W. "Dubya"

Bush, Henry Kissinger, John "McCan't" McCain, and others), set the tone in his front yard. While some observers interpret the garden art as angry, provocative pieces, and others construe them as a call to action for citizens, Jim considers them therapy above all else.

"I'm not really that political," he explains. "I'm just trying to retain what little sanity I have." For a moment, let's give him the benefit of the doubt. This is a guy who is active in the notoriously eccentric West Coast art car scene, who created a dog-shaped mailbox for his local letter carrier, and who celebrates *The Simpsons* creator Matt Groening's Portland heritage with a large mural of Krusty the Clown on his garage.

Skinner's humorous and outspoken personality also shines through in his bawdier art. As the sign over his front gate indicates, Skinner has named his property Brahalla. He denies that this reveals any personal fixation with women's undergarments. "I was just looking to name it something funny and figured I'd play with the word *Valhalla*," he says. "I just figure if it amuses me, it'll amuse someone else."

He has an eighteen-inch satellite dish bolted to the side of the house. It probably serves no purpose other than to hold a sculpture of a breast. A casting of a topless bust of Lady Liberty hangs a few feet away. We recall seeing more breast-themed curios throughout the home. (Thanks for the mammaries, Jim!)

Male anatomy is celebrated, too, inside and outside Skinner's house. "John C. Gnomes," an adult twist on lawn gnomes, watches over a flower patch. Castings of goofy-grinning phallic creatures serve as hose guards around his tomato plants.

This all fits in with a larger focus of Skinner's, which is roasting as many sacred cows as he can. The way he sees it, "People get all worked up over symbols to the point where they're ready to die for them. That's just nuts!"

No nuttier, perhaps, than Skinner's erotic religious art. Take the life-sized naked Jesus on a cross labeled with the acronym AIDS instead of INRI. Jim has also cast rubber adult novelties with a crucifixion theme, anatomically correct Virgin Mary sculptures, and several other pieces that neither the ecclesiastical crowd nor our editors would

We're not sure if the neighborhood is more enlightened by his efforts, but it's certainly weirder!

approve of us describing. It's sufficient to say that there's something to offend almost everyone at the Skinner house, and he wouldn't have it any other way.

A few years ago, Skinner's previous residence in southwest Portland was widely known for the same kinds of offbeat and excessive displays as at Brahalla. In fact, that property was referred to by some as the Institute of Questionable Art, a name that Skinner has carried over to Brahalla as a sort of umbrella brand for all of his pieces and displays.

Brahalla is constantly in flux; new art is added or altered on Skinner's whims, always attracting the Weird Eye and giving character to the neighborhood—for better or worse, depending on your outlook.

The Brahalla Effect
Jim Skinner has emboldened some of his neighbors to promote their own causes on their properties. In fact, during our visit, the house next door had a colorful display of flags on the porch—including an old Soviet Union flag hanging next to the Stars and Stripes.

Treasures of "Tim Bucktoo"

Tim Tharp's family has owned a 666-acre valley (hmmm . . .) in Willamina since it was granted to his ancestors by President Andrew Johnson in 1866. The property has hosted generations of local and family history, including, according to Tharp, his mother's claim that she saw a flying saucer overhead sometime in the late 1940s.

While this particular incident does not seem to have been recorded within the larger body of Oregon UFO lore (up until now—perhaps it was part of the UFO flap of 1947, covered in the Unexplained Phenomena chapter), a small part of Tharp's property is recognized for a different kind of quirkiness.

Around the hillside where he built his dream home, he has begun an as-yet modest art yard with lots of future potential. The property, which he named Tim Bucktoo, began taking shape about twenty years ago when he spotted a large decorative martini glass in Portland. "I fell in love with it," says Tharp. "And I decided to build my own."

Build it he did. In fact, he built several over the years, to replace older models as they got worn or damaged. The current one stands proudly in front of his home. It is made of wood, stands twenty-five feet tall, and is strung with

lights for easy spotting at night from Highway 18, the main road in front of the house.

Tharp works mainly as a lumber broker, but has always exercised a healthy creative side. Several years back, he painted his childhood home, a farmhouse directly across the valley, a patriotic red, white, and blue. He laments, "My wife hated it. She eventually made me paint over it, and warned me not to do anything to our new house when we started building it."

So far the warning has been heeded; Tharp has not applied any unusual color schemes to the house since they moved in fifteen years ago. But the call of the weird has sometimes beckoned, and Tharp has answered it elsewhere around his property. After the martini glass, he erected a twenty-foot-tall Route 66 sign as a tribute to the Mother Road and his as-yet unfulfilled wish of traveling it.

Car culture got further tweaked at Tim Bucktoo. Years ago, when a blown engine stranded a frustrated motorist on Highway 18, he signed his Dodge Aries K over to Tharp. Intending to make a statement about the high number of fatality accidents along the highway, he used a bulldozer to half-bury the car in a dirt mound. He then placed a dummy hanging out of the driver's-side window.

Motorists on the highway slowed down to look at Tharp's handiwork. They seemingly understood the implied warning, except for one lady who mistook the scene for an actual accident and phoned 911. Emergency responders rushed over and realized what it really was. They suggested to Tharp that although his sense of humor was appreciated and his good intentions were understood, they would be forced to fine him heavily if this kept occurring. The Dodge found its way to the scrap heap, but Tharp was determined to produce an even wilder and more eye-catching car display.

Procuring a 1950s Studebaker, he revisited the American flag theme by painting the car like Old Glory, also adding menacing sharklike teeth to the grill. To increase its visibility, he asked some local heavy machinery operators to place it in a tree. The Studebaker remains there among the branches and has become a local icon. It is perhaps Tharp's most popular piece.

He later indulged in some personal nostalgia: his fondness for the animated Beatles film *Yellow Submarine*. Not only did he paint a portrait of the Dreadful Flying Glove on the side of a shed, he also commissioned a large plywood cutout of the submarine itself. It stands a few hundred yards from the house, near the Route 66 sign.

Although his wife forbade him from doing anything too drastic to the house itself, some pieces seem to be creeping closer. A small-scale Statue of Liberty replica stands at the edge of the driveway, its base doubling as a storage port. A realistic plaster alligator guards a flower bed at the front walk.

A few playful displays have also been added to the backyard, most notably a tree made to look like a harp and a water fountain made from an old satellite dish.

Apparently, Tharp plays it smart in reconciling this kind of decoration with his wife's concerns. "I set up a lot of this stuff while she's away on business," he explains with a mischievous gleam.

We can only hope he continues to get away with it. There is plenty of room for more folk art and many other themes to explore. And so we say, go for the gusto, Tim! With a little effort, Tim Bucktoo could become the largest art yard in *Weird Oregon*!

Weird Oregon Sits in the Freaky Room

Early in 2008, several people asked us at *Weird Oregon* about the historic Anchor Inn, probably the oldest surviving hotel or motel in Lincoln City. The oldest portion, the main lodge, was built in the late 1930s or early 1940s. After World War II, the owners built several bungalow-style rooms off of the main lodge to accommodate the increased tourist traffic. Unfortunately, over the years it had become run down, until the present owners bought it in 2006. The innkeepers allowed us to stay, even though they were really not open for business. They did wonders, restoring some of the original features like cedar shingle siding, but also remodeling several of the rooms in different themes.

They showed us the ceiling in one of the guest rooms. The owner had an artist from the Oregon Museum of Science and Industry paint a starscape. You can't see it during the day or when the lights are on. You have to wait until it gets dark; then the stars come out.

In the hallway, a cigar store Indian guards one room, while historic photos, including several autographed ones

from the old *Batman* series, hang on the walls. They would not sell us the one signed by Catwoman, Julie Newmar. The lounge reminded us of something from the *Gilligan's Island* show, where the castaways periodically set up a tiki-style bar. There are bamboo hula girl curtains there, as well as in several of the cabins, built off of the main lodge.

Probably the most interesting room at the Anchor Inn, at least to *Weird Oregon* readers, would be the Lillian Suite, also known as the Freaky Room. As the owners remodeled the inn, sometimes they had decorating plans for certain rooms, while other rooms developed their own character as if by magic. In the Freaky Room, the walls gradually became covered with a series of disturbing pictures and prints, including very old paintings of children dressed in seventeenth-century costume, whose eyes seem to follow you around the room. There are also prints of people attending wakes, and an inspirational poster of a young soldier who stayed at his post and was mortally wounded in battle. The African fetish masks only add to the atmosphere. But the most interesting piece of furniture is Bob's chair.

Bob was one of the inn's cooks. He was friendly enough, but sometimes he kept to himself. No one thought anything about it when he left work one evening and wasn't seen for a day or two. That is, until it was his turn to cook breakfast for a charity group of little old ladies. The first time the owners knew something was wrong was when the first of the ladies arrived, and Bob was not in the kitchen cooking breakfast. The owner sent one of the staff to Bob's room to get him up and cooking.

She knocked on the door, but there was no answer. She heard the sound of the television on, and knocked louder. No answer. She got a passkey, let herself in, and saw Bob sitting on his recliner, watching TV. He did not move as she walked in his room. She started in on old Bob: "Bob!

You're supposed to be cooking breakfast for this ladies group right now! Bob! Look at me when I'm talking to you!" She reached out and touched Bob to get his attention. He slumped over, she screamed, and the owner came running.

Many plays have been written about what happens in a restaurant or hotel when someone finds a dead body. This situation seemed like something out of Neil Simon. They were pretty certain that two days earlier, Bob had got off work, turned on the television, sat down, and died within minutes. The 911 operator was not so sure when the restaurant staff called emergency services. "Touch his neck, and try to find his pulse," the operator directed.

"I already touched him," the woman who found Bob said to the others gathered around the chair. "One of you try to find his pulse."

"Hey, I'm the boss—that's why I have employees, to do things like this," the owner evaded. Eventually the ambulance arrived and they removed Bob, but even this was far from dignified. With the breakfast service delayed, several of the members of the ladies' club went in search of the owner or were looking around doorways as the paramedics took Bob out the side entrance.

After things quieted down, it just seemed natural that they put Bob's chair in the Freaky Room. *Weird Oregon* asked the owners what Bob would have thought. Apparently Bob had a great sense of humor, and the owners thought that Bob would have loved it. No one has ever claimed that Bob still haunts his chair, though some guests do not sit in it. Others spend quite a few minutes sitting there, perhaps hoping for a visit from Bob.

To make reservations to sit in Bob's chair, visit www.historicanchorinn.com.

Weird Oregon *Update*: Recently the Anchor Inn had to get rid of Bob's chair and remove the African fetish mask. Apparently some guests were . . . disturbed . . . by the unique decor. The manager told us that they took Bob's chair to a yard sale with a sign that said, FREE, SOMEONE DIED IN THIS CHAIR. Perhaps we were wrong about Oregonians being weird? Maybe not. After all, someone took Bob's chair.

Roadside Oddities

Ah, the roadside. Is anyone still unaware of the potential it holds for shared cultural experiences? Whether we're talking popular hangouts, whimsical monuments, offbeat advertising, or out-there art, the roadside is often the podium at which society voices its quirky sensibilities. This is true of many locales, and Oregon does not disappoint—just ask Paul Bunyan, who has at least two statues of himself in the Beaver State.

I-5 is the state's main artery and passes through its most populated areas, so most of Oregon's roadside oddities tend to be located within a few miles of it. Of course, this isn't to say that there aren't roads in eastern Oregon or along the coast with their own unique surprises. We present here a select few examples to get you started on your own offbeat sightseeing adventure. We're confident that there are many more along the way, and if you see them, you know what to do.

If these various displays attract our attention and inspire us to take a closer look, they've successfully done their job. If this chapter encourages you to actively seek them out, understand their cultural significance, and share any others you find, we've successfully done ours.

Bunyans of the Beaver State

It's only natural that Oregon, with its deep-rooted (pun intended) timber industry, would honor Paul Bunyan. Joining dozens of similar tributes around the United States, at least two roadside statues of America's mythical giant lumberjack can be found in the state. A third statue honoring a Bunyan sibling further demonstrates Oregon's longstanding appreciation of lumbermen great and small.

Muffler Bunyan

Muffler Men—those gigantic fiberglass statues that serve as attention grabbers for repair shops, car dealerships, and other businesses—are to roadside culture as apple pie is to America. Think about it: If they hadn't been invented, there may very well have been a sense of something missing among all the neon signs, mimetic architecture, and other gimmicks along the road. As a concept in kitsch, oversize representations of ourselves just seem appropriate and inevitable.

Muffler Men were first manufactured in the early 1960s by International Fiberglass of Venice, California. It all started with a likeness of Paul Bunyan created for a cafe in Flagstaff, Arizona. That's right: The giant lumberjack not only inspired the Muffler Men but provided the original mold used to make most of the others that followed.

In Grants Pass, you can get a pretty good idea of what that first fiberglass Bunyan looked like, as one of his many clones stands astride a utility pole at the Cedarwood Saloon (1345 Redwood Avenue, a block or two north of Highway 199). At fifteen feet tall, this statue was once decked out as a blond miner, complete with a giant pickaxe and a mine cart full of (fake) gold at his feet.

When Bruce and Tamerie Mesman bought the Cedarwood in 1991, a property dispute caused an irate neighbor to have the statue yanked from its berth with a truck and dragged across the street. Although the statue was scraped and scuffed, the harsh treatment was arguably a blessing in disguise.

This is because the Mesmans took advantage of the opportunity to have the miner restored to his true "Bunyanosity" and mounted him in front of the saloon. He has maintained this identity and location ever since. Sadly, this has not made him immune from suffering further indignities over the years. Vehicular collisions, BB gun assaults, and even a decapitation by windstorm have all left their mark on the steadfast lumberjack. Regardless, we can all find inspiration in the fact that, with stubborn resolve and prompt repairs, ol' Paul still stands tall, with beer and pride on tap!

From Lumberjack to Bouncer?

Portland's Kenton neighborhood pays its tribute to the lumberjack with a thirty-seven-foot-tall grinning behemoth—one of a handful of Paul Bunyans that aren't Muffler Men. Made of iron and plaster, it was built by the Kenton Businessmen's Club in 1959. Its purposes were to commemorate Oregon's centennial, honor the state's timber industry, and, strategically placed at the corner of Interstate and Denver Avenues, act as Portland's official greeter for Washingtonians. (In the days before I-5 was built, Interstate Avenue served as the main connection between Portland and its neighbors to the north.)

Bunyan was eventually moved about fifty feet from his original location to make way for a rail station. He's freshened up with a fresh coat of paint on occasion, and as of this writing he watches over the "Dancin' Bare" strip club across the street. No wonder he's grinning!

An irate neighbor yanked the statue from its berth and dragged it across the street.

In His Brother's Shadow

Frank Stallone. Billy Carter. Zeppo Marx. Tito Jackson. Roger Clinton. The world is full of guys whose personal achievements are overshadowed by those of their more prominent brothers. Perhaps some of them can find their niche in Oregon, as one Bunyan sibling has. The city of Butte Falls honors Paul's lesser-known brother, Ralph. A statue of the six-foot-tall everyman lumberjack holds a place of honor in City Park. He was carved from wood (go figure) by the late Bill Edmondson, a local logger.

Ralph stoically stands on a stump, looking a bit stressed, probably with good reason. Besides a likely inferiority complex (imagine how sibling rivalry with brother Paul must pan out), he is a frequent target of vandalism. A chain-link fence erected around him provides limited protection. Either way, the tiny town maintains him with pride. As far as Butte Falls is concerned, Portland and Grants Pass can keep their respective Paul Bunyans. Here, they celebrate the little guy!

Butte Falls is the only U.S. town that is completely surrounded by a fence. This is because it is located right in the middle of an open cattle range. The fence is there to keep the cattle out (or the people in, depending on whom you ask). The population remains steadily in the four hundreds, as the fence tends to limit expansion.

A Stone Age Front Man

The caveman statue on NW Sixth Street is Grants Pass's greeter and mascot. At eighteen feet tall, the animal-skin-wearing, club-wielding Neanderthal looks like he means business. As well he should, since that's what he was put there to promote: local business.

Any doubts about this fiberglass fellow as a symbol of the local economy are quickly dispelled with a look at local enterprise and infrastructure. In Grants Pass, you can knock down some pins at Caveman Bowl or go swimming at Caveman Pool. For booking vacations, there are two Caveman Travel Agencies and a Caveman RV. If the motor home breaks down, call Caveman Towing and Repair, or visit Caveman Auto Parts to fix it yourself. Back on the road, you cross the Rogue River on Caveman Bridge. (Are you noticing a pattern yet?)

The caveman theme started decades ago to promote the Oregon Caves, thirty miles to the south, and the now defunct Oregon Caveman Club, founded in 1922. Members, which included civic and business leaders, attended parades and other functions in animal skin uniforms, hamming it up as only "prehistoric" males could.

Unfortunately, on Independence Day 2004, someone expressed contempt for the statue by lighting it on fire. But by the following year, the caveman, now covered with a flame-retardant coating, was repaired and back on his pedestal. Which just goes to show, you can't keep the big lug down.

The Oregon Caveman Club has attracted its fair share of prominent guests over the years. Politicians Ronald Reagan, John (and Jackie) Kennedy, and would-be Truman defeater Thomas Dewey are counted among the luminaries who spent time in Grants Pass.

Three years after Dewey's visit, newspapers in the USSR used photographs of Dewey and members of the Oregon Cavemen to document American poverty (the animal-skin tunics were the giveaway). Dewey was identified as an "anti-religious leader," while a Caveman parade became a revolt of "peasants." The gathering was supposedly a protest against "religious feudalism" propagated by capitalist priests.

In response, the Cavemen raised funds for the Crusade for Freedom, to encourage more accurate news reporting within Iron Curtain countries.

It's Hip to Be (at the) Square

In 1984, construction was completed on Portland's 48,000-square-foot plaza, Pioneer Courthouse Square. A favorite gathering spot for all sorts of folks, the square has deservedly been nicknamed Portland's Living Room. Today it's hard to imagine the downtown area without this central hub, which was named after the federal court building at its eastern end.

Between the 1850s and the early 1980s the space was consecutively occupied by a school, a hotel, and a parking garage. In the 1970s, the property was privately owned, but it was eventually purchased and developed by the city at a cost of $7.3 million. Public support was key in building the square. Its completion was seen as a victory for the common man over the powerful because then mayor Frank Ivancie and an alliance of local business owners stymied its development for a while, fearing it would attract transients.

In accordance with the popular bumper sticker directive, "Keep Portland Weird," Pioneer Courthouse Square offers its fair share of quirkiness. For example . . .

Celebrity Bricks

One of the ways Portlanders helped fund the square's construction was by selling engraved bricks. At $15 per brick, the Friends of Pioneer Square citizens group sold about fifty thousand of them, amounting to $750,000 toward the square's completion. These days, bricks are still being added to the upper level. You can buy your own, but inflation has upped the price of each brick to $100. Usually, the purchaser will have their own name, or that of a loved one, inscribed on it. However, there are a few "celebrity bricks" dispersed throughout the square. Look around and you might find familiar names such as President Ronald Reagan, Bilbo Baggins, Carrie Fisher, Dan Rather, Barbara Walters, Bruce Springsteen, and others. Most spectacularly of all, even God and Jesus Christ seem to have purchased bricks!

The Echo Chamber

If you see someone standing in the mini-amphitheater at the northwest corner of the square, and he seems to be shouting to himself, give him the benefit of the doubt. Chances are he's not crazy; he's probably just conducting an auditory experiment. Standing on the central marble stone in the rounded corner and vocalizing toward the steps produces a strong reverberating echo. There are elementary scientific principles at work here; they just seem out of place in this urban environment. Odder still, the echo isn't audible from a few feet away, or even from a little off-center!

The Mile Post Sign

Need to canter to Casablanca or trot to Timbuktu? This helpful sign post will point your way there and to numerous other exotic destinations around the world, including nine sister cities.

The Weather Machine

Fate is often cruel to meteorologists. When the weather doesn't match their predictions, they're often branded as being unreliable, or liars, or both. Enter the Weather Machine, a pole-mounted contraption designed to take much of the heat off of beleaguered human weather readers. A series of light bulbs run up the pole and progressively light up as the temperature warms. Every day at noon, amid a spray of mist and a lively fanfare, the Weather Machine proclaims the day's

outlook through one of three painted icons that pop out of its crowning globe: a dragon for heavy rain, a heron for light rain, and a sun for, well, sunny weather.

As with most places, some locals who hang around Pioneer Courthouse Square contribute considerably to its weird vibe—sometimes even more so than the architectural and decorative elements. The presence of street performers, vagrants, and all manner of odd characters is yet another reason to appreciate the square's ambiance. If you want to experience Portland at its most unfettered, this is the place to go!

Jug of Jugs

As Portland is a city well known for its strip clubs, there's a nice touch of innuendo inherent in running one inside a massive jug. (Is all this *Weird* stuff getting to us, or what?) This jug-shaped building on NE Sandy Boulevard was built in 1928 and initially hosted an auto repair shop. Later, it served as a diner, a tavern, and assorted other businesses. The jug's current incarnation as the Pirate's Cove strip club is its second stint as an "adult" venue. It's delightfully seedy inside . . . or, uh, so we're told. Its spherical "cork" was painted as an eight-ball for quite some time and was considered a local icon in its own right.

Caddy Shake (and Burgers, and Fries)

Today's high gas prices can make motorists nostalgic for the classic days of car culture. In the cruising heyday of the 1950s, gas was cheap, cars were big, and diners on the main drag were the preferred hangout for young Americans. In Salem, you can get a taste of these simpler times at Rock-n-Rogers 50s Diner. It's on Market Street; you'll know it by the vintage pink Cadillac perched atop a pedestal in the parking lot.

The diner opened in 1987; the Cadillac, minus its motor and other innards, was mounted by the Martin Brothers Sign Company, a local firm well known for its eye-catching creations. Neon lettering and accents on the car assure that the diner's kitschy ambiance is maintained, even enhanced, after dark.

This Rock-n-Rogers is one of two in Salem. The other is on Commercial Street and, alas, does not use a car as a sign. Fortunately, the interiors of both locations are decorated with a quirky mix of mid-twentieth-century record albums, appliances, magazine advertisements, and other knick-knacks. Either location is worth a look, and the food is great. Drop in for a classic milkshake and burger, as seeking out roadside oddities can be hungry work. (We ought to know!)

Voodoo Doughnuts

Weird Oregon wants to know: How many readers are tired of too-sweet, too-greasy doughnuts made by some pastry chains? Did you know that Portland, Oregon, has a special doughnut shop where the cooks may add a special bit of magic to their food? It's called Voodoo Doughnuts.

Voodoo Doughnuts is a little hard to find if you do not know where it is, because of the discreet sign above the front door of their little lobby. Sometimes their front door is closed but their to-go window is unlocked, because they operate twenty-four hours a day. Rather than simple cake doughnuts or apple fritters, Voodoo Doughnuts has a specialty line of unique pastries.

These include many items like the maple bar (with two stripes of bacon), the Grape Ape, the Triple Chocolate Penetration, and their signature treat, the Voodoo Doughnut. It is shaped like a human voodoo doll and filled with raspberry jelly. It comes with pretzel sticks, which can be used to stab the voodoo doughnut. This is a favorite at office meetings, where *Weird Oregon* understands some workers imagine the doughnut is their boss.

They do more than sell pastries at Voodoo Doughnuts. Lovers can be married while standing in front of the giant doughnut for a modest fee, which pays for the minister and coffee and doughnuts for ten. Want to learn Swahili? They give free classes every Monday night, starting at 9 P.M. If you can eat their Tex-ASS doughnut in under ninety seconds, it's free—but you have to pay for it first. They will reimburse you afterward if you can keep it down. They have Club Doughnut, which is a twelve-foot-high stage. Every Tuesday and Wednesday night they have live local bands play live concerts. However, not all of their doughnutarian concoctions have gone over big. They had a doughnut glazed with Pepto-Bismol and Nyquil, until someone

with the Food and Drug Administration pointed out that it was illegal to mix food and drugs . . .

Voodoo Doughnut is located at 22 SW Third Avenue in downtown Portland.

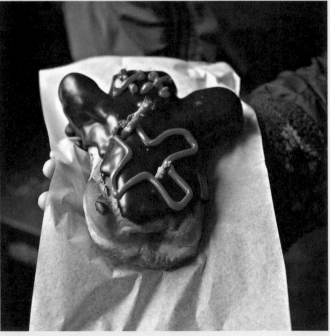

Developing a Bomber Complex

There are any number of things a reasonable person wouldn't expect to find while traveling down strip mall–lined McLoughlin Boulevard in Milwaukie. A World War II–era B-17 bomber might certainly be counted among them, were it not for the fact that one has occupied space along the road since 1947.

The old warplane, affectionately nicknamed the *Lacey Lady,* is the main attraction at what is called the Bomber Complex. A family business that now consists primarily of a restaurant and souvenir shop, it is actually best known for the gas station that occupied the property until 1991. Credit for this roadside oddity goes to Art Lacey, the original owner of the gas station. In the mid-1940s, the former army engineer was mulling over gimmicks to attract customers. As an aviation buff (with limited flying experience but high aspirations), his mind naturally turned to doing something airplane-related.

B-17 Flying Fortresses had more than proved their worth in World War II, particularly in bombing German industrial targets. Well more than twelve thousand of the bombers, of multiple variations, were built at Boeing and Lockheed Vega between 1935 and 1945. Now, in peacetime, the military was burdened with too many to maintain. Although the B-17s were still mechanically sound, the U.S. Army Air Forces declared them obsolete and began retiring them. Lacey decided to save one from the scrap heap and mount it over his gas station.

The Hazardous Acquisition

He traveled to Altus Air Force Base in Oklahoma, where he inquired about the planes and explained his intentions. Eventually, air force personnel were suitably convinced of Lacey's sincerity (and sanity) at wanting to buy a surplus bomber. The purchase price was a relatively paltry (even in 1940s terms) $13,750. Not a bad deal for a plane that initially cost the government $350,000!

Despite his lack of experience in flying—he had logged only eight hours in a cockpit while in the military—Lacey fully intended to fly the B-17 back home himself. He hired a few local farmhands to help him "un-pickle" the plane and get it ready to fly. When it came time to engage in a short test flight, Lacey lacked a copilot, which USAAF regulations required. He found the next best thing: a mannequin he topped with a flight cap and sat in the copilot's seat!

As it happened, however, the mannequin knew even less about flying than Lacey. The test flight went okay, but the landing was problematic: Neither Lacey nor the mannequin was able to lower the landing gear. They crash-landed on the airplane's belly, damaging another B-17 in the process. Lacey emerged unscathed, though understandably shaken. History does not record whether the mannequin was as lucky.

Fortunately the base was willing to write off the mishap as "wind damage" to the two planes and allowed him to replace his wrecked B-17 with another. This time he contacted two buddies from Portland—experienced pilots—to help him fly the plane home.

The Perilous Journey

Experienced pilots or not, the flight back to Oregon was just as, if not more, fraught with danger. After a refueling stop in California, the three embarked on a northward flight following the Sierra Nevada mountains. During one of Lacey's turns at the controls (while the others slept), he flew into a major snowstorm. With almost zero visibility, he descended until he could get a better view. Before too long, he had to abruptly pull up just as he was about to crash into a mountain—a rather dangerous and structurally stressful maneuver to pull with a B-17.

Soon realizing they were lost, the not-quite navigators

buzzed a small town in order to read street signs and determine where they were. They eventually realized they were over Fall River Mills, California, about one hundred miles off course. They continued along their way, leaving some startled and very confused locals in their wake.

Lacey and friends flew level with the treetops all the way to Klamath Falls, refueled again, and then ran into another snowstorm halfway to Bend. Once more, Lacey flew the plane low, at a steady eight hundred feet, until he landed at Troutdale Airport.

The FAA would've surely had their heads for these aerial antics had they not occurred eleven years prior to its founding!

The Final Haul

As capable at low altitudes as Lacey's B-17 had proven itself, it was inadvisable to simply fly it to Milwaukie, taxi down McLoughlin Boulevard, and pull into the gas station. Lacey instead sought a permit from the Oregon State Highway Department to move the plane by truck. The unusual request was mired in bureaucracy as it moved up the chain of command as far as the governor's office.

Tired of waiting and determined to move the plane, Lacey arranged for it to be hauled the twenty-plus miles at 2:00 A.M. on a Saturday morning. Four trucks carried the B-17, taking up the entire width of the route; at one point, a bus had to run up on the curb to let it pass. Lacey was fined a whopping $10 for transporting a wide load without a permit.

Afterward it was just a matter of bolting the *Lacey Lady* above the gas pumps—a relatively easy task compared to the challenge of getting it there in the first place. The display became an immediate hit and has been a favorite of roadside culture enthusiasts ever since.

As of this writing, local businesses are sponsoring Wings of Freedom, a major restoration project for Art Lacey's B-17 Flying Fortress. The goal is to restore the bomber to its former glory, piece by piece, and build a more protective environment for its display. As you can see, when *Weird*

Oregon visited, the nose section had been completely removed. The good news is that each separate piece will be available for viewing at the complex as its restoration is completed. In other words, there's no need to wait until the entire plane is rebuilt in order to be impressed with the restoration, although you won't see the *Lacey Lady* in one piece until some time in the future.

Regardless, she serves as a fitting tribute not only to the man whose determination brought her to Milwaukie, but also to the Greatest Generation, who defended freedom with her and later filled their gas tanks in her shadow.

The FAA would've surely had their heads for these aerial antics had they not occurred eleven years prior to its founding!

Bomber Complex Totem

Although the *Lacey Lady* is the main attraction at the Bomber Complex, there are other worthwhile sights on the grounds. For instance, a colorful totem pole pays tribute to Native American craftsmanship, and a nearby red, white, and blue signpost conveniently points you toward such varied locations as the North and South Poles, Normandy, and Berlin. If you decide to follow one or more of these signs to its destination, don't forget to send us pictures of any roadside oddities you might find there!

Lady Liberty of the Parking Lot

As far as iconic Americana goes, the Statue of Liberty is certainly among the most powerful symbols we have. The classic visual associated with the statue is one of downtrodden immigrants arriving in New York Harbor by ship. Seeing the statue for the first time near the Manhattan skyline, the soon-to-be Americans look on with profound hope, eager to make new lives for themselves in a land of opportunity.

Here is something to ponder, however: If immigrants arrived not on ships through New York Harbor, but on buses through Milwaukie, Oregon, and if Lady Liberty were much smaller and located in a parking lot, would she still have the same impact?

Decide for yourself! Partially hidden behind a strip mall just two miles south of the Bomber Complex is a replica of the Statue of Liberty. It's on the west side of McLoughlin Boulevard, just north of Roethe Road.

While the original statue is 115 feet tall, this shorter Lady Liberty measures about 60 (including pedestal). She was placed here in March 2005 with some difficulty. As the statue, which is wired for nighttime lighting, was being lifted into place, a piece of her crown broke off, causing an electrical fire on her head. It must have been an awkward moment for the owner of the strip mall, who is reportedly of Middle Eastern descent and had the statue added partly to demonstrate his loyalty to post–9/11 America.

Lady Liberty was promptly repaired and has since stood her ground with grace and dignity, regardless of her unusual location. A plaque on her base, beneath a sculpted eagle, reads:

Liberty
Freedom for all Nations
Freedom for all People
Let Freedom Ring

Okay, even we admit that this replica of Lady Liberty may not be as awe-inspiring as the original. But the burger joints, car lots, supermarkets, and other typical sprawl along McLoughlin Boulevard sure give immigrants a more direct and immediate look at modern America.

Finger Food Family Values

The 1950s and 1960s were an era of prolific development of advertising mascots. Many of these characters, such as Mr. Clean, Ronald McDonald, and the Raid Roaches, have been used to the present day. Others were not as enduring, but remain nostalgic icons of their heyday. If they're lucky, some in this latter group even find continued popularity among select groups of fans.

Such is the case with the happy brood known as the Burger Family. As representatives of the nationwide A&W restaurant chain, these cartoony figures decorated the exteriors of many locations to advertise their yummy burgers, refreshing root beer, and family-friendly atmosphere.

By the time the A&W restaurant at SE Tualatin Highway and Thirteenth Avenue in Hillsboro closed in 1984, its Burger Family held much sentimental value for the community. They had even been placed on the Hillsboro Cultural Resource Inventory a year earlier as "unique remnants of the drive-in culture of the 1960s." Even so, their journey from fast food hucksters to their current role as greeters at the Shute Park Aquatic and Recreation Center was not without uncertainty.

The Hillsboro Burgers—Papa, Mama, Teen, and Baby—first appeared in the late 1950s in the restaurant parking lot. All was well until they suffered their first crisis in 1979: Teen mysteriously vanished. He was later found up the flagpole of Lincoln High School, where it was determined that he had been stolen by a few considerably more mischievous teens. Unfortunately, this adventure left him too damaged to put back on display. He went into storage behind the restaurant and eventually disappeared again.

Was he disposed of? Did somebody else take him? Did he leave of his own accord? The answer remains uncertain, but many claim to have seen Hillsboro's Teen Burger at other businesses throughout Oregon.

When the restaurant closed, Mama and Baby were removed, and Papa was moved to another spot on the property. The Burger Family's future looked bleak until 1986, when Papa Aldo's Take and Bake Pizza stepped in. The local franchise, located on SE Tenth Avenue, purchased Papa, Mama, and Baby, repainting them to look Italian. Their hamburgers were made to resemble pizzas, courtesy of a few local art students. They were then relocated to the Papa Aldo's parking lot. The trio remained here until the pizzeria was sold in 1990, and the former owner donated them to the city.

After three years of restoration (again by local art students) and temporary display across the street from the pizzeria, the Burgers were finally placed at their (allegedly) permanent home at Shute Park. Teen even made a return of sorts: An orphaned Teen from Longview, Washington, was adopted to replace his long-lost Hillsboro counterpart. Baby disappeared for a while in 2008 after someone presumably tried using her burger as a seat and broke off her arm. Not to worry: She has been repaired and is back with the family along SE Tenth Avenue.

Here the Burgers remain, representatives of a bygone fun-loving era and ambassadors of good will for Hillsboro. Their incredible family bond and their ability to triumph over adversity beg the eternal question: Would you like fries with that?

Photos courtesy of Robyn Rawls and the Hillsboro Parks and Recreation Department.

The Old Volks (Motor) Home

Here's a novel idea for the budget-conscious RVer: Combine a travel trailer with one of the world's most popular compact cars! It may be a bit cramped, but no other motor home could top the gas mileage! A custom VW Beetle/RV combo turns heads toward Hillsboro RV Supply, at 4173 Tualatin Valley Highway (about a mile from the Burger Family).

Come to think of it, do circus clowns go RVing?

The Last of the Thunderbeasts

Eons ago (from about 1962 to the late 1990s), prehistoric beasts roamed Klamath County. On second thought, "roamed" may not be entirely accurate. Lingered around? Nah . . . It would be best to say they stood very still, attracting tourists to a remote corner of the state. After all, these beasts were made of concrete, which made lingering, let alone roaming, kind of difficult.

They were located in the high desert in Chiloquin. Their home, Thunderbeast Park, was once a lively diversion from a drive down scrub pine-lined Highway 97 (an "are we there yet" stretch of road if ever there was one). Like similar dinosaur parks around the country, its kitschy confines were fun for the whole family, if only moderately educational.

Thunderbeast Park's concrete sculptures represented twelve different kinds of animals from long before the park, or even modern man, took up space in Chiloquin. Interestingly, none of Thunderbeast Park's painted concrete critters were "A-list" dinosaurs. Instead, most were based on lesser-known prehistoric animals like the dinohyus, the glyptodont, and the uintatherium. A few better-known beasts were also present, such as a saber-toothed tiger and a dodo bird.

Ernie Nelson, who created Prehistoric Gardens in Port Orford (see the Personalized Properties chapter), reportedly designed these sculptures, although he did not build them.

Just as life-forms emerge, thrive, and disappear through different paleontologic periods, so too did Thunderbeast Park. It succumbed to a gradual decline through the 1980s and 1990s. By 1996, the park was out of business. It seemed sadly appropriate that these sculptures faced extinction as they slowly crumbled in their abandoned habitat.

To the displeasure of enthusiasts, the property was eventually sold to new owners with no interest in reopening a dinosaur park. Instead, in 2000 it was transformed into Hub City Chrome, a shop specializing in truck supplies and accessories. Most, but not all, of the sculptures were removed from the premises. Today, the most obvious indication of the property's former purpose is the remaining Thunderbeast out in front: a gigantic black-and-white paraceratherium.

While this particular sculpture looks somewhat bovine, the real creatures that inspired it were massive predecessors of the rhinoceros. Observers might sense a certain nobility of purpose in this concrete version. It represents both the largest land mammal ever known and a much-beloved but long-gone roadside attraction. It's as if it were holding down the fort, maintaining a lonely vigil for its lost concrete brethren in case they should ever return.

Is the paraceratherium what it appears to be: the sole survivor of Thunderbeast Park? Perhaps not. Rumor has it that a couple of other creatures still stand their ground out back, behind the gate, among the trees. We can only hope that someone at Hub City Chrome recognizes the kitschy value of these concrete dinosaurs and reconsiders adding more. With a bit of luck and a little vision, the current state of the former Thunderbeast Park can become a temporary season of hardship, rather than a lasting extinction.

Eh . . . Look up, Doc!

Remember the classic movie Harvey? Perhaps Elwood P. Dowd, the mild-mannered alcoholic who claimed to see a giant invisible rabbit, would not have been considered a crank if his sister had simply moved them to Aloha. Then again, this notion is a bit anachronistic, as the giant rabbit in Aloha came later, inspired by and named partly after Dowd's *pooka* friend.

In any case, here's Aloha's giant rabbit—all twenty-six feet and one-and-a-quarter tons of him. This Harvey greets customers at Harvey Marine, a boat supply and repair shop located at 21250 Tualatin Valley Highway. Owner Ed Harvey added the big bunny in the 1960s, after a customer abandoned a fiberglass Muffler Man that had been repaired at the shop. (Those guys can sure come in handy!)

Harvey (the man) had always been fond of *Harvey* (the movie) and, since his business was called Harvey Marine, he thought of a way to use the Muffler Man as a mascot. He fashioned a fiberglass rabbit head and, like a modern-day Dr. Moreau, merged it with the Muffler Man body to create the somewhat disturbing, yet strangely appealing, hybrid.

Harvey has been a local favorite ever since, inspiring such beliefs as honking at him brings good luck and waving at him prevents flat tires. He has gotten letters from fans and, surprisingly, once received several get-well cards after vandals ripped off one of his ears.

Harvey is well known for celebrating holidays by holding appropriate props like an American flag, an oversize Valentine's heart, a Christmas tree, and more. In fact, there was one holiday he celebrated a little *too* well. In 1987, Harvey's big bunny noggin was looking a bit weather worn and was in need of a touch-up. The task required that it be removed, and it was decided that the most appropriate time for this would be around Halloween. For a short time

Harvey stood decapitated, holding a large pumpkin a la the Headless Horseman of Sleepy Hollow.

This variation on Harvey, essentially a headless giant, proved too frightening for area children. Nightmares supposedly reached distressing proportions, and parents demanded an explanation. The local media had a field day with the story. Fortunately, the repairs were quickly finished and a freshly recapitated Harvey soon traded his pumpkin for a Thanksgiving turkey.

Since then, the popular roadside sentinel has kept his head about him, remaining at his post, larger than life in both size and appeal.

Bigtime Snacking in Portland

Anybody hungry? Let's share a snack in the spirit of *Weird Oregon.* Today's offering: sliced bread and soda! We can think of weirder food-and-drink combinations, but probably none more convenient for anyone seeking roadside oddities in Portland. This is because two of the city's most popular icons—a giant, rotating bag of premium white bread and an oversize bottle of a popular soft drink—are located within a couple blocks of each other.

First, we offer a "toast" to the Franz Bakery. Located on the corner of NE Twelfth Avenue and Flanders Street, it has been in operation since 1912. The building was among the first of numerous bakeries to be started or acquired across the Northwest by the Franz family. While the company is currently the largest supplier of baked goods in the Northwest and their products are mainstays of most supermarkets, most impressive to us is the eye-catching large-scale replica bread package spinning lazily over their outlet store.

Meanwhile, on a rooftop two blocks southeast, near the corner of NE Fourteenth Avenue and Couch Street, a large 7UP bottle overlooks the industrial central east side. This tribute to lemon-lime refreshment and its three-sided base have seen better days, but they still remind admirers of simpler times when soft drinks came in twelve-ounce glass bottles and cost substantially less than they do today. The "retro cool" art deco building hosting them has impressed many a roadside pilgrim, as well.

The bottle was not originally atop this building, however. Its first home was decidedly weirder. Read on . . .

The Hidden Milk Bottle Building

Would you believe that the 7UP bottle was once a roadside oddity on top of another roadside oddity? Several years ago, it and a couple of similarly weather-beaten 7UP billboards sat atop the distinctive cylindrical tower in the heart of Portland's Hollywood neighborhood. The structure, part of the building at Thirty-seventh Avenue and Sandy Boulevard, now sports two flashy Budweiser signs. While the architecture and signage are certainly eye-catching, it's not the outward appearance, but rather what's inside, that really counts!

What many people may not realize is that the tower hides a piece of classic mimetic architecture. Built in 1926, the building originally housed the Steigerwald Dairy. Like many dairies from that era, part of the building was built in the shape of a giant milk bottle in order to attract customers. When the dairy closed in 1936, Pabco Paint moved in and the bottle was altered to resemble two stacked paint cans. To achieve this, a new exterior wall was built at the point where the building starts tapering to form the neck of the "bottle." It rises straight up at the same circumference as the base and is topped by another, smaller cylinder. In effect, the original bottle building was hidden, intact, inside a tower!

By the 1940s, Pabco Paint had left the building, along with the tower's paint can motif, and the building looked much as it does today. The 7UP bottle and billboards were soon installed and remained into the 1990s. Through the years, it has housed various shops and (as can be expected—this *is* Portland, after all) a strip club.

Luckily, the building's original milk bottle is not entirely relegated to old memories and historical photographs. Thanks to the foresight of those who built the tower, tall, narrow windows were installed near the top. Through them, the tapered white neck of the giant bottle is still visible today.

The World's Tallest Barber Pole

One of our companion volumes, *Weird Minnesota*, contains a short profile of the William Marvy Company, the last mass producer of barber poles in the Americas. They ushered in a barber pole renaissance in the 1950s, when the venerated symbol had largely fallen out of use. But why bring this up here, in *Weird Oregon*?

Because we just can't help but wonder what the Marvy Company's staff would make of Forest Grove's version of the classic icon. Their barber pole, proudly proclaimed the world's tallest, measures about 17.5 times the size of the William Marvy Company's biggest commercial model!

It's an appropriate landmark for a town nicknamed Ballad Town USA for its deep appreciation of old-fashioned barbershop quartet singing. The World's Tallest Barber Pole was the brainchild of Chuck Olson, one such balladeer. When the Barbershop Harmony Society decided to hold its 1973 convention in Portland, Olson recalled another convention years earlier in San Antonio, Texas. That time, San Antonio's barbershop harmonizers erected a much-admired forty-foot barber pole near the Alamo.

Olson figured that a convention in the heart of timber country warranted an even more impressive display. He and some fellow area "barbershopers" procured a seventy-foot-tall wooden pole and proceeded to paint on traditional red, white, and blue spiral barbershop stripes. Attendees of the Portland convention were suitably impressed. Olson and company returned as hometown heroes and arranged to put the pole on permanent display. As stated on its sign (which was missing when *Weird Oregon* paid a visit, probably to protect it from nearby construction), it's dedicated to Forest Grove "for the continuing preservation and encouragement of barbershop quartet singing."

Look for it in Lincoln Park, near the scoreboard on the football field. It often pulls double-duty as a flagpole.

Candle Colossi

The towns of Damascus and Scappoose, twenty-odd miles southeast and northwest of Portland, respectively, are big on old-fashioned lighting. We mean *really* big: Each town sports its own giant candle!

Damascus's giant candle, rising twenty-one feet and made of stuccoed steel and concrete, stands on Highway 212 in front of the fire department. It replaces a twenty-ton wax predecessor, which was molded inside several oil drums welded end-to-end. This original candle was placed in the downtown area in 1959 to commemorate Oregon's centennial. Lit for one hundred days, the locals liked it so much that they decided to keep it beyond the centennial festivities. However, its

melting wax proved a bit messy, so the good folks of Damascus erected the more durable version in 1962. Sadly, a good amount of the original candle's "weird factor" was lost in the transition, as the newer "candle" resembles little more than a pillar. Still, we give credit to its designers for attempting to simulate melted wax with concrete.

Scappoose's fifty-foot-tall, eighteen-foot-diameter Peace Candle of the World is nine years younger, constructed in 1971 as an advertising landmark for a local candle factory. The factory had set up shop on a farm, and the candle was made by covering an old silo with 45,000 pounds of wax and adding a large wick on top. As with the Damascus candle, it was decided that this setup was probably too literal for the long term, and the wax and wick were eventually replaced with more conventional construction materials. A gas flame was briefly installed, but it proved too costly and was replaced with the current animated neon lighting. For us, the Peace Candle triggered a bittersweet feeling of vanishing Americana, standing as it is among a cluster of small country shops across the road from newer encroaching shopping centers.

Welcome to Scappoose

Established in 1921

Peace Candle of The World

Personally Dedicated by Governor Tom McCall May 9, 1971
in front of a large group of Scappoose Citizens.

History with a View

What do Rome, Italy, and Astoria, Oregon, have in common? The answer stands atop Coxcomb Hill, Astoria's highest point at some 600 feet above sea level. Rising a further 125 feet is the Astoria Column: a unique American monument inspired by an ancient Roman original.

In A.D. 113, the height of the Roman Empire, a marble tower was erected to commemorate Marcus Traianus, otherwise known as Emperor Trajan. Trajan's Column, as it's called, is known for its bas-relief etchings depicting the emperor's military victories against the Dacians of Eastern Europe. Added with a technique known as sgraffito, the intricate etchings spiral up the column in a continuous strip, depicting the battles in chronological order.

Astorians decided to build their own version of Trajan's Column, an effort that came to fruition in 1926. The project was funded by the Great Northern Railroad and Victor Astor, grandson of John Jacob Astor, the millionaire founder of the Pacific Fur Trading Company. (His local trading post, Fort Astor, developed into Astoria.) Concrete was substituted for marble and painted reliefs of local history replaced depictions of Trajan's conquests, but the Astoria Column's dimensions more or less match those of its Roman inspiration.

Credit for the column's design goes to Electus D. Litchfield and Attilio Pusterla, two men with impeccable credentials. Litchfield was a prominent architect from New York City; Pusterla a well-known and highly regarded muralist. The fourteen upward-spiraling scenes on the Astoria Column begin with a native wilderness at the bottom and end with the building of a railroad on top. In between are several renderings of the Lewis and Clark expedition and the Pacific Fur Trading Company's voyage from New York to establish Fort Astor. (Never let it be said that the railroad and the Astor family shied away from reciprocative back-patting!)

Inside, a 164-step spiral staircase leads to an observation deck with panoramic views of the Columbia River, Young's Bay, the Astoria Bridge, and even Mount St. Helens and Mount Ranier in Washington.

By the 1990s, the Astoria Column was showing clear signs of a seventy-year lack of upkeep. (About the only enhancement made was the installation of a small television transmitter in 1949.) The bas relief was worn, and the paint was almost completely faded in places. The community banded together to arrange a major restoration and hired a group of internationally renowned experts. The restoration was completed in 1997, with stunning results.

Not weird, but historically significant: A canoe, located near the base of the Astoria Column, marks the burial spot of Chief Comcomly of the Chinook Nation. Described as "a shrewd old savage with but one eye" by Washington Irving, Chief Comcomly assisted the Lewis and Clark expedition and was instrumental in helping John Astor establish his interests in the area. The chief died in 1830, probably from malaria. History records that five years later, a doctor working for the Hudson's Bay Company stole his skull and sent it to Scotland for study.

The Astoria Column is located at the end of Coxcomb Drive, east of downtown. There's a parking fee, imposed with its own quirky charm: At press time, it cost only $1 for a yearlong pass. Balsa wood gliders can also be purchased from a nearby vendor for launching from the observation deck.

Where does one find ghosts? Where people live, or have lived in the past. *Weird Oregon* found more than one haunted building, like Portland's White Eagle Saloon, where shanghaiers and ladies of the night plied their trades for decades. In Old Town Portland, ghost seekers increase their chances of seeing spooky things, such as the ghostly appearance of actor Charles Laughton, who died before he could play King Lear at the Oregon Shakespeare Festival. Farther west, several of Oregon's lighthouses have a reputation for being haunted, as does the grand Egyptian Theatre in small and conservative Coos Bay.

Of course, the way from Portland to the coast is guarded by the Bandage Man. And to the east, at least one hotel still hosts a guest—or ghost?—or two who have never left.

Oregon Caves Chateau

Many marriages end when either the husband or wife cheats. However, the typical cheater usually waits at least until the honeymoon is over to embark on an affair. Unfortunately for Elisabeth, her husband did not wait that long when they honeymooned at the Oregon Caves Chateau. In her despair over the incident, Elisabeth died—but never left. She still makes herself known to other women at Oregon Caves. (See the Ancient Mysteries chapter.) As if to balance this tragedy, a husband died on his honeymoon in the Oregon Caves, and his presence too has been seen and felt.

In 1934, the six-story Chateau was built near the entrance to the Oregon Caves National Monument. The ten-sided log lodge spans a small ravine and workers diverted a stream to form a catch pool, which in turn flows through the main dining room to entice young lovers.

Weird Oregon spoke with Anne, a Chateau employee, about Elisabeth, who committed suicide by either slitting her wrists in the bathroom or hanging herself—no one knows for sure. Elisabeth's ghost has remained in the suite that is now the subdivided Room 309/310. In 2005, an angry guest staying in Elisabeth's rooms came down to the lobby and accused the staff of playing a trick on his family. His daughter's cries from the smaller bedroom had awakened him. She yelled that there was blood all over her bed comforter. The staff went up to the room and inspected it with the guest. Everything was clean. No blood. Still, the family refused to stay there.

On another night, a woman staying in a third-floor room contacted the front desk, complaining that her electric blanket was too hot and that she could not find the control to turn it down. The desk clerk told the woman that they did not have any electric blankets at the Chateau. The guest looked down at her feet and saw balls of light hovering above them. She woke her husband, who also saw the lights. Other people reported having their feet tickled.

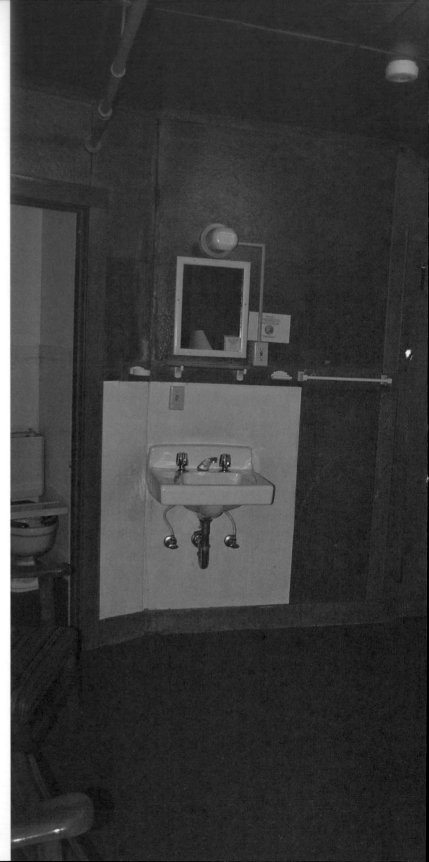

One gentleman sat down on his bed, and a few seconds later he felt someone sit down next to him. Someone invisible. At another time, a male guest saw several articles of women's clothing, including old-style shoes, under his bed. He went down to the front desk to ask who was checked into his room but was told he was the only guest. When he went back to the room, the only clothing there was his own.

When a former cook made a remark about ghostly Elizabeth, a paper towel roll jumped off its rack and flew past his head. He apologized, and they seemed to get along better after that.

Elisabeth is not the only ghost at the Chateau. One day a staffer opened a small maid's closet on the main floor. It was locked, so she had to use her keys. She was surprised to see a small man standing inside, wearing rough work clothes and an old-fashioned cap. He tipped his hat at her and walked down the hall. When she tried to find the man, he had vanished.

Shortly after she was hired by the Chateau, Pam was working in the dining room. She set down a small container of butter in front of a dining family and then watched it slide across the table. Pam thought that maybe it had some moisture on its bottom. She wiped the bottom off and put it down again, only to watch it fly across the room. Trying to be nonchalant, she got another container of butter for her stunned customers.

Oregon Caves Outfitters currently runs the Chateau under contract with the National Park Service. They keep a "guest ghost book" in the lobby, where guests and staff alike can write down accounts of odd things happening there, or read what happened to others.

Fit for a Pharaoh: The Coos Bay Egyptian Theatre

The Egyptian Theatre is the jewel of Coos Bay's downtown cultural center. For decades it was a place for the young and old to gather.

In 1925, the little city of Coos Bay saw the opening of the theater. However, the Egyptian was almost never built. In those days, there were several ordinances against building frivolous things like ornate movie theaters. The Egyptian started out as a large garage and auto service station, but the architects had designed it so that it could be converted into a theater after the ordinances changed.

Theater managers had known that there were dressing rooms in the upper levels, behind the stage. But some believe that there are others, down below the stage. We were shown a series of loose planks that might lead down to the legendary dressing rooms. No one has had the time to investigate—yet. Perhaps they are afraid that this might upset Maggie, the long-ago seamstress whose presence has been felt in the upper dressing rooms.

Others have been standing on the stage when someone has touched or nudged them from behind the curtain. When they investigated, the backstage area was always empty. Legend has it that one of the stagehands was killed many years ago when he fell off a raised catwalk. There was also a dark stain on the stage below the catwalk, removed only with a lot of work.

On the main floor, some of the original chairs are still in place, though mostly as displays, since modern folk are generally larger and would not be comfortable sitting in those chairs for long periods. This did not affect the ghostly man in black, who was often seen sitting in the back of the theater. Over the years, many people saw him, and when they approached he would vanish. When workers removed his chair for restoration, the spirit was seen sitting comfortably in the air, as if his chair were still there.

The theater employees led us up one of the two sets of stairs, which met in a kind of lobby behind the balcony seating. This was where the men's and ladies' rooms were located. Many people have reported seeing the ghost of a woman wearing an usherette's uniform walking around there. (An usherette's uniform would have been a typical theater employee's garment in the 1940s.)

Recent paranormal investigations may have detected a ghostly undercurrent in the balcony and elsewhere around the Egyptian Theatre. According to one investigator, there are three spirits locked into some kind of spiritual prison, with a young woman confined to the balcony by a malevolent male spirit. All is not lost, though, since she is kept company and protected by another male spirit. No one seems to know if the three people involved in this spiritual triangle died in the theater. Since renovation started, the spirits seemed

to have quieted down, though one investigator has a recording of a little boy saying, "Don't be afraid; we're not evil."

See classic movies and the spirits at 229 S. Broadway, Highway 101 in Coos Bay, or visit www.egyptian-theatre. com. For more on the theater haunting, visit the Curious Country Web site at http://curious_country.wakingrem.com.

Weirdness at Old Town Pizza

Portland Walking Tours gave *Weird Oregon*'s Al Eufrasio a peek at the world's largest oyster cracker, old buildings with cast-iron exteriors, and an alternative health shop with wall-to-wall exotic cures. (Powdered rhino horn, anyone?) But the final stop was a bit weirder. We'll let him elaborate. . . .

Nina Gets the Shaft

Although these days Old Town Pizza is known as a trendy restaurant-bar, it was once the lobby of the Merchant Hotel, built in the 1880s at Second Avenue and Davis Street.

In 1900, the Merchant was a base of operations for people involved in the "world's oldest profession." Nina, one of the working girls living there, informed on pimps who ran their affairs from the building. Shortly thereafter, she died in a suspicious fall down the hotel's elevator shaft. Stories persist that her spirit remains behind, sensed on occasion by both employees and customers of Old Town Pizza: a cold spot, a sudden twinge of unease, a shadow seen indirectly. Most tangibly, her name is etched into a brick. Did someone living carve it there as a memorial, or was it Nina's way of making herself known? I wondered.

The Darkness Below

The pizza parlor's basement holds decades-old secrets. Tour groups negotiate the back stairs, flanked by narrow bare-brick walls, with cheap plastic flashlights run by half-dead batteries. The air is still and musty. Tour guides explain that tunnels running parallel to us were used for illicit purposes: shanghaiing (see the Fabled People and Places chapter) and booze smuggling.

As my tour group began heading back upstairs, I lagged behind, wanting to snap a couple of pictures. As I raised my camera, two things happened simultaneously: My flashlight batteries fully died, and the door closed behind the exiting tour group.

I briefly pictured an employee, or another tour group, entering the basement sometime later and finding a skeleton in a *Weird U.S.* T-shirt, clutching a camera. Inspection of the camera's memory card would reveal a few final photos of some ghostly horror approaching from deep within the tunnels. It would resemble a Victorian prostitute, limbs twisted and broken from a horrible plunge down an elevator shaft.

Was my imagined scenario coming true? Fortunately, no. It was just the tour guide, patiently holding the door open as I tried shaking off the creeps.

Visit www.portlandwalkingtours.com for full tour schedule.

N-I-N-A

I am a paranormal enthusiast and a tour guide for Portland Walking Tours. We've been experiencing phenomena in the basement of the old Merchant Hotel building, seemingly ever since we started speaking directly to the spirit we call Nina. We've heard a girl's voice, felt breezes, and had all the tour guests get goose bumps. I've left out Scrabble tiles randomly on a chair before I lock up, and I ask Nina to try to leave a message. When I return, letters have often moved slightly. On a recent tour, in front of the group, I was explaining the experiment and asked Nina to spell her name as I randomly mixed the tiles on the chair. As soon as I lifted my hand, everyone pointed out that right in the middle of the tiles N-I-N-A was spelled out in a straight line. During these experiences we are always detecting huge spikes in the electromagnetic field, which indicates an unknown energy force. I've had even more frightening encounters after locking up at night, and will no longer step foot down there alone. —*Leigh Ann W.*

Ghost of Charles Laughton

Ashland, Oregon, hosts the Oregon Shakespeare Festival, probably the largest festival of its kind outside of Stratford-upon-Avon, England. The centerpiece of Ashland's theaters is the Elizabethan Stage, modeled after London's 1599 Fortune Theatre. This cultural icon sprouted from an idea by a local man named Angus Bowmer.

In the years since the festival began, many world-famous actors and actresses have traveled there to play their favorite parts. At least one wanted a role so badly that even death has not stopped him from visiting—and staying—in Ashland.

According to communications manager Amy Richard, Angus Bowmer wrote to English-born actor Charles Laughton, who begged to play King Lear in the 1963 festival. (He'd been Lear at Stratford in 1959.)

Laughton died in 1962, before he could play the part. But his spirit apparently still lives on at the festival. According to what Angus Bowmer wrote in his book, "Each year the familiar ghost that nightly sighs through our theatre is . . . Mr. Charles Laughton."

Bandage Man

For many years, Oregon residents have had terrifying encounters with an entity that has come to be known as Bandage Man. Most reports of him place Bandage Man hiding in the woods on either side of the overpass at the junction of Highways 101 and 26, between Seaside and Cannon Beach. People driving that stretch of road at night in pick-up trucks or open-top vehicles should beware. Bandage Man jumps from the woods into the back of the truck, pounds on the cab and back windows, and jumps out as the vehicle passes through the woods at the other end of the overpass. He supposedly leaves behind a bloody bandage or the smell of rotting flesh.

There are various stories about the origin of Bandage Man. There is a constant theme in the Bandage Man tale as it goes backward in time. The most recent theory is that Bandage Man is some kind of space alien that landed or crashed along the Oregon Coast. It was injured in the crash, or later by hunters, and it is hiding out, waiting for the mother ship to pick it up. Another similar story holds that it is actually a Bigfoot, also injured by hunters, who were transporting it from the woods to Cannon Beach or Seaside. It escaped confinement and is now hanging around the area to take vengeance on those who injured it. People have also suggested it is the phantom of an escaped mental patient, a mummy from a freak show that came to life, and so on. Perhaps the oldest story is true, that Bandage Man is the ghost of an injured logger.

People traveling along the Oregon coast in the past few years have noticed new logging activity along the Coast Mountain Range. Most of this logging is taking place in new growth at the site of an old fire known as the Tillamook Burn. In August 1933, logging operations near the Oregon coast started a fire that burned for three weeks, charring more than 260,000 acres (over 400 square miles) of timberland, killing 11 billion board feet of timber trees. The same land burned three more times, in 1939, 1945, and 1951, though none of the later fires was as large as the first. In 1948, Oregon began reforesting the land, which grew into the forest that is being cut today.

Amazingly, only one person died fighting the 1933 fire, and *Weird Oregon* does not know whether any others died in the later fires or harvesting the dead timber, though it seems likely. If Bandage Man exists, he may be the spirit of one of those unfortunate men, killed in a logging accident. His friends would have tried to take him from the woods to the nearest doctor, in Cannon Beach or Seaside, but the man died, perhaps on the overpass.

Weird Oregon contacted the Oregon State Police, who had never heard of him, and when we stopped to take pictures of the road intersection, we spoke with a local property owner who looked old enough to remember the last fire in the Tillamook Burn. He edged away from us after we asked whether he or anyone he knew had encountered a specter leaving behind bloody bandages.

Unwanted Memento

Me and my girlfriend stopped by the side of Highway 101 in Cannon Beach and we were getting "intimate" when all of a sudden a man covered in bandages and smelling like rotten flesh flung open the door of my car, pulled my girlfriend out, and then started attacking me. I was lucky to kick him off. He started running down the road, and I never saw him again. But the next morning I checked the inside of my car and it still smelled like rotting flesh. I bent over my backseat and found a piece of what looked like part of the man's bandages. Can you tell me what I saw? —*Aaron D.*

Haunted Lighthouses on the Central Oregon Coast

It is almost expected that lighthouses are haunted. This is based in part on the lonely existence of lighthouse keepers. Many of them have gone insane from the isolation or from watching too many ships wrecked upon the shores they guarded. Three of Oregon's central coast lighthouses, at Yaquina Bay, Yaquina Head, and Heceta Head, all have reputations for being haunted, based on stories of madness and tragedy.

The Yaquina Bay Lighthouse

Visitors to the Yaquina Bay lighthouse in Newport are surprised to see that it is a two-story wooden caretaker's house with a three-story wooden tower attached. It does not resemble the stone-and-brick structures most people expect. Soon after the lighthouse was built, it was obvious that it was too far inside Yaquina Bay for its beacon to help ships along the coast navigate safely. It was replaced less than three years later by the nearby Yaquina Head lighthouse, its light extinguished in 1874. The lighthouse was used for only three years.

According to folklore, at least one ghost inhabits the Yaquina Bay lighthouse. Shortly after the lighthouse ceased operations in 1874, a group of local young people discovered a secret wall panel and metal door in an upper-story closet. Inside the door they found a tunnel or chute leading down. After they left, one of the members said she had left her handkerchief in the lighthouse. She went inside alone, but her friends followed her a few minutes later after hearing her scream.

Inside they found a trail of blood drops leading upstairs and a pool of warm blood on the floor of one of the upstairs bedrooms. They saw her handkerchief lying on the floor of the closet where they found the hidden door. She was never seen again. Rumors continued for a hundred years about strange lights and figures seen at night in the old lighthouse.

If the story seems like a work of fiction, it is. In 1899, Lischen Miller wrote a story for *Pacific Monthly*, detailing a story of terror and suspense along the Oregon coast. She picked the Yaquina Bay lighthouse as the setting for her tale.

Many visitors have reported seeing strange figures or lights in the top of the three-story lighthouse tower, even after the lighthouse beacon was turned off. According to some of the staff at the lighthouse, this was due to camera flash reflections. *Weird Oregon* spoke with some of the volunteers and learned of other stories. One of the volunteers was in the basement cleaning up after the lighthouse closed. He heard the sound of footsteps walking on the first floor above him. He went up to investigate but found the place empty.

Learn more about the Yaquina Bay lighthouse at www.yaquinalights.org/ybay.html.

Yaquina Head Lighthouse

The U.S. Light-House Board built Yaquina Head Lighthouse. The lighthouse beacon is located at the top of a ninety-three-foot brick tower, perched on an eighty-four-foot-high cliff. The lighthouse was completed in 1873.

The first ghost story dated to the tower's construction. The tower was built with inner and outer brick walls, and a hollow space the builders filled with rubble. This allowed the tower to bend a bit in high winds, rather than cracking and breaking. They had to add the fill all at one time to ensure it would pack tightly. When they opened the hoppers, one of the workmen fell inside, and the others could not get him out in time. Supposedly, he can be heard tapping on the lighthouse walls on quiet days, hoping someone will get him out.

According to some stories posted at the lighthouse visitor's center, the second ghost is Henry Higgins, an assistant lighthouse keeper. According to the stories, sometime in the 1930s the head keeper went into Newport for a drink, leaving Henry and another keeper at the lighthouse. The other keeper drank himself into a stupor, leaving Higgins to carry several cans of oil up the 114 steps to the top of the tower. Higgins had a heart attack and died. Ever since, people have heard Higgins walking up the stairs and have felt his presence on the landing where he died.

Weird Oregon author Jeff Davis asked an employee inside the visitor's center about any spirits. The man looked around carefully before replying. Seeing that there was no one nearby, he replied that he had been in the lighthouse alone and had felt something. And no one would confirm or deny the stories of the workman legend says was buried inside the tower.

For more information about the Yaquina Head lighthouse, visit www.yaquinalights.org/yhead.html.

Heceta Head Lighthouse

The Heceta Head lighthouse near Yachats, built in 1893, is the most expensive lighthouse built along the Oregon coast. It also has the most powerful beacon and is the most photographed lighthouse in Oregon, if not the entire United States. Despite its relative youth— it is the youngest of the three lighthouses— it also is probably the most haunted lighthouse on the Oregon coast. Fortunately for *Weird Oregon* readers, it is also open to the public, as a bed-and-breakfast.

Technically, the lightkeeper's quarters are haunted, not the lighthouse—nor is the lighthouse open to bed-and-breakfast guests. Stories first arose in the 1970s, when Lane Community College leased the building as an extension campus. The most dramatic stories date to 1976, when workers began repairing the building. One of the carpenters was in the attic replacing several broken windowpanes when he felt a cold wind behind him. He turned around and saw a middle-aged woman floating in the air. Her old-fashioned dress was pressed against her by the wind. She opened her arms toward the man. Somehow he made his way past her, down the attic stairs, and out of the building without hurting himself. He never came back, so she visited him in his dreams for the next four nights.

They called her Rue, though historians believe that this may be the spirit of Mrs. DeRoy, wife of a past lighthouse keeper, who was obsessed with keeping the house clean. One night the innkeepers heard the sound of someone in the attic walking around and apparently using a broom. The next morning they went up to the attic and saw that all the glass was swept into a neat pile.

Rue may also be the ghostly lady seen standing outside, over the grave of a child nearby.

More than a decade ago, the Lane Community College lease ended and the U.S. Forest Service let the building be turned into a bed-and-breakfast. The innkeepers keep a ghost log for guests to record odd happenings. Some guests have reported the scent of flowers or rose perfume. Others have entered their rooms to see an imprint on their beds, as if someone had been lying there only seconds before.

Make a reservation to see for yourself at www.hecetalighthouse.com.

Cornelius Pass Roadhouse

Some years ago, Oregon's own McMenamins began buying old and decrepit buildings, and rehabilitating them into a growing chain of microbrew pubs and hotels. It is no wonder that some of their properties are haunted. They have a staff of artists whose aim is to beautify the walls of these properties with artwork that tells the story of the places, the McMenamins, and local history. Sometimes the forces of the paranormal and artwork combine to either create or explore ghostly legends.

Robert Imbrie built the Italianate farmhouse along Cornelius Pass Road, near Hillsboro, between 1863 and 1866. He needed a new house not just because he had twelve children, but also because he wanted to make a statement. At that time, the area was farmland and forest, and most of the homes were built of logs or rough wood planks. Building such an ornate house showed everyone that the Imbrie family

could afford the best and also ensured that the house would survive for more than a hundred years; long after the other ones were demolished. According to legend, one day three of the Imbrie children, two girls and a teenage boy, were playing in the attic when the boy fell down the stairs to his death. This story has been illustrated by the McMenamins' artists. There is a painting of the younger sister at the top of the attic stairs. There is another of saddened parents standing above the upstairs fireplace. Hidden in a closet next to the fireplace is a third painting of a young woman hiding, her eyes filled with tears. This young woman is supposed to haunt the halls of the mansion, perhaps looking for forgiveness—and her brother.

According to at least one member of the Imbrie family, this tragedy never happened and the house was not haunted. However, over the years, several McMenamins employees have reported odd things. Several noted cold spots throughout the house. A few of these were explained away as drafts created by the kitchen ventilation system, but this does not explain the cold spot located on the attic stairs. Servers claim to have seen glasses sitting on tables shatter, even though no one was near the table.

In the late 1990s, the Cornelius Pass Roadhouse manager walked through the building, making sure all of the appliances and lights were turned off and that the doors and windows were locked. His last duty before leaving was to turn on the burglar alarm. Normally this happened without incident. Twice, however, he went

through his routine, secured the building, and got in his car to drive home as usual, only to see, when he turned around to look at the building before driving away, that all of the lights were turned on.

The Number Thirteen Paranormal Group of Portland learned that three Imbrie children were buried in a nearby cemetery, one of them a teenage boy. Founder Lisa Branum decided to test the legend.

They tried experimenting with electronic voice phenomena, asking questions while using a digital audio recorder, pausing for a response, and then listening to the recording later. Sometimes

paranormal investigators do seem to get responses on the recording that they did not hear when they made the recording, as happened at the Cornelius Pass Roadhouse. Near the fireplace, one of the investigators asked, "Are you an Imbrie?" Upon replaying the recording they heard a voice whisper, "Aye."

The next question was, "Are you protecting your home?" The same voice whispered back slowly. During this session, several members of the group felt as if someone touched them. Of course this could have been their own imaginations or the drafts caused by the ventilation system—or there might have been someone, perhaps Robert Imbrie, standing over them.

Perhaps the best evidence of hauntings at the roadhouse is not due to any investigation, but is in the reaction of people who visit there and know nothing of the legends. Tim, Lisa Branum's husband, now works at the Cornelius Pass Roadhouse. He spoke with a waitress, who told him a little girl walked up to her and said, "I like this place, but not the ghost here."

The Cornelius Pass Roadhouse is located at 4045 NW Cornelius Pass Road in Hillsboro and is online at www. mcmenamins.com. The Number Thirteen Paranormal Group of Oregon's findings is on the Internet at http:// home.comcast.net/~branum6125/site/?/home/.

The White Eagle Saloon

When the McMenamins bought the White Eagle Saloon a few years ago, they knew in advance that they purchased one of Portland's most famous haunts. In 1872, the area east of the Willamette River was the town of Albina. Most of the people who settled there were German, Russian, and Polish. Russell Street was the toughest street in Albina. Thirty saloons lined Russell Street, from what is now Interstate Avenue east to Martin Luther King Way. Eventually, the city of Portland annexed Albina. The White Eagle Saloon is a survivor of those early days.

According to a past owner, there has been a saloon on the same site since the mid-1800s, but the present brick saloon and café was built between 1905 and 1906. Surviving records for the White Eagle go back to 1906. It was known as the B. Soboleski and Company Saloon, owned by Barney Soboleski and William Hryszko. Modern visitors to the White Eagle admire the huge nineteenth-century oak bar with columns bracketing a large mirror. Another original feature is less easy to see: the open urinal running at the foot of the bar.

Depending on custom, there was a difference between a bar, a tavern, and a saloon. Most people agree that a saloon meant that women were not allowed, except for employees. It was a man's domain. Customers could use the urinal, rather than risk losing their place at the bar or having their drinks stolen. Although the urinal has been filled in and covered over, there are some historic pictures of it hanging on the walls of the present-day White Eagle.

There were several ten-by-ten-foot rooms sometimes called cribs on the top floor of the saloon. The owners and staff lived in some of these rooms, and rented the rest out to various workmen, and perhaps working women. According to rumors and legends that many serious historians consider absurd, the top floor of the White Eagle was a brothel staffed by white prostitutes, while black and Asian prostitutes served customers in the basement. This would explain why several people have reported seeing a woman leaning out of the upper floor window in the 1970s and 1980s, after the upper floor had been closed off and abandoned. Some people believe she is the ghost of a prostitute named Rose, who may have been kept company by the ghost of Sam Worek.

According to one legend, Sam Worek was abandoned near the tavern when he was a child. Sam was more or less adopted by the Hryszko family and worked at the saloon in return for room, board, and a small salary. In the 1950s, the owners were closing off the upper floor, and Sam had to find a new place to live. But before he could move, Sam died in his sleep. When they sealed off the upper floor, the owners left his possessions in his room.

According to others, Sam was an adult when he came to the White Eagle. He was an excellent cook, but had a weakness for the bottle. When he went on a bender, he would disappear for days or weeks at a time. When he returned, he would go back to his kitchen until the next time the bottle called. He was in his sixties or seventies when he died. A picture hangs in the White Eagle that shows the Hryszko family and an adult Sam posing for the camera.

In the 1990s, the McMenamins brewpub chain purchased the White Eagle and restored the upper floor, opening it up as a European-style hotel. Their artists named Room 2 "Sam's Room" through Room 3 appears to have been built for a long-term boarder.

There are many, many stories of ghosts and the strange at the White Eagle Saloon. *Weird Oregon* heard about "flying" mustard jugs and a Room 3 poltergeist.

Not even the ladies' bathroom is entirely safe from this nuisance ghost. According to a past owner, a female patron was using the ladies' room. She had entered with a friend. The first patron was sitting in the stall, when a wad of (clean) toilet paper came over the stall wall and hit her. She soon found herself involved in a furious toilet paper fight. When she finished, she found that her friend had left the bathroom a few minutes earlier. So who was in the other stall?

Ghosts of Carl Road

Growing up in Woodburn, it would be impossible not to hear about the ghosts of Carl Road. From a very young age, probably from the time I was in second grade, people talked about the road and the evil orchard that stood alongside it.

The road is long and desolate, quiet and dark. The legend most commonly associated with it is that a strange, forbidding phantom, dressed in all white, haunts the aforementioned orchard. It seemed like everyone in my town knew about this ghost and believed in it, and that a sizable number had seen it with their own eyes. Growing up, I was completely terrified of Carl Road and particularly that orchard.

When I was in high school, and some of my older friends got their driver's licenses, it became a pretty consistent ritual that at the end of our nights, we'd take a trip down Carl Road to see if we couldn't spot the ghost for ourselves.

Those first trips were filled with tension—the orchard is definitely a quiet, creepy place, and I was downright hyperventilating. We would pull up with our headlights off, then walk through the trees with only the sound of leaves crunching beneath our feet, waiting for the sudden moment when the ghost would jump out at me.

But unfortunately for me, that never happened. In all my visits to the orchard, I never saw the ghost. After a couple of years, I went from being scared by older friends to trying to scare younger friends. We would drive our freshman friends out there, telling them of all the times we had seen the ghost, getting them worked up and ready for a fright. But then something happened during my senior year.

I had become friends with a girl, Maddy, who lived on one end of Carl Road. Her house was not anything particularly scary. We went out one night, on a double date with a couple guys from a neighboring town. Unfortunately our dates were basically a couple of meatheads who only wanted to talk about themselves and their heroic adventures in sports. Maddy and I ditched the guys after dinner and headed back to her place, where we had decided to sleep that night, as her parents weren't home.

As a kind of rite of passage, we stopped at the orchard on our way back. But something was wrong there—it was just too quiet, and the air was really still. About three that morning, I woke up on her pull-out couch, sweating. I got out of bed and looked around—I swear I thought someone was in the room with me. After a moment or two, I calmed down and laughed it off—after all this time, I couldn't believe that I of all people was having nightmares about Carl Road.

Then, I heard Maddy's door open. "Elle, did you see it too?"

"Did I see what?"

Just then, I swear to God, a white light shined into the living room, and slowly crept from window to window. This was on the side of the house facing away from the road, so it was definitely not a car. And the light was too white and too widespread for it to be a flashlight or anything along those lines. On top of that, the whole atmosphere in the room had become completely oppressive and terrifying. I was frozen where I stood and all my hair stood up on end.

The light passed and the air came back into our lungs. Both of us burst out crying. We hadn't been drinking or anything. Both of us swore up and down that it was the ghost, following us home from the orchard.

When I hear people telling each other that there's no such thing as ghosts, and that Carl Road isn't scary at all, I tell them to think twice—because I for one, will never take that orchard for granted again. —*Ellie Spring*

The Wolf Creek Inn Still Howls

The Wolf Creek Inn was built in 1883 and served for many years as a stagecoach stop along the sixteen-day trip from San Francisco to Portland. Somehow the inn survived the end of the stagecoaches, the arrival of the railroads, and even the invention of the superhighway. It hosted simple folk, like gold miners and merchants, as well as the rich and famous, people like Jack London and Clark Gable. Even though the Wolf Creek Inn is no longer along main travel routes, it is Oregon's oldest operating inn, hosting living guests—and maybe old guests who have not checked out.

Wolf Creek, located a few miles north of Ashland, has been a waypoint for travelers since the 1850s. Many people saw a lot of wolves in the area, and they named the stream, and eventually the little town that grew up around it, Wolf Creek. Wolf Creek grew up after gold was discovered in northern California and southern Oregon, as miners and the people who served their needs traveled between claims. One of their stops was the Six Bit House, built near the site of the present-day Wolf Creek Inn.

According to legends, the Six Bit House got its name when some gold miners decided to hang a Native American who was at the inn, drinking. They placed the young man on a horse under a tree, with a noose around his neck and the other end of the rope tied to a large branch. Before they could swat the horse, the owner of the inn came running out toward them, yelling. He ordered them not to hang the man until he collected the seventy-five cents, or six bits, that the doomed man owed as a bar bill. They searched him, found the money, and then hanged the unfortunate man.

The Six Bit House was eventually abandoned, and guests instead came to stay at the Wolf Creek Tavern as it was known then. Henry Smith built it in 1883 and it was much nicer than the infamous Six Bit House. He found many skilled craftsmen and paid them very well for building him build a beautiful restaurant and inn. Even after the gold ran out and the stagecoaches stopped running, the inn survived. Railroads have passed through Wolf Creek since the 1850s, but in 1887, the Oregon and California Railroad lines began stopping in Wolf Creek. When the old highway was built in the 1920s, it passed through Wolf Creek, and many tired drivers stopped there. Business was so good that the owner built a wing of guest rooms in 1925.

Following World War II, the pace in America became faster, and more people traveled between Oregon and California by airplane. When I-5 was built, fewer cars stopped here, and business shrank. Fortunately, the State of Oregon purchased the Wolf Creek Inn in the 1970s and restored it. The inn, decorated in early-twentieth-century style, is now open year-round. It attracts guests who want to relive an era with less stress and more flavor. Perhaps the historic aura around Wolf Creek has kept some past guests and employees around.

With a name like Wolf Creek, there are many legends surrounding the town and inn. The most shocking tale involves werewolves and, oddly, vampires. Periodically stories spread across the Internet of werewolves hunting or haunting the hills above Wolf Creek. One Web site devoted to cataloging haunted places across the country stated that many people have seen a vampiric batlike creature, with blood dripping out of its mouth, in the vicinity. It stated that the creature was seen along the nearby highway, where it chased cars and attacked a couple of hikers, leaving marks on their necks. So far, Weird Oregon has not found any newspaper accounts that confirm this story, but believes that there is something at the Wolf Creek Inn.

In 2007, Cougar and Fox from the Shamans and Spirit Warrior Society, spent a few days at the inn, investigating the stories of hauntings. They experienced several different paranormal events, and may have even activated dormant hauntings.

Cougar and Fox spent one night in the Clark Gable suite. In the past, many guests and the staff reported smelling cigar smoke in the men's room, near the bathroom of the Clark Gable suite. The Wolf Creek Inn has been smoke-free for many years, but it happened often enough that they could not blame it on someone breaking the rules. When they arrived, Cougar and Fox walked around the hotel, and Cougar smelled smoke in the same area, before anyone told him about the legends of ghostly smokers. Later they smelled a sweet perfume in their suite, and Cougar briefly saw a figure in their bathtub, though he could not tell if it was a man or woman.

People have seen a man reflected in the mirror in the men's bathroom on the second floor. Some romantics believe that this may be the ghost of Jack London, who once stayed and wrote here, though it is not proven. The innkeepers have a radio in their office. In the past, the staff rented the radio to guests for an extra fee. More recently, the staff watched the radio dials move on their own, until someone taped the dials down so they would not move anymore.

An earlier guest who stayed in Room 5 reported seeing a female apparition come into his room. She shifted his blankets and massaged his feet before she disappeared. She may have been the same ghostly woman Cougar saw in various places in the inn. He saw her once in Room 5, and described her as being in her early twenties and wearing a blue and white dress with a short stand-up collar and a white apron. Later he had a vision of her with some kind of cloth around her neck, falling or jumping down a flight of stairs. He speculated that these were the servant's stairs in the back of the inn, which are off-limits because they are so steep. He believed that she could have been a servant girl who stayed only because she desperately needed a job. Other people believe that she may have been the daughter of Henry Smith, who is supposed to have committed suicide in the Wolf Creek Inn.

Perhaps the most frightening vision Cougar saw was outside the Wolf Creek Inn. About a hundred yards away from the present inn, he found an old tree that he believed marked the site of the Six Bit House. Cougar saw a vision of a young Native American man, sitting on a ghostly horse. The man had a rope around his neck, but strangely, the other end of the rope did not end on one of the tree branches. Instead it was hanging in the air. After a closer look at the tree, Cougar saw where a large tree branch had been sawn off, in a position such that in the past, the rest of the tree limb must have grown to where the rope hung on empty air. The vision lasted a few seconds then flashed forward to the man's body hanging from the tree for several days as a tourist attraction.

Shamans Cougar and Fox saw and experienced many other strange things at the Wolf Creek Inn—too many to list here.

Ignore That Big Red Man in the Window

When I was about twelve I checked out a book from the school library about the "urban myths" of Oregon. They were all pretty lame. But one has stuck in my mind ever since.

Here's how it goes. A long time ago, in the 1870s, the logging industry was booming. In a small logging community there was the legend of Big Red, also known as the Bandage Man. Big Red had been a logger, and was a big, burly, horribly mean man. Not surprisingly, he was also a loner and a semi-hermit. He made his money by chopping down fir trees to sell, often for firewood or Christmas trees. His bad temper made him unpopular, but he kept it up.

In those days, they used huge two-man saws to cut down trees that were taller than the average man. Big red wanted to sell quite a bit of lumber and needed help, but nobody volunteered. Big Red was not given his name for nothing, so he felt he could handle the saw by himself. When he began to saw, he rested the saw against a tree branch, stepped the wrong way and sheared the skin off his body.

He was not dead, but soon would be unless he got help. He staggered into town near the window of the saloon. It was pouring down rain and he began to plead for help and bang against the windows. But the people inside hated Big Red, and ignored him completely. They went back to their drinks until they finally saw him no longer.

They went out later that night to try and find his corpse, but it was not there. Since that time they claim that if you go into that area at night you can still hear the dying wails of Big Red, but be forewarned, his ghost will wreak vengeance, a vengeance that is said to claim all those who refused to help him that night in the 1870s. —*Angela*

The Hot Springs and Tunnel 13

My friends and I discovered this old hot spring that used to be a hotel and was turned into a hospital a while back.

Anyway, the first time I went there I found a room where there was nothing but papers all over the floor. They were the nurse's notes of medication given to the patients there. It was really strange because it seemed as though the drugs were experimental. The patients' health fluctuated greatly from one day to the next. The strangest thing was that I wanted to take some of those notes and research the drugs to see what they were. Well the next night I decided to do this but I couldn't find the room. It was weird.

Then another time we went, most of the people we went with were in the old surgery room while we were next door. There was no one else in the house, and upstairs we heard a table or something like it being moved across the floor. The weird thing was that whatever was moving it walked on four legs because of the way its feet were hitting the ground. The people in the surgery room didn't hear it. Another time there was a rocking chair in front of this window, and the next day we couldn't even find the chair anywhere in the house. They say the ghosts are from the patients in the hospital but who really knows? The hot spring is located in La Grande, Oregon.

Another place my friends and I went to was what they call Tunnel 13 in Ashland, Oregon. The story is that it was the location of the last train robbery in Oregon. Evidently it was a robbery gone wrong, and instead of blowing up the tracks they blew up the train— and all the passengers of the train haunt that tunnel. The story states that you can hear the cries of the children in the tunnels and a woman wearing red paces the entrance of the tunnel. When we went I didn't hear anything or see anything but I did smell smoke in one spot in the tunnel. The weird thing is I was the only one that could smell it. It smelled as though someone had just put out a campfire and it was still smoldering If I stepped just one step forward or backwards I couldn't smell it anymore. It was quite a strange experience, especially since it was such a strong smell and no one else with me was able to smell it. —*Joelene*

Pizza Girl Murder

I'm not sure if there is any haunted background to this story but it is something you'll want to check out if you come to Salem, Oregon. Back on the night of July 4, 1982, a pizza delivery girl named Sherry Fyerly was lured onto a gravel road thinking she was delivering a pizza to someone. She was abducted and the case went unsolved for twenty-five years until the killer, who was already in jail for other crimes, confessed to it in December 2007.

If you go to the gravel road where the abduction took place, there is a little memorial with a cross for her. It's in a very eerie area, at least at night. I remember when my friends and I were probably in middle or high school and we were riding our bikes there and accidently came across the area where she got abducted. Back then there was just a sign there that said "I was abducted here." —*Nick*

Cemetery Safari

ow people treat their dead, both at burial and afterward, reveals a lot about their culture. Were the rich buried with the poor? Do the graves of the famous share space with the infamous? Oregon prides itself on its democratic past and present. In places like Lone Fir Cemetery in Portland, madams and shanghaiers share space with politicians and the wealthy. Many of Portland's historic and modern celebrities like Virgil Earp and Lyle Alzado rest in beautiful River View Cemetery. Dr. John McLoughlin and his wife rest just outside their Oregon City home, and recently, a few people preferred to have their cremated remains rest in a battered lighthouse in Tillamook Bay, much to the dismay of some relatives.

Most would agree that the grave of one child is more tragic than those of a dozen adults. Three children from the same family all died and rest together at Stayton Cemetery, while four boys from the Mill Creek reformatory face one another in fellowship.

Perhaps the most tragic grave marker of all commemorates the victims of a Christmas Eve fire in Silver Lake that killed forty people in a matter of minutes. Tragedies just as dark may have caused spirits like the legendary witch of Lafayette Cemetery to attack intruders, while something dark just watches and waits at Linkville Cemetery. And while some people perform voodoo rituals at Portland's Columbian Cemetery, the State of Oregon still hopes to reunite the remains of several thousand people who died at mental health facilities with those loved ones who may have forgotten their existence. This all shows that Oregon cares for and about her dead, in many and diverse ways.

As always, if you visit any of the cemeteries mentioned in *Weird Oregon,* or anywhere else, we ask that you act respectfully. Try to stay on any paths or walkways and do not damage any headstones or take any offerings or mementos away. Please treat the graves as if the person resting there is someone you cared deeply about.

Lafayette Cemetery

Today, visitors in little Lafayette are impressed with the fact that the town still retains its small-town feel, in the midst of the rapidly growing wine country of Yamhill County. Few of them realize that Lafayette's small-town feel has lasted a long time, but perhaps not all of it is as pastoral as the rows of grape vines might suggest.

Joel Perkins founded Lafayette along an important Native American trail network in 1847 as a kind of commercial waypoint. It took a few years to get going, but in the 1850s it grew quickly and became the county seat, and it remained so for several decades. At that time, each county in Oregon was responsible for executing its own condemned prisoners, and there was allegedly a hanging tree, located near Lafayette Cemetery, where prisoners were executed. The tree has long since been cut down. Perhaps. Stories have grown about a witch who was hung by townsfolk and buried in the cemetery. Of course, in a town as old as Lafayette there are several cemeteries, so which one is haunted? The two major candidates for the haunted witch's cemetery are Pioneer Cemetery, established in 1852, and Masonic Cemetery, established in 1855.

Weird Oregon received several e-mails from Lisa A. and her friend, Lisa B. The two Lisas believe that Masonic Cemetery is very haunted:

When my friend and I went out during the day, we discovered one of the graves—only one!—had been dug at. We supposed it was an animal? The name on the grave was Lxxx something. I read the legend about the witch of Lafayette coming out of her grave and chasing people around the tombstones, scratching people. But no one seems clear on exactly which cemetery she is buried in . . . Hmmm. The grave looked like something was digging down though. "It" (the digger) had actually turned back some Visqueen (plastic sheeting) with several inches of dirt on top. It was definitely odd.

My son and I decided to go back, me with my digital camera, him with a video tape recorder. Again, I didn't catch anything with the camera, but Andrew (my son) had an experience. He was filming and standing near a grave, when he suddenly said he felt super cold and all of the hairs stood up on the back of his neck. We wrapped it up and went back to my house to analyze the film and photos. We hooked up the video recorder to my TV so we could use the volume and WOW! We heard the sound of a male adult voice say repeatedly, at least four or five times "Leave" very loudly on the audio portion. (We didn't catch anything on film, rats!) A split second after we heard the last "Leave" spoken was when Andrew had his creepy feeling.

*A girlfriend and I went back to
Lafayette Cemetery No. 3 the Friday after
Thanksgiving. It was during the day this
time, and we both had digital recorders.
My friend didn't get anything on hers.
. . . I don't think we got anything this
visit. Theory: Both times we captured
something on tape, I was accompanied by
men who held the recorders. Since it was
not customary to permit women to join
the Masons (just the husbands were given
actual membership), maybe the spirits were
reluctant to communicate because we are
women?*

*Lisa and I went alone two weekends
ago. I captured some EVP on my recorder,
but it did not record on my friend's. We both
had our recorders on and we were standing
in front of a plot that held two little girls.
We both stood there at the same time with
our recorders, while I asked questions such
as, "Is there anyone here?" and "What is
your name?"*

*We captured from my recorder, but
not hers, a child's voice that sounds like a
little girl saying, "Mama, don't leave," or
"Mama, don't leave me."*

*It sends chills up my spine and makes
me so sad every time I hear it! Why only my
recorder? —Lisa A.*

Unfortunately, as often happens in the cases of
cemeteries said to be haunted, Lafayette's cemeteries have
suffered from their legends. Pioneer Cemetery is fairly well
maintained and exists along a fairly well-traveled road. At
the same time, Masonic Cemetery is along a route that
used to be popular but is now a back road, and graveyard
maintenance was irregular. It began to look haunted, which
attracted thrill seekers. As stories of paranormal incidents
and investigations grew on the Internet, thrill seekers turned
into vandals. Although Lisa A. thought an animal could have
partially dug up the grave she saw, it was probably someone
on a witch hunt.

Many of the people in Lafayette and nearby towns are
descendents of people in Masonic Cemetery. After the recent
vandalism, it has been posted NO TRESPASSING, and the
people living along the cemetery road have called the police
to report any strangers entering the cemetery.

Canterbury Cemetery

Hey *Weird Oregon,*
I was driving by some church on Canterbury Lane
in Tigard when I had to stop. Y'see it was night
time, and even though there are a lot of houses out
that way now, the old cemetery is dark at night.
Anyway, I stopped because I saw a bunch of green
lights in the cemetery, moving around, like they
were flying. At first they were all moving around
in different directions, but they started coming
together and moved like a cloud. I opened my door,
and was going to investigate when I heard a bunch
of noise, like an animal or crazy person howling at
the top of their lungs. I got back into my car and
drove away. —*Mitch*

A Missing Link at the Linkville Cemetery?

The city of Klamath Falls has had some serious ups and downs in its history. Based on some of the stories heard by *Weird Oregon,* it may have the most ghosts per capita of any city in Oregon, especially in one of its oldest cemeteries, Linkville.

When settler George Nurse platted his new town in 1867, he called it Linkville, after the river and falls located along the city he laid out. The Klamath tribe may have thought Nurse was crazy to start a town there. They regularly witnessed what they thought were supernatural events in the

area. They called the area Yulalona, referring to the way the Linkville River flowed upstream when high winds blew in from the south. There were several geothermal springs in the area, which some of the early settlers diverted to heat their homes. Over the years there were ups and downs in the town, which was renamed Klamath Falls around 1892.

Klamath Falls grew up around the cemetery, which has become something of an oasis, with paths winding around mature trees and, for the most part, well-tended landscaping. Based on looks alone, it hardly seemed to be the site of a haunting, yet recently there were rumors that people passing by at night saw a grave glowing bright green every full moon. Most could not say which grave it was, because they were too frightened to come too close. Other people reported hearing strange noises and lights in various other locations as well.

In August 2006, a Klamath Falls–based paranormal group, Haunted Hunters, investigated Linkville Cemetery. After gaining permission to investigate the cemetery, the team spent some time preparing for their evening investigation. There were several open drains and potential hazards in the graveyard, so the team went into the cemetery during the day and placed several reflective markers to show hazards as well as define a perimeter for the investigation. Later that night the rest of the team arrived with special gear, including audio recorders, camcorders, still cameras, and their senses.

They set up a base camp as a control center and sent two two-person teams into the test area to see if they could get any response from any paranormal entities. It was not easy. They stumbled when avoiding several out-of-place tombstones, and the heavy winds interfered with their audio recordings. Dust carried on the wind also interfered with them capturing any undisputed paranormal video footage with their cameras. Worst of all, they had to move cautiously to avoid being sprayed by the family of skunks who shared the cemetery with them that night. Every thirty minutes, the teams returned to the base camp, and two more teams went out.

Interestingly, even though they did not discuss their findings at the time, most of the teams reported feeling uneasy, like they were being watched when they were near the center of the cemetery. Also, when they were in one corner of the cemetery, some of the teams heard low voices. At first, it sounded like whispering, but later the voices became louder, and one of the camcorders caught what may have been a voice calling to them.

Ghosts at the McLoughlin Graves

Every year, thousands of people visit the Dr. John McLoughlin House and his grave in Oregon City. People have called McLoughlin the Father of Oregon, because if it weren't for his influence, the Oregon Territory might not have become part of the United States. He did this in spite of the fact that as the chief factor (regional manager) of the British-owned Hudson's Bay Company, McLoughlin should have kept American settlers out.

Some visitors to the house have sworn that they have seen the ghosts of Dr. and Mrs. McLoughlin walking along the path that leads from their graves to the house. Inside the house, other visitors and staff have seen the disembodied shadow or outline of a tall man. One of the staff heard furniture being shifted around in the upper story of the house. When she went upstairs to investigate, she found that all of the furniture in the master bedroom had been

rearranged. According to others, on the anniversary of McLoughlin's death, September 3, a ray of sunlight shines through the parlor window onto a portrait of the doctor. When this happens, the portrait glows.

McLoughlin was a complicated man, having many values that were ahead of his time. Like many who started in the lower ranks of the Hudson's Bay Company, McLoughlin was born in Canada of French-Irish descent. Unlike many of his coworkers who were illiterate and born into the fur trade, he was educated as a physician before he joined the company. He rose up through the ranks, eventually becoming the chief factor of Oregon Country for the company in 1824. At that time, the United States and Great Britain were negotiating for future control of the area, and McLoughlin moved his chief post from Astoria, building Fort Vancouver on the north bank of the Columbia River, opposite where the Columbia and Willamette Rivers met.

He did this to draw a line. The British would take all the land north of the Columbia River, leaving the land south of the river to the United States. Future events showed that this early move did not work. Eventually the United States gained ownership of all the land north of the Columbia to the present border with Canada. This was due in part to McLoughlin's overwhelming sense of humanity.

McLoughlin was born into a Catholic family, and, though raised as a Protestant, he eventually returned to his Catholic heritage. Like many early settlers, his wife, Marguerite, was part Native American. Unlike most frontiersmen, he was happily married and did not abandon her in favor of a white wife later in life. McLoughlin was six foot four inches tall and had prematurely gray hair. The Native Americans he dealt with called him Great Eagle because of his fairness and dignified bearing. McLoughlin aided many American pioneers after many of them nearly starved upon arriving in Oregon. He did not stop them from settling in what would become Washington, and the Hudson's Bay Company eventually forced him to retire.

McLoughlin filed a land claim and helped plan the community of Oregon City as the logical capitol for the American settlers. In 1846, he retired to Oregon City and began sponsoring local commerce like fishing, sawmills, and a store. He donated three hundred building lots to private parties, as well as a school and several different churches. He loaned money to many people and practiced medicine for free. In 1847, the pope made him a member of the Knighthood of Saint Gregory for his humanitarian acts.

Unfortunately, many of the American settlers distrusted McLoughlin because he used to work for the Hudson's Bay Company. Many people borrowed money and never repaid it; some bragged it was because he was a foreigner. Even though McLoughlin eventually became a U.S. citizen, his enemies were able to have his original land claim dissolved, because he was not a citizen when he filed the claim. Fortunately, no one tried enforcing the dissolution of McLoughlin's claim.

Despite this, McLoughlin was a leader in American society, until his death in 1857 at the age of seventy-two. He and Marguerite were buried at St. John the Apostle Catholic Church. The church was demolished and rebuilt in 1948, and their bodies were moved with it. McLoughlin's house was also moved. It had stood on the lower banks of the Willamette River until 1909, when it was scheduled to be demolished. As one of the largest houses in old Oregon City, it had been used as a private residence, a boardinghouse, and possibly even a brothel. Many thought it would have been a good thing to tear it down, but the McLoughlin Memorial Association had it moved to a new location overlooking the river. They restored it and operated it as a museum for several decades. In 1970, they moved the McLoughlins' graves onto the grounds of the house. In 2003, the National Park Service took over the McLoughlin House, as part of the Fort Vancouver National Historic Site.

You can see the McLoughlins' graves (and perhaps catch a glimpse of their ghosts) by visiting the McLoughlin House at 713 Center Street, Oregon City.

Forgotten but Not Abandoned: The Oregon State Asylum Dead

In the 1970s, in Oregon and across the United States, many government-run facilities that treated the mentally ill began closing. New trends in mental health treatment mandated a change to smaller, community-based treatment centers. At Oregon's state mental health hospitals, this change helped expose a problem that was decades in the making. What was to be done with the remains of those people who died while in the custody and care of the State of Oregon?

In 1883, the Oregon State Insane Asylum opened its doors. It closed in 1913, thirty years later. Over those decades, more than a thousand people died there, many of whose bodies were not claimed by family for burial somewhere else. The cemetery on the asylum grounds filled rather quickly. This abandonment by relatives was not unusual at the time. In some cases, the families of the dead patients lived across the state and could not afford the cost of having the body shipped home. In many other cases, the families simply did not want the bodies of their supposed loved ones returned.

Some people at the hospital had severe mental illnesses that needed special care. However, in those days, the number of ways to earn a trip to the Oregon State Insane Asylum were many.

In 1913, when the original asylum was shut down, the state decided to put the graveyard land to another use. They ordered the asylum staff to dig up the graves, and posted a public notice for people to claim their dead relatives. Some of them did, but most did not. It took a year to exhume the unclaimed bodies, cremate them, and store them in quart-sized copper cans. At the time of the cremation, employees labeled each can with a number and data that could be cross-referenced with a log of patient's names.

The oldest patient buried in the asylum cemetery was ninety-four years old, and the youngest was four years old. After 1908, when the Institute for the Feeble-Minded opened, children went there instead. Some of the odd deaths recorded at the Oregon State Insane Asylum included those of Eva York, who drowned in her bathtub when she had an epileptic seizure in 1896, and a man who jumped out of a third-floor window, but many died of natural causes. In the end, officials dug up 1,539 burials at the old asylum.

The hospital continued cremating the remains of any unclaimed patient until the mid-1970s. At first this was done on the hospital grounds, in a crematorium that may have been attached to the smokestack of the incinerator called Steiner's Chimney, after a past superintendent. For a while, the urns were stored in a basement at the Oregon State Hospital. However, in 1976 the hospital created a series of vaults around a fishpond, which they called the Memorial Circle, and interred the urns there. In 2000, the State of Oregon began closing its larger facilities and disposing of land, including the Memorial Circle. Workers examined the 3,489 (or was it 3,490?) unclaimed urns and found that many of them had corroded after water leaked out of the fish pond, and about a third of the labels had fallen off or rotted away. They returned the cremains to an indoor storage room and tried to figure out what to do with them.

In 2003, Salem author Capi Lynn learned of the situation and wrote articles about it for the Salem *Statesman Journal.* Over the next three years, the same situation arose in different locations across the United States, and the fate of Oregon's abandoned dead became a national news story. The Oregon state legislature called for greater outreach on the part of the hospital to families. This happened, but several families who contacted the state hospital for information were stymied by laws designed to protect patient identity. In 2007, the Oregon state legislature passed laws that would require hospital officials to disclose names and dates to people applying for information about dead relatives. Until then, the State of Oregon continues to care for the remains of her citizens who may have been forgotten by their families, but not abandoned by all.

Lost Boys at the Mill Creek Reformatory

These days, most state welfare organizations do not like to run large institutions for abandoned or orphaned children. Instead, they prefer to place children in foster care or small facilities. That is because in the past, large (and cheap) reformatories were run more like prisons, where older children bullied and abused younger ones under the authority of uncaring adults. *Weird Oregon* was very sad when we learned of a graveyard where four teenage boys died and were buried outside of what was the Oregon State Reform School, near Salem, Oregon.

These four teenagers were Bennie Jackson, Hiram McRae, James O'Brien, and Frank Dilley, and they all died within a two-year period. The first three died in 1908, and Dilley died in 1910. Many rumors and legends surrounded the graves of these four. The reformatory was a hard place, and someone suggested that the staff killed Jackson, McRae, and O'Brien during an uprising of the reformatory inmates. Other stories suggest that there was a fire and that the boys who died in 1908 perished after rescuing several of the younger ones. Then there's a more mundane theory that all four perished in a series of epidemics like influenza or tuberculosis.

Author Capi Lynn spoke with *Weird Oregon* about many of her investigations. She said she had spoken with Oregon state authorities about the boys and their graveyard. There was no record of any kind of an inmate uprising, but there was a fire at the reformatory in 1908. However, a check of each boy's records showed that none of them died in tragic or heroic circumstances; common illnesses ended their lives. Dilley and Jackson died of tuberculosis, McRae died of diphtheria, and O'Brien died of an internal hemorrhage, complicated by a high fever. State authorities suggested that none of the four boys had any family, so the staff buried them in the reformatory cemetery.

Despite these mundane explanations, visitors to the cemetery may notice a few strange things. For one, the four gravestones all face one another, as if the boys are somehow still together after all these years. None of the tombstones are original. The first grave markers were probably wood, and they were replaced with concrete in the mid-1900s. While this in itself is not too strange, there are some oddities about the new stones. For one thing, the *y* in Dilley's name is backward. For some reason, they left off an *m* in McRae's name, too. Was there some special meaning in the grave placement and spelling errors? Perhaps someone practiced in anagrams or code breaking will find that there is something to these other legends of fires and inmate uprising.

After Lynn's investigation, the errors on the tombstones were corrected. Inmate work crews from the nearby Mill Creek Correctional Facility keep the cemetery itself in good condition. The cemetery is not easy to find, however, located uphill from the correctional facility, south of Gath Road, near the old pig barns.

Portland's Many Missing Dead

As Oregon's largest city, and one of its oldest, Portland has several cemeteries that serve its people. Over the years, as Portland grew, it swallowed up many smaller communities, adding their deceased residents as well as the living. Many smaller family plots have disappeared under later development. This is especially true in the case of cemeteries dating back to Portland's founding, in 1844. Portland's first public cemetery, Lone Fir, did not officially open until 1866. Before then, people were buried in family plots or the yards of pioneer churches, which are now gone. According to some estimates, there are as many as ten thousand unmarked or lost graves in and around Portland's many cemeteries—about average for a city of its size—so *Weird Oregon* suggests you walk carefully wherever you go along Portland's many busy streets.

Lone Fir Cemetery

Lone Fir Cemetery has the honor of being Portland's oldest surviving public cemetery. It began as a private family plot on the Stephens family homestead. Although the Stephens family sold their land in 1854, they made the buyer, Colburn Barrell, promise to maintain the family graves. Barrell had a steamboat that exploded on the Willamette River. He buried the casualties in the same plot, and in 1866 added twenty acres to the cemetery land and sold plots for $10 each. Over the years, the cemetery changed hands several times, going from a group of private investors to Multnomah County and eventually to Metro authority in 2007.

More than twenty-five thousand people have been buried at Lone Fir. It was Portland's main cemetery for several decades. Oddly, in the early days, most of Portland's

businesses and people lived on the west bank of the Willamette River, while Lone Fir Cemetery is located on the east bank. Whenever there was a burial, the body and party of mourners usually traveled across the river on the Stark Street Ferry. This ferry operated from 1855 to 1895, and charged a modest toll for foot passengers. Horses and riders cost a bit more, and wagons cost more than that. Corpses crossed the river for free.

Many of early Portland's rich and famous were buried at Lone Fir Cemetery. That is, until River View Cemetery opened on the west bank of the Willamette in 1882. After that, many of the rich preferred staying closer to downtown Portland, leaving Lone Fir to less wealthy folk, including many of Portland's Chinese immigrants. In 1947, Multnomah County removed many bodies from a portion of the cemetery used mostly by the Chinese and constructed a building on top of them. In 2005, the government learned that they had not removed all of the bodies when they tried to sell the land to developers. The controversy continues to this day.

River View Cemetery

By 1879, many Portlanders were tired of sending their loved ones across the Willamette River for burial. Perhaps they did not like the similarity with the Greek belief in the god Charon, who rowed the dead across the River Styx, never to return. It was obvious that Lone Fir Cemetery would fill up eventually, so some of Portland's citizens started looking for land to start a cemetery on the west bank of the Willamette. A dozen of Portland's financial leaders put up $140,000 to buy a three-hundred-acre wooded tract south of Portland. In 1882, with the help of the Ladd and Tilton Bank, they opened River View Cemetery. A nonprofit cemetery association grew to run and administer it. They set a rule whereby 30 percent of all space sales went into an endowment fund to preserve the cemetery. In the following years, many of Portland's wealthiest businesspeople and politicians and their families were buried there, as well as several national celebrities.

One of River View Cemetery's more famous residents is nineteenth-century lawman and wanderer Virgil Earp. His life and travels were long, and it is interesting that he was buried in Portland after visiting the city only once while he was alive. He ended up there because a long-lost descendent read about him in a newspaper.

In 1861, Earp married Ellen Rysdam in a whirlwind courtship on the eve of the Civil War. Their daughter, Nellie Jane, was born in July 1862, two weeks before Earp left to fight for the Union against the Confederacy. He did not return for three years, and when he did, Earp found that his wife had left. Sometime in 1863, Ellen heard he had died in the fighting, and she and her family headed west, where Ellen married twice, once in Walla Walla, Washington, and then in Portland in 1867. For some reason, Earp did not try to find Ellen or Nellie. Perhaps he suffered from the wanderlust that many Civil War veterans seemed to have after traveling and fighting. Instead, he headed southwest, where he divided his time between activities like ranching, gold mining, running saloons, and, most famously, being a lawman.

In 1881, Earp and several of his brothers settled in Tombstone, Arizona. Earp had two jobs, one as the

deputy federal marshal and a second as Tombstone's city marshal. He and his brothers made enemies of a group of men called the Cow-Boys, led by Ike Clanton. While the Cow-Boys mostly worked at the Clanton ranch as employees, there was evidence that they made more money by cattle rustling and robbery. Things came to a head that October, when the Earps and the Clanton gang had their famous shoot-out at the OK Corral. Earp was unwounded in the gunfight, but nearly died in an ambush later that year. Although he survived, the doctor removed large bone fragments from Earp's left arm. A few months later, he and his third wife, Allie, left Tombstone. Despite being crippled in his left arm, Earp was an active man, and he held many other jobs as a lawman over the next decades.

In 1898, Earp was working on his ranch in Arizona when he received a letter from Portland, Oregon. The writer, Mrs. Nellie Law, was his daughter, whom he had not seen since she was two weeks old. She had recently seen a newspaper story about Earp's shoot-out nearly twenty years earlier and wanted to know if he was her father. In April 1899, Earp and his wife traveled to Portland, where he was reunited with his daughter and first wife. He remained in Portland for several days before returning home. In October 1905, Earp died of pneumonia, and Allie sent his body to Portland, where his daughter buried him in her family plot. Their decades-long separation has now been ended by an eternity of togetherness.

One twentieth-century "cowboy" buried in River View Cemetery is National Football League player Lyle Alzado. Alzado played professional football for the Los Angeles Raiders, Cleveland Browns, and Denver Broncos in his fifteen-year career. He played in two Super Bowls and, as a defensive lineman and tackle, racked up nearly a thousand tackles and more than a hundred sacks. In addition to a football player, Alzado was also a successful professional boxer and had a budding career as an actor. Unfortunately, his physical attributes and success came in part from a twenty-year addiction to steroids, which probably led to his dying of brain cancer at the age of forty-three. Before he died, Alzado pleaded with people not to travel the path he did.

Baseball player Carl Mays also is buried at River View Cemetery. Mays was pitching in a Major League Baseball game against the Cleveland Indians when he hit a batter, Ray Chapman, in the head, killing him. That has been the only fatality in the major league to date, and it slowly eroded Mays's fifteen-year career. Everywhere he went, people whispered about the accident, some hinting it was intentional.

Another River View notable is Henry Weinhard. At one point, the governor accused Weinhard of ruining the state. His crime? Brewing beer. Weinhard arrived in Portland in 1856 and, over a period of six years, he worked and operated breweries in Washington and Oregon before finally settling down at Portland's First Avenue and Davis Street. Over the decades, his business grew and expanded several times. In 1899, its production was at 100,000 barrels of beer a year. Weinhard died in 1904; after that, his empire grew, shrank, and changed hands several times. The Henry Weinhard label is now produced in other locations, his Portland brewery complex demolished in favor of upscale urban planning. We wonder what Weinhard thinks of that from his final resting spot at River View.

Unlike many cemeteries in the United States today, River View is well maintained, and the Cemetery Association is proactive in taking care of their charges. They offer guided tours, requesting only a donation, and have an online cemetery tour on their Web site at www.riverviewcemetery.org.

Columbian Cemetery

In the late 1800s, the North Portland neighborhood was an up-and-coming place to live. Many merchants and sailors who worked along the Willamette River built fine homes along or near Interstate Avenue. Over the years though, as river traffic lessened, North Portland became less wealthy and less important. The history of Columbian Cemetery followed this same trend.

The cemetery was founded by Civil War veteran Capt. Lewis Love and is owned in trust by the descendents of the five thousand or so people buried there. *Weird Oregon* recommends against visiting this cemetery at night. Cemetery caretakers frequently find evidence of drug use and odd activities among the headstones. Several of the headstones were toppled over, and in 2004 they found the carcass of a chicken that had been decapitated over one grave in a voodoo or Santeria ceremony.

Despite these incursions, there is an active Columbian Cemetery Association that keeps up the graves and grounds, and raises money from donations and sales from their online store at www.columbiancemetery.org.

Silver Lake Cemetery

In the 1890s, the little town of Silver Lake was growing, against bad odds. The U. S. government had opened up the highlands of south-central Oregon to settlers a few years earlier. The pioneers who took up land claims there battled hot dry summers and very cold winters, eking out a living in the arid soils. Even so, as the Christmas of 1894 approached, word went out that there would be a huge Christmas Eve celebration in Clayton Hall, on the second floor of one of Silver Lake's two stores. People came from their isolated farms, some on foot, others by horseback. Some people traveled more than thirty miles in buckboard wagons, risking their lives from frostbite as they made their way through snowdrifts blown by high winds.

All of Silver Lake's 50 residents attended, in addition to 100 to 150 other guests. Everyone had a great time by all accounts, singing, dancing, and eating, until the party was nearly over. One of the guests got up and accidentally bumped into a lamp hanging from the low ceiling. The fuel oil in the reservoir emptied directly into the flame burner, which flared up and caught the ceiling on fire. Someone yelled, "Fire!" and everyone panicked as they tried to get out of the second-floor hall. Within minutes, the entire building was in flames.

When the fire died down, the survivors looked through the ashes and counted forty bodies. They could not identify anyone positively; the fire had been so hot that the bodies were carbonized. When the survivors tried to pick up the bodies, they crumbled into dust. It was midwinter, and they could not dig enough graves in the frozen ground to bury them all. Carefully the survivors gathered up the remains of their anonymous loved ones and put them into five large caskets. They buried these sad remains in a common grave in their little cemetery. In the three months that followed, another three people died, bringing the grand total to forty-three, which was about 20 percent of the population within a thirty-mile radius of Silver Lake. Their names were all inscribed on the single monument raised over their common grave in 1898.

Silver Lake and its cemetery are located east of Chemult, Oregon, and U.S. Highway 97. It is not easy to get to. You can take either Oregon State Highway 31 from the north, or State Highway 4 from the south. The cemetery is located near the intersection of State Highway 4 and State Highway 5, just east of Silver Lake.

Stayton Cemetery

Pioneer life in nineteenth-century Oregon was difficult. The work was hard, and people were often isolated on their large homesteads. Despite the isolation on these farms, regular gatherings—such as church on Sunday—brought people together to exchange news, help, and sometimes diseases. Because of poor hygiene, but mostly because of inadequate medicine, many diseases plagued the early pioneers. Cholera struck everyone equally: rich and poor, male and female, old and young alike. More tragic were the diseases that always seemed to attack the young, like diphtheria.

Between 1980 and 2000, there were only fifty-two reported cases of diphtheria in the United States. In the early 1920s, there were about 150,000 cases of diphtheria, which may not sound like many in a nation of millions, but most of the people who got it were children, and more than 10 percent of them died of the disease. It was a terrible illness for parents to watch their children suffer from, as their necks swelled up, and slowly, ever so slowly, their windpipes were sealed shut by a crust

the infection created inside their throats. There was nothing that people could do about it for years, until a doctor in the late 1880s invented a series of tubes that could be put down the throats of diphtheria sufferers to keep them from suffocating. It took many years for a vaccine to be developed. Unfortunately the vaccine came too late for the Grier family.

In December 1885, the Griers spent a lot of time together in their small cabin. One of the Grier children got diphtheria—probably at church—and it spread quickly. Between December 16 and December 31, William, Christopher, and Mary Grier all died of diphtheria. All three were buried in Stayton Pioneer Cemetery, and as a testament to the family tragedy, all three are remembered on a single stone. The real tragedy is that too many families lost all of their children in the same way, and stones like this may exist in many of Oregon's pioneer cemeteries.

The town of Stayton is located about twelve miles southeast of Salem, on Highway 22. The cemetery itself is located on Boedigheimer Road, about a third of a mile north of its junction with Highway 22.

Tillamook Rock Lighthouse

When the U.S. government decided to build a lighthouse in Tillamook Bay, they may have made a mistake. The island where the Tillamook Rock lighthouse stands is a sacred place to Native Americans. According to legend, the rock was home to *Elip Tillicum,* powerful spirits who would wreck the canoe of anyone who came to the rocky island. In 1879, a wave swept the master mason hired to oversee construction of the lighthouse off the rock, the day he began work. The lighthouse was dedicated in January 1881. It saved many lives over the years, but it always seemed to exact a human toll—and today it literally houses death.

It was run by several rotating teams of lighthouse keepers. It was a lonely existence; the crews remained on the island for months at a time, in part because it was so dangerous for boats to land there. They landed people and supplies on the island using a crane built on Tillamook Rock, until a storm destroyed the crane in 1934. In some storms, the waves were so high that they actually flooded the lighthouse when they broke over the top of the lighthouse tower. The keepers nearly drowned several times when the ocean level rose, flooding the lower part of the tower at the same time as waves crashed over the top of the lighthouse, flooding it from above.

During those storms, and on ordinary nights too, the lighthouse keepers often saw ships wrecked but were powerless to stop it. On one memorable occasion, they watched the ocean currents bring a very old abandoned ship toward them. It came so close that it brushed the rock. The keepers tried lowering one of their members onto the ship using the crane. Perhaps fortunately, the man did not make it on board the ship. Several of the keepers mentioned hearing eerie noises at night and seeing shadows of people on the island, even when all of the keepers were accounted for. It is no wonder that there are legends that the lighthouse is haunted.

The lighthouse operated until September 1957, when the light was finally turned off in favor of other lights and beacons. Then the government sold the island, and ownership passed to a series of private parties. In 1980, a group of real

estate investors bought the island. They received a license to refurbish the lighthouse building and reopen it as giant columbarium, a place to store urns filled with human ashes. When they opened Eternity at Sea for business, the owners said they had sealed all of the windows and lined the walls of the lighthouse with niches, which were ready to receive thousands of "honorary lighthouse keepers."

Their advertisements stated: "We accept keepers from anywhere in the world, and we hope that you and your heirs will visit this beautiful end of the Lewis and Clark Trail for many vacations before taking up residency." Perhaps as many as one hundred people decided that they wanted to be keepers, but not all of them made it to their final resting place.

The official records are confusing, but in 1999, the Eternity at Sea people did not reapply for their license. Despite this, they continued operations until 2005, when they reapplied, and things began coming to a head. The Oregon Cemetery Board did not renew the license. After

discussions, which were quite heated, the board held a formal investigation. The Cemetery Board learned that instead of filling the lighthouse with niches, the owners had set up shelves using boards laid across bricks. The roof leaked, and of the thirty or so urns placed there, two had been stolen by vandals. It was several months before the columbarium managers found the damage. In that time, several birds had entered, built nests, and fouled inside the building. Records were not well kept, and the company bank account held only a few hundred dollars.

During the investigation and for a short time afterward, the Eternity at Sea Web site still operated. It offered discounts for people putting themselves on a waiting list of future "keepers." In October 2007, Eternity at Sea announced they were planning a million-dollar renovation and reapplication for their permit. In early 2008, advertisements for future keepers ceased, and as *Weird Oregon* goes to press, the Eternity at Sea Web site at www.worldlights.com promises, "We are back soon!"

Strange Sounds at Dibble Cemetery

The small Clackamas County town of Molalla seems quiet enough. With around six thousand residents, the town is known for its plentiful outdoor activities, as well as the Molalla Buckeroo Rodeo. In most ways, Molalla is small-town life personified. Yes, things are certainly quiet here—except of course, in the notorious Dibble Cemetery, where it seems that things never quiet down.

For many years, stories have been told that something strange is going on at Dibble Cemetery. Some say the cemetery is severely haunted; others swear that some sort of unidentified natural phenomenon takes place there. But there's one thing that all seem to agree on: On quiet nights, an incessant howling noise emanates creepily from somewhere within the depths of the graveyard.

Ebenezer Chapel

Along an isolated avenue known as Webfoot Road, in the small Yamhill County town of Dayton, stands Odell Cemetery. This small graveyard may seem unassuming at first glance, but to locals, it's anything but. They know that Odell Cemetery is also known as Ebenezer Cemetery, and within its borders stands the infamous Ebenezer Chapel, regarded as one of the most haunted spots in all of Oregon.

Ebenezer Chapel was originally constructed in the 1850s and rebuilt in the 1920s. Eventually it was abandoned, and many ghost stories still surround this place.

According to stories, the reverend at Ebenezer was a charismatic preacher with a devoted flock of followers. But unlike most preachers, he was not looking to spread the good word of God. Instead, he was looking to bring his faithful closer and closer to him—so that he might betray them in the most heinous of ways.

It turns out that this preacher was actually the leader of a mysterious and enigmatic cult. One day, he and his darker cultish followers kidnapped the congregation. They took the children to the attic of the chapel and killed them. After that, Ebenezer disappeared.

The chapel sits, abandoned and crumbling, out in the woods deep within its cemetery. It lays gutted and vandalized by those who make their way out to the chapel to investigate the many rumors of hauntings attached to it. Sunken graves, some dating back to the early nineteenth century, still surround the chapel. It is a visually intimidating haunted site.

A visit to Ebenezer Chapel, surrounded by graves and crumbling in an isolated patch of forest, can be a truly terrifying experience. Many have heard voices yell from deep within the abandoned chapel. Others have felt cold spots, even on warm summer days. Some locals, who have grown up hearing of the abandoned chapel, refused to visit the place.

He Just Did It

In Nehalem Cemetery stands a grave so bold, a grave that stands out so clearly among the rest, that you'd think it was designed by an advertising agent.

You'd be right. This grave marks the remains of Robert Jay Strasser, the ad man who helped create Nike's "Just Do It" campaign and the Air Jordan craze before moving on to help revitalize the Adidas brand of sneakers.

Child-sized Adidas shoes hang from the trees surrounding Strasser's grave, and loved ones leave decorations, bottles, and other trinkets nearby. The tombstone is an impressive boulder, split down the middle, engraved with Strasser's own words. Here is a sampling:

Rob's Words

Here lies a man bigger than life,
A builder of teams, a dreamer
   of dreams.
A visionary who saw around corners
   of stone,
A friend who protected strangers
   as well as his own.
Passionate and warm, loyal and kind,
Generous of heart, brilliant of mind,
He loved and was loved for all that
   he gave
And that love will live on, far beyond
   this grave.

Tragic Tombstone Tales

STAN SHATTUCK WAS HUNG BY MISTAKE

IOOF Cemetery, Coburg

DENNIS OWRE
1955 — 1994
OFF ON ANOTHER ADVENTURE

St. Patrick's Historic Cemetery, Canby

ALMA D. MARKEE
1894 — 1984

DEATH IS A JOURNEY
AND YOU KNOW HOW I LOVE TO TRAVEL

St. Mary's Cemetery, Stayton

ROBERT L. SAYER

OCT. 19
1951

BAHA'I

JULY 4
1991

REMEMBER
NO MATTER WHERE YOU GO, THERE YOU ARE

Pleasant Hill Cemetery, Pleasant Hill

I AM Phenomenal
Jody E. White
April 8, 1960 - May 17, 2005

I'll be back in two shakes
of a lamb's tail.

River View Cemetery, Portland

Let the Games Begin!

Columbia Memorial Gardens, St. Helens

Lone Fir Cemetery, Portland

Ocean View Cemetery, Warrenton

Agency Mission Cemetery, Mission

Off-Limits and All But Forgotten

Like many progressive places, Oregon and Oregonians are very quick to build things to suit their needs. Most of these places remain in use for years, but eventually some outlive their usefulness and are abandoned. In some cases, like the Hot Lake Hotel, they have been rescued and put to other purposes.

In other cases, however, they remain vacant and sit year after year, left to the elements, like the forlorn Cape Arago Lighthouse. A few other places, like Camp Adair and the Mission Mill in Salem, have changed uses but still retain some of the mystique of their past aura. The memory of some places, like the Trojan Nuclear Reactor and the Fairview Training Center, will linger on for years, though many people would prefer to forget them. Then there are other sites, like the Bull Run Reservoir, that will remain off-limits and objects of speculation for years to come.

Hot Lake Hotel

Many people believe that hot springs are supernatural places. Of all the places in Oregon that are rumored to be haunted, the Hot Lake Hotel in La Grande probably has the greatest reputation. Nearby hot springs attract many visitors, and for decades a hospital operated inside the hotel. When it went bust and sat vacant for years, the legends grew about ghosts and other odd doings.

No one knows for sure how long the La Grande hot springs have been active, possibly longer than people have lived in North America. Today two thousand gallons of 190–205°F water pour out of the hot springs every minute, roughly 2.9 million gallons every day. In 1812 fur traders visited the hot springs, following in the footsteps of many Native Americans. As time passed, pioneers following the Oregon Trail stopped there to rest their weary bones in its healing waters. Some of the pioneers stayed there and built the first hotel in 1864. It grew, and quickly supported a store, blacksmith shop, bathhouses, and other businesses. As the first indoor mall, some called it the "Town Under One Roof."

In 1884 the Union Pacific Railroad lines passed through La Grande, and a station was built near the hot springs. By 1901 the hot springs' owners incorporated their business and attracted shareholders, who built a new hotel and facilities in 1903. In 1908 they built a three-story brick facility, and in 1917 Dr. William Phy purchased the facility. In addition to a hotel, Phy enlarged the scope of the business to include a sanitarium as well as a

resort. At that time, a sanitarium was not a place for people with mental illnesses; it was a facility for people with specific physical ailments to be healed. People believed that the hot springs' water and mud could cure a variety of illnesses, including tuberculosis and even syphilis.

The expanded facilities included a kitchen, a dining room, modern bathhouses, greenhouses, and a dairy. There were guest rooms on the second floor and a hospital on the third floor that boasted modern equipment like an X-ray machine (Phy was a pioneer in radiation treatment for some illnesses). Phy promoted the Hot Lake property as the Mayo Clinic of the West, and it served an average of 124 guests each day. Unfortunately, Phy died in 1931, and his son, who inherited the business, died two years later.

The fortunes of the Hot Lake Hotel declined during the Great Depression. In 1934, a fire destroyed most of the wooden portions of the complex. In 1943, the railroad abandoned its station near the hot springs, and a new highway bypassed the hotel in 1951. Unable to attract visitors, in 1953 the facility was converted into a nursing home, which closed in 1975.

The Hot Lake Hotel and lands passed through various hands. Many ghost stories began to circulate. Perhaps the most interesting ghost was attached to a piano at the hotel. According to legend, a piano was purchased for the original hotel complex and had been owned by Robert E. Lee's in-laws. A caretaker reported hearing the piano playing on the third floor, with no pianist.

Perhaps the most frightening stories were about Phy and his successors. According to these stories, they experimented on their clientele, sometimes performing operations without anesthesia. There were other stories that rich patients came to the facility for abortions. One caretaker claimed to have heard a woman's screams coming from the third-floor operating room. Perhaps some nursing home residents did not leave after the business closed in the 1970s. Many visitors found wheelchairs moved in and out of locked rooms and claimed to have heard the ghostly sound of wheels going up and down wheelchair ramps. On the grounds themselves, others believed that they saw the ghost of a Japanese gardener who committed suicide there. A television show even featured it as one of the most haunted places in the United States.

Over the years, the elements and vandals took their toll on the Hot Lake Hotel building. It was in danger of being torn down when Lee and David Manuel purchased the property in 2003. After years of work, they reopened the property in 2005 as the Hot Lake Springs Gallery and Foundry. Their plans include many artistic and historic displays, as well as possibly opening part of the building to overnight guests. Reporters have asked the Manuels if they have experienced anything supernatural. The Manuels replied negatively but may be trying to distance their work from the negative press that still clings to the Hot Lake Hotel.

Take exit 265 off I-84, near La Grande, to see the renovation in action, or visit www.hotlakesprings.com for more information.

Unfair Practice at the Fairview Training Center

Crumbling walls and discarded gurneys. Patient files scattered across dust-laden floors. These are standard sights at many of our nation's abandoned mental hospitals, including Salem's Fairview Training Center, possibly the most sadistic hospital of all.

As one former patient recalls, "My parents took me out to Fairview, and a gateway to hell opened up."

Founded in 1907 as the State Institution for the Feeble Minded, what later became known as the Fairview Training Center first opened its doors in 1908 for the "training, care and custody of feeble-minded, idiotic and epileptic persons." The 672-acre institution received many of its original patients from the Oregon State Hospital, which was the setting of the 1975 film *One Flew Over the Cuckoo's Nest*, starring Jack Nicholson.

At the time of Fairview's opening, the prevailing attitude of society toward people with mental disabilities was that they were better off living with their own kind. But it wasn't just the mentally disabled who were sequestered at Fairview. Orphans, promiscuous girls, and hitchhikers were also

committed. The focus of the facility was to train patients to do physical labor despite their handicaps. Animal and vegetable farms were located on site, and patients grew the majority of the food they consumed. This seemed, for all intents and purposes, to be a well-intentioned, productive program.

In 1923 the facility embraced eugenics, the belief that individuals with certain undesirable qualities should not be allowed to breed, for fear of further genetic spreading of those qualities. This philosophy defined the behavior of many American hospitals during the twentieth century. It was also co-opted by the Nazis and used as the basis for murdering large segments of their population.

The Board of Eugenics encouraged the "sterilization of all feeble-minded, insane, epileptics, habitual criminals, moral degenerates, and sexual perverts who are a menace to society." Fairview pursued eugenics feverishly in the form of forced sterilizations that defined the institution for decades. In the 1920s the patient population soared from 389 patients to 950, and by 1929 more than 300 of those patients had been sterilized. By law, patients were supposed to sign waivers stating they willingly agreed to the procedures, but coercion seems far more likely. Sterilization was frequently used as a condition of release from the institution or a punishment for misbehavior.

The 1950s and 1960s were marked by intense overcrowding. By 1963 the population reached an all-time high of nearly three thousand, the largest population in the state. The overburdened staff simply could not keep tabs on all the inmates in their care, and consequently escapes from the institution did occur. One resident who escaped in 1956 stole a gun and shot a group of kids in Salem. In 1967 another escapee set several fires throughout surrounding communities. A 1969 fire that destroyed Byrd Cottage, an intensive-care unit

housing mainly older bed-ridden men, killed three patients and seriously injured nine others. The physically disabled residents were trapped in the burning building because the doors to their wards were not wide enough to accommodate their rolling beds.

Straitjackets, handcuffs, leg shackles, and even cages were used to restrain patients. Cottage windows had prisonlike bars on them. Cafeterias doled out "institutional mush" with oversized spoons to expedite the process of

feeding the thousands of residents. Psychotropic drugs were employed liberally throughout the 1960s and 1970s.

In 1984, the U.S. Health Care Financing Administration looked into how Fairview was operating and threatened to cut off all federal funding to the hospital. The state scrambled to throw money into fixing Fairview, but in 1985 the U.S. Justice Department got involved. They deemed the conditions at Fairview to be life threatening and, in fact, went so far as to act as coplaintiff in a suit against the facility along with an organization representing the disabled and the parents of some Fairview residents. Medicaid cut off all funding to Fairview through most of 1987. Again, the state threw money at the problem, making physical improvements to the site as well as hiring new staff, including a required human rights representative.

The repercussions of this lawsuit would be felt at Fairview for many years, right up to its closing in 2000. After many attempts at fixing Fairview's facilities and operating procedures, it was decided that the facility was still committing outright civil rights violations and that the hospital provided no sense of safety to its patients, who were in harm's way on a daily basis. The last patients left Fairview in mid-February of that year, followed shortly thereafter by all the employees. It still stands closed.

What exactly was going on at Fairview that attracted such attention, finally forcing it to close? One of the glaring flaws in Fairview's sterilization program was that it continued for far too long. The last sterilization was performed at the facility in 1983. This is well after the tide had turned against eugenics as a popular practice. In 1974, a federal judge ruled in favor of patients who had been administered sterilizations during a class action lawsuit, and in 1975 the *New York Times Magazine* published an exposé on the practice and its faults. Yet, for close to a full decade after that, Fairview was still sterilizing its patients. All told, nearly three thousand patients were sterilized during the six decades that Fairview administered the procedures.

Even more disturbing were the reasons the sterilizations were ordered. Simple misbehavior could lead to permanent sterilization. Researchers found that more than a hundred teenage girls were forced into hysterectomies for very minor transgressions.

For men, the cruelty was perhaps even more severe. While vasectomy was the common method of sterilization in most hospitals nationwide, Fairview leaned more toward castration as their preferred method of sterilizing male patients. In the early days of eugenics at Fairview, nonconsensual castrations were routinely required for homosexual men. These methods, as well as the incredibly flexible standards for what constituted who was marked for sterilization, are at the core of Fairview's mistreatment.

By 2002, many former patients had organized themselves and were demanding an apology. In December of that year, Oregon governor John Kitzhaber obliged them. "Today, I am here to acknowledge a great wrong done to more than 2,600 Oregonians over a period of about 60 years, forced sterilization in accordance with a doctrine

called eugenics. . . ." he was quoted as saying in the *Inclusion Daily Express*, a newspaper focused on protecting the disabled. "The time has come to apologize for misdeeds that resulted from widespread misconceptions, ignorance, and bigotry. It's the right thing to do, the just thing to do. . . . Our hearts are heavy for the pain you endured."

Oregon became the second state (after Virginia) to issue an apology for eugenics. Thirty-one other states promoted similar programs and have yet to issue formal apologies.

Many came forward around the time of Kitzhaber's apology to tell their stories of life at Fairview. One of them was Kevin Trowbridge, who told a reporter from the *Statesman Journal* about his experience of being sterilized at Fairview after being tricked into signing papers authorizing the procedure. "They threatened me. I couldn't get out," he said. "Sometimes, I still have nightmares about it."

Kenneth Newman and his wife, Shirley, were Fairview residents, both coerced into sterilizations. "It was terrible, living in a place like that, an institution," Shirley Newman told the *Inclusion Daily Express*. "I never did anything wrong."

The Ghosts of Fairview

Since 2000, Fairview has sat abandoned and crumbling. In that time, developers have debated exactly what to do with the site. By and large, the former hospital's only visitors have been a few brave souls whose curiosity has led them to explore its hulking, silent depths. Not surprisingly, many visitors to the site have reported back that there are a series of strange phenomena at the old hospital.

Many have reported seeing ghostly figures wandering the fields that surround the abandoned buildings. This is not surprising—in the course of its history, many patients died as residents, sometimes because they lived out their natural lives here, and sometimes because of botched

medical procedures. Oftentimes, patients were abandoned at Fairview by their families, who did not want to raise disabled children, and no one claimed the bodies of these patients upon their deaths. They were buried as paupers in these same fields. Now, their tormented souls are said to still wander here.

Reports from within the buildings have yielded harrowing tales as well. There are numerous legends of walls within the buildings that bleed, as well as furniture that moves around the desolate halls on its own. Strange noises are heard with alarming frequency by visitors, at all times of day and night. With all of the pain and suffering that took place within these buildings, it is not surprising to hear that ghosts linger here—maybe they are still seeking the attention and care that was not provided to them during their lives at the Fairview Training Center.

If there has ever been a place where psychic remnants of a troubled past would exist, it is the Fairview Training Center. During its operation, it was a place where people's physical and mental health was toyed with. Since its abandonment, it stands as a monument to thousands of untold horrors. No wonder it is regarded as one of the most haunted places in the entire state of Oregon.

From Lobotomies to Lattes, Dammasch Mental Hospital

Mental illness used to be something shameful. Mentally ill people were put in institutions where they were hidden from view. Although many family members wanted to simply forget the mentally ill, others wanted their loved ones cured. The workers at the institutions may have burned out, but most wanted their charges healthy. As costs rose and as American society turned to drugs as cures, many mental institutions were shut down and the properties sold. In some of Oregon's upscale neighborhoods, people are now sipping designer coffee in the same spots where others suffered mental illnesses, like Dammasch Hospital.

In 1951, Oregon authorized the construction of a 460-bed hospital to care for and treat "persons affected with mental illness of the aged." They selected a 490-acre piece of ground in what was rural Wilsonville. In 1961, the facility was opened as the Ferdinand Dammasch State Hospital, named after the legislator and physician who promoted its construction. In its time, there were humorous stories of some patient escapades, such as the Russian sailor who defected from a Soviet fishing vessel in 1989. Once he gained asylum, he went on a binge and ended up running naked down the streets of Rockaway. Then there was the inmate who took advantage of walking unsupervised on the hospital grounds. He jumped into a car and took it for a joyride around Wilsonville, with the owner's son in the back seat, before returning to the hospital.

Just as there were humorous tales, there were other more serious stories associated with Dammasch. Although medical science had given up wholesale lobotomies to treat mental illness by the 1960s, rumors persist that they continued at Dammasch. They were still practicing electroshock and insulin "therapy" in the early days at Dammasch, and into the 1970s and 1980s experimental psychotropic drugs were given to patients. Oregon's mental health community had a long tradition of practicing eugenics, which meant forced sterilization of those whom doctors deemed to be "feeble minded" or to have some "defect" that could be passed on to future generations. Several children were sterilized at Dammasch.

Although the year-round inmate population of Dammasch averaged around three hundred people, the cost per patient rose every year. In the 1980s, the state legislature debated closing Dammasch and other large facilities in favor of powerful drugs and short-term-stay group homes. The debate continued as state asylum populations shrank. Health-care workers at Dammasch made impassioned appeals for the continuation of their facility. They pointed out that many of their inmates released to the streets added to a growing homeless population. Unfortunately for their pleas, Dammasch suffered a terrible tragedy. In 1993, two patients died while eating, and another died after staff placed him on his face, with hands secured behind him, and the man suffocated. The staff blamed the death on personnel cuts, but the end for the hospital was in sight.

In 1995, the last patients were released or sent to other facilities. The governor, Barbara Roberts, issued an apology on behalf of the State of Oregon to people who were mistreated by the doctors and staff at Dammasch. The buildings sat vacant for several years. Over the next decade there were many plans, including turning the place into a women's prison. Local homeowners objected, as well as businesses whose basements intersected a long tunnel running under Dammasch. This tunnel ran more than a mile underground, connecting all of the buildings that used to belong to the hospital complex and carrying electricity, steam, and probably patients at one time. According to rumor, the facility was designed to be used as a fallout shelter during the cold war—and something seemed to remain behind there, as well as in the main building.

picture what looked like mist, even though the air was clear. One of them had a tape recorder on, and he said, "I see you!" Later when he played the tape back, he heard a man's reply: "I felt you!"

In another case, a construction foreman was working in a storage area, cleaning up some broken glass. After working quietly for some time, he jumped when he heard a loud slamming. He was the only one in the building. He walked around, and when he turned a corner, the doors to the service elevator stood open. He knew that the elevator had been shut down, and when he had walked into the building, they'd been closed.

Although most of the expensive medical equipment was removed when the place shut down, the staff left so quickly that furniture and records were left behind. Vandals, curiosity seekers, and ghost hunters managed to find their way into Dammasch. Some found the tunnel complex locked up, so they shot their way through locked doors. Others found the upper operating rooms, where children and adults alike had been sterilized. Other forced surgical procedures may have taken place there as well, as indicated by the leather-strapped table (designed to hold the patient immobile).

Some people reported seeing a man walking around outside without a flashlight. When people tried to catch him, he disappeared into the darkness. In 2004, several ghost hunters visited Dammasch, and one captured in a

It is hard to tell what may happen to the spirits and aura left behind on the Dammasch complex. The city of Wilsonville eventually gained control of the complex and transferred it to the Villebois planned community development project. This has been a growing trend, developers buying land and properties in or near large cities, like old asylums or prisons, and turning them into upscale townhouse communities. Will there be a latte stand with comfy chairs on the same site where patients used to writhe in pain during convulsive therapy? How will the past collide with the present there?

Playing Dammasch

Most of the music venues in Portland were not interested in punk (or postpunk) in 1980. So our band, the Kinetics, took what opportunities came along. We played colleges, antidraft rallies, whatever. Then one day I got it into my head that we should play Dammasch State Hospital.

Our bass player, Jerry, got the gig together somehow. He arranged that we would share the bill with Smegma, a local art/free jazz/noise combo.

Dammasch had a presence in our community and not just because of *One Flew over the Cuckoo's Nest* by Ken Kesey. Live long enough in Portland in the right

scene of castoffs, weirdos, and artists, and you'll meet someone who has done some time in the state mental ward.

It felt like it was out in the country, rather isolated, with trees dotting the grounds in an attempt to soften the stark brick buildings. We were a little uneasy as we drove up. They assigned us to playing the "Multipurpose Room." As we set up the stage, people wandered in and out. I kept thinking that they must have been "crazy," but they were about as crazy as many of the people who lived in Northwest Portland at that time.

They were the best audience I ever played to. First of all, they were remarkably present and kind, even though the performance was not our best. It was the only gig I ever did in which I received bouquets from the audience. I was able to talk to a lot of the patients; many of them had just been dumped off by their families. I saw people in wheelchairs who might have had disabilities, but not necessarily mental ones. I saw teenagers who were just being teenagers, but they were too much trouble for their parents. So there they were.

They all received an amazing amount of drugs. If they refused, they would be injected. Everyone wanted pot. They also wanted handshakes and kisses. There we obliged. —*Eva Lake*

Umatilla Chemical Depot

Travelers driving along I-84 in eastern Oregon barely seem to notice the squat lumps sticking out of the flat ground as they pass between tiny Boardman and Stanfield. If they turn north on I-82, they might notice that what had looked like little lumps in the ground from a distance are really gigantic concrete bunkers. There are 1,001 of them, surrounded by a vast chain link fence. This is the Umatilla Chemical Depot, and it would be safer to just drive away.

In World War I, the Germans used chemical weapons like mustard gas on the battlefield. In World War II, the Allies worried they would use them again. Allies produced chemical weapons but vowed to use them only if the Germans did first.

Before World War II began, the U.S. government was preparing for chemical warfare. In 1941, they established the Umatilla Army Depot as a storage facility for war supplies, ranging from blankets to bullets. Over the years after the war, they constructed the giant concrete bunkers, half buried in the ground and covered with turf. In 1962, they began storing chemical munitions at Umatilla. Eventually, 12 percent of the United States chemical arsenal was stored at the depot.

This included more than fifteen thousand artillery shells filled with the nerve agent sarin, as well as containers of the nerve agent VX. These poisons were invented by chemists trying to develop insecticides. The results were too dangerous for public use—both substances kill by stopping the body's central nervous system from sending impulses to control the body's muscles. People suffering from nerve agent poisoning die because they cannot control their own breathing. Both sarin and VX can be used as either a gas or a liquid absorbed through the skin. It would take between two and twenty milligrams (the difference between a very small and a small drop) of either chemical to kill the average man.

In addition to the nerve agents, the government also stored several ton-sized containers of the mustard gas HD at Umatilla. HD does not kill in itself; it is a blister agent. A small drop of liquid HD on the skin will cause a blister about the size of a silver dollar. When used as a gas, it can

cause blistering in the lungs or blindness. HD can last for decades, and artillery shells and gas containers are still found on World War I battlefields.

In the early 1990s, the army decided to close the facility, and by 1994, everything but the chemical weapons had been sent elsewhere. At the same time, across the world, many nations were debating destroying all of the world's supply of chemical weapons. The United States and 187 other countries signed the Chemical Weapons Convention, agreeing to destroy their aging stockpiles. At Umatilla and several other locations, the government built destruction facilities that used incinerators and filtration systems to burn up the chemicals, turning them into (relatively) harmless byproducts.

Umatilla finally began destroying the chemicals in 2004. In the interim years, workers had to double- and triple-check their safety procedures, in case of a chemical leak. The surrounding communities planned evacuations in case winds brought clouds of poison gas, and environmentalists sued for adequate plans for waste disposal. Eventually they formalized plans, the lawsuits were settled, and the army began destroying the chemical stockpiles at Umatilla.

In September 2007, they announced that they had safely destroyed 1,014 tons of sarin nerve agent. This was about 25 percent of the total chemical stockpile at Umatilla. Late in December 2008, they announced that they had destroyed the last of the VX nerve agent. The last of the mustard/blister agent will be destroyed by 2012.

Hunkered in the Bunkers

I remember being in the army in the 1980s. I was stationed at Fort Lewis, Washington, but every now and then, we would pick up and go on field problems somewhere else. It seemed for a while like every month they took us to the Umatilla Depot, where we played war around all of those giant bunkers. It was miserable: either wet and cold, or windy, dry, and cold. Some of us hunkered down against the bunkers to stay out of the wind, and sometimes a couple of the more curious guys tried to get into one of the bunkers. Years later I found out what was inside of some of those bunkers. I guess we were lucky we did not get in. —*Dale*

Camp Adair

During World War II, Camp Adair was the second largest "city" in Oregon. Within three years of the end of the war, the camp dwindled away as most of the land and buildings were sold off. The remnants became a National Guard facility, but, unlike old memories, some old soldiers have not faded away.

In the 1880s, the area between Corvallis and Eugene was settled by a mix of small family farms and isolated lumber camps. Town sites were few and scattered, with Corvallis being the largest. During the Great Depression the area was hit very hard—banks foreclosed on mortgaged family farms, and many timber mills shut down. Although many people moved away, some stayed and made a go on their farms and other properties. When the Depression ended, many of the surviving farms flourished, and some expanded in the wide empty lands around them. In 1941, the War Department announced that they wanted to build a training camp in western Oregon.

A few months before the Japanese attack on Pearl Harbor, the local newspapers announced that the Corvallis area would be the army training site. Five days after Pearl Harbor, Congress approved the funds, and construction began on Camp Adair—good for Corvallis, perhaps, but not so good for many of its rural inhabitants. In a wartime panic, the government claims agents condemned many farms to make way for Camp Adair. Property owners complained about graft and low settlement prices. Some people refused to leave farms that had been in their families for decades, and the government forcibly evicted them. A few committed suicide, while others just seemed to fade away and die. Whole communities disappeared into what became a forty-four-thousand-acre military camp.

Thousands of workers arrived in the area to build 1,800 buildings, including warehouses, barracks, chapels,

recreation facilities, and a hospital. By the summer of 1942, most of the major construction at Camp Adair was completed, and the army training cadre arrived. They were followed by the new soldiers of four infantry divisions, each about fifteen thousand soldiers. After six months at Camp Adair, these units left, completing their training in a variety of climates from Alaska to Arizona, before going on to war.

During the war, the hospital at Camp Adair grew. Many sailors and marines suffered severe burns in the fierce fighting against the Japanese in the Pacific, and more than three thousand came to Camp Adair to recover or, unfortunately, die. In addition, there are records of at least one military airplane crashing at Camp Adair. The military put up fences and guard towers around some of the barracks, turning part of Adair into a prisoner-of-war camp. Most of those prisoners returned to their own countries after the war. Some of them became sick and died in their own infirmary-type hospital.

It was not always possible to return U.S. service members' or prisoners' bodies to their families in a timely manner. Some were buried in the post cemetery, while others were cremated in a large incinerator near the hospital and their ashes were returned through the Red Cross.

Shortly after the end of World War II, the recovering sailors and marines were sent to hospitals nearer their homes. The POW camp was disbanded, and the prisoners were sent home. Some of the military land was sold, as were most of the buildings. The central core of Camp Adair remained as a U.S. Air Force base and training area. In 1969, the air force closed its facilities and sold much of the land. The town of Adair Village grew out of the last land sale, and was incorporated in 1976. Its town hall is one of the original camp buildings.

Soldiers and Sailors Remain at Camp Adair

Some people think that the spirits of soldiers who stayed at Camp Adair haunt an airplane hangar, the old hospital building, and the prisoner's clinic building. One person reported people hearing cries of pain or suffering from the hospital. Other stories told of the nearby crematorium, with visions of transparent mourners holding vigils around the now cold building.

Weird Oregon spoke with Christina, a paranormal investigator who was curious about the tales of ghostly prisoners still in the hospital. She decided to see if they were true. In April 2001, Christina visited the hangar and POW clinic. The clinic building was set apart from most of the other buildings, in what was then an open field. It was in a decrepit state. Many of the windows were broken and boarded up. Even though there was equipment stored inside, it had been a long time since anyone had opened the rusty locks that secured the doors. As Christina walked up to the building, she heard the sound of heavy footsteps and clanking inside the supposedly deserted building.

Christina put a small tape recorder on the window ledge, inside the building, and walked around the open field for about sixty minutes, keeping the building in sight for the entire time. At the end of an hour or so, she retrieved her tape recorder and took it home, where she listened to it. At first, there was nothing remarkable, but around seven minutes into the recording, it sounded like someone stood very close to the microphone, breathing hard. About thirty-five minutes into the tape there was a sound like old-fashioned metal bedsprings squeaking for a few seconds.

This sound repeated several times, and one time the squeaking continued for about twenty seconds.

Christina had a good look inside the building. When it was a soldiers' barracks and clinic, there would have been metal-spring beds inside. When Christina was there, there were no beds, just some wooden storage shelves and equipment.

The remaining core of Camp Adair still exists as a training area for the Oregon State National Guard. Some of the buildings have been torn down and others are slowly decaying. Since 9/11, hasn't been easy to get into Camp Adair.

For more information, the Benton County Historical Society in Philomath (www.bentoncountymuseum.org) and the Albany Regional Museum (www.armuseum.com) have large exhibits on life at Camp Adair.

Foiled by the Camp Adair Fog

My name is John and I am conducting research on Camp Adair and the POW camp there. I was able to find out where the hospital used to be. In addition I gained access to the smoke stack where bodies were burned. Pretty creepy being inside. I have taken pictures, but a pretty strange thing happened to the cameras. I was carrying a Kodak digital camera and a Panasonic broadcast DVR, and I was able to get inside shots of one of the infirmaries. While taking pictures, as I stuck the camera inside, the lens got all foggy instantly! Same with the video camera. I know enough of video basics that if the temp outside is low and the inside temp is high, fog will occur in matter of seconds on the focusing lens. But this—I have never seen anything like this. —*John G.*

Missionaries Remain In Salem's Mission Mill Museum

The Mission Mill Museum is located on Mill Street in Salem, focusing on the closed Thomas Kay Woolen Mills, but the museum grounds have become a refuge for many of Salem's historic homes—and perhaps some of the early pioneers are still around.

The woolen mill was built in 1889 and processed much of the wool harvested in eastern Oregon. It operated for several more decades, before synthetic fabrics replaced wool in American clothing. The Kay family continued to run the mill until 1958, finally shutting its doors in 1962. The museum opened in 1964 to show the public the interesting history of the Thomas Kay Woolen Mills.

Over time, several historic homes and a church were moved to the museum grounds to protect them from demolition. They include the Methodist Parsonage, originally built in 1841; the Jason Lee House, dating to 1841; the John D. Boon House, built in 1847; and the Pleasant Grove Presbyterian Church, which was consecrated in 1858.

On certain days, the museum provides tour guides who lead visitors from building to building. If there are no tour guides, paying visitors are loaned a passkey that will let them into the various historic buildings.

Other Ghosts at the Mission Mill Museum

On weekends, volunteers sometimes demonstrate how to make woolen goods on the still-operational equipment. A museum employee told *Weird Oregon* that if you are on the third floor of the museum and stand in the right place, you can feel the vibrations of the water turbine— even if the water wheel is not turning. Is this some kind of ghostly replay of past activities? The mill used to run twelve hours a day, six days a week.

Several bridges run across the stream that supplies water to the mill. Some people claim that they have heard the ghostly echo of a murder committed by a past employee who drowned his wife in the millstream near the Mentzer Machine Shop.

More than one staff member told *Weird Oregon* that they had heard a service being given in the old church. Once one of these staff members entered, he saw a ghostly light suspended in midair.

The most interesting ghost is not very old. One of the old mill workers became a museum volunteer and security guard in his later years. He frequently put on displays of mill work in addition to keeping the parking lot secure. Apparently he stopped people who were littering or doing other naughty things in the parking lot, only to disappear after delivering his warning.

Jason Lee's Children?

It was raining hard when my wife, Janine, and I visited the Jason Lee House. I thought I'd heard a child or children's voices coming from inside the house, and someone walking up the stairs inside. Janine had heard children's voices, too.

Inside the house, we thought we heard a thump from upstairs but found no one there. Later a museum staff member told us that a psychic had detected the spirit of a young girl inhabiting the house, mainly on the second floor, where she had lived. She had a mischievous sense of humor, and would sometimes play with visitors or laugh when the tour guides got the historic facts wrong about the house.

They also told us of the security guard who'd paused outside the house when he saw a light shining from the second-floor windows—even though he had turned the lights off earlier. After turning off the lights again and resetting the alarm, he paused outside to look up at the second-floor windows again. One of the curtains was pulled aside then fell back over the window a few seconds later.

So who still inhabits the Jason Lee House? Is it one of the many children who lived there over the years? What about Lucy Thompson Lee, who died shortly after giving birth there? —*Jeff Davis*

Cape Arago Lighthouse Cursed?

The Cape Arago lighthouse on Gregory Point Island was built in 1934, but long before that, the Coos tribe had named the place Chief's Island and designated it as a sacred place. In the past, there was a village on the island and a burial ground.

The federal government prohibited the Native Americans from using the burial ground after the construction of the first lighthouse in 1866. The current lighthouse is the third—the first two having fallen victim to erosion and the elements.

A bridge from the mainland to the island was constructed in 1898. Unfortunately, a few days before it was completed, lighthouse keeper Thomas Wyman, his daughter, and two other people tried crossing to the island on the old tramway, a winch-powered cable car suspended between two towers. The cable snapped, and they fell sixty feet into the rocky channel below. No one died, but Wyman eventually lost a leg from the accident.

In 2006, the government decommissioned the lighthouse, and the lights were removed. The sandstone island is slowly shrinking. After every storm, local residents check to see how much of it remains.

The island and lighthouse are not open to the public, but they're viewable from Sunset Bay State Park, just south of Charleston. The 1898 footbridge, leading from the mainland to the island, still exists but is blocked off and unsafe.

Bull Run Reservoir

Bull Run Reservoir is one of Oregon's most "off-limits" places, by the decree of two U.S. presidents. And it is probably going to stay that way.

In the late 1800s, Portland's city planners were trying to figure out a way to supply water for the growing city. They identified a large natural lake on the western slopes of Mount Hood, and in 1882 President Benjamin Harrison established the Bull Run Reserve, clearing the way to construct more than thirty miles of water lines from the lake to Portland. It also forbade any settlement in or around the lake and surrounding watershed. Portland received its first Bull Run water in 1895, and people immediately noticed that cases of diseases like cholera decreased in the city.

In 1904, President Theodore Roosevelt made trespassing at Bull Run a federal offense.

While most cities in the United States constructed massive underground cisterns, or aboveground water towers, Portland is still old-fashioned. Bull Run's reservoirs are open-air and aboveground. In recent years there have been homeland security concerns that terrorists might try to poison the city's water supply. However, the only recent threat was a 2008 incident involving a couple of skinny-dippers.

Beware the Fate of the Trojan Nuclear Reactor

Sometimes Oregon's showcases of progress have not stood well against changing times and attitudes. Take the Trojan Nuclear Reactor, the only commercial nuclear reactor in Oregon. For many years, the 499-foot-high cooling tower was a familiar landmark. Although it emitted a cloud of steam for a few years while it operated, for far longer it stood cold, like some kind of Victorian folly, a structure with no purpose.

Work on the Trojan reactor began in 1970, costing $450 million, then supplying electricity by late December 1975. In 1978, a major earthquake fault line was discovered near the reactor, as were several construction errors. In 1992, one of the steam generator tubes developed a crack and leaked radioactive water and Portland General Electric shut it down.

The reactor sat unused but not unwatched. In 2005, the reactor slowly traveled by barge more than 250 miles up the Columbia River to the Hanford Nuclear Reservation, in Washington, where it was buried in a forty-five-foot-deep pit.

Finally, on May 21, 2006, Portland General Electric imploded the tower. The best estimates suggest that decommissioning and demolishing Trojan has cost as much as it did to build.

INDEX
Page numbers in bold refer to photos and illustrations.

WEiRD OREGON

ACKNOWLEDGMENTS

Jeff's Acknowledgments

Writing my portions of *Weird Oregon* was a kind of marathon. I wrote five chapters in a little less than three months. This meant a few trips across the Cascades, between snowstorms. A lot of people helped. I am sure I will miss a few who deserve acknowledgment; sorry if I do. Thanks to my wife for feeding the cats and waiting for me to return from the trips. And to Tim and Veronica in Lincoln City, for letting me crash on their couch so many times. It was more comfortable than it looked.

For archaeology and history information, thanks to: Dennis Jenkins and Pamela Endzweig of the University of Oregon; Hank at the Fort Rock Valley Historical Society; Nancy Nelson; Oregon State Parks; Pat Fine, Oregon Caves National Monument, their guides, and everyone at the Chateau; and Scott Williams (good luck with the Nehalem wax). For help and photos of the Oregon Trail, thanks Carmagene Uhalde, Linda Turner, and Kathy Bowman of the Columbia Gorge Discovery Center. Then there was Michael Dryden, archaeologist at the Mt. Hood National Forest.

There are plenty of man-made and natural wonders in Oregon. Thanks Christian Gurling of the Tillamook Naval Air Museum, Nicole Wahlberg at the Evergreen Aviation and Space Museum, and Bob Ward for his contributions on Francis Drake at Whale Cove. And not to forget Jennifer Day of the Portland Water Bureau. Some of the places for *Weird Oregon* had to wait until the spring melt, such as places like the Cloud Cap Inn on Mount Hood. Which reminds me, thanks to the Crag Rats on the Mountain. Thanks to Cistie Shaffer, of the Fossil Public School District, and everyone at the Fossil Beds National Monument, especially for the "fanged" photos. Thanks Dave Grimes of the Crater Lake National Park, and David Potter at Smith Rock Climbing Guides.

For paranormal and cemetery information, thanks ghost hunters Lisa Amato, Lisa Branum, Catherine Duncan of the Trails End Paranormal, Wendy at the Fulton House B&B, Cougar and Fox at the Shamanistic Society, Alison Kastner of Oregon Paranormal Investigations, Kristi Cardwell of Haunted Hunters, Teri Fisher and everyone at the Egyptian Theatre in Coos Bay, as well as paranormalist Ann Fillmore, Chelsea LaPan, Barbara Sidway of the Geiser Grand Hotel, and Amy Richard of the Oregon Shakespeare Festival. Thanks Burt Hendrix and all the ladies at Riverview Cemetery for helping locate some interesting gravesites. Thanks Capi Lynn, author, reporter, and weirdo (in the best sense of the word,) for her help in relocating some historic graves and graveyards.

There are some interesting people in Oregon. Among them are Tia Rich, hypnotherapist and birth coach, and genius Mike Richardson and Jacquelene Cohen at Darkhorse Comics.

WEIRD
OREGON

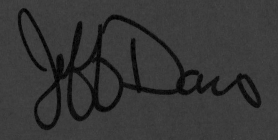